The Relational Map
A practical guide to improving all your relationships

BOB LEINBERGER

Copyright © Bob Leinberger, 2023
All Rights Reserved

This book is subject to the condition that no part of this book is to be reproduced, transmitted in any form or by any means; electronic or mechanical, stored in a retrieval system, photocopied, recorded, scanned, or otherwise. Any of these actions require the proper written permission of the author.

FIRST EDITION

ISBN 978-1-961749-73-3 (paperback)

ISBN 978-1-961749-74-0 (hardcover)

Scriptures taken from the Holy Bible, New International Version®, NIV®. Copyright © 1973, 1978, 1984, 2011 by Biblica, Inc.™ Used by permission of Zondervan. All rights reserved worldwide. www.zondervan.com. The "NIV" and "New International Version" are trademarks registered in the United States Patent and Trademark Office by Biblica, Inc.™

Front and back cover design: Steve Siewert of Thirst-Creative

*To my wife Darlene,
for her incredible patience,
meaningful encouragement,
timely challenges,
and remarkable support.*

*She has been my greatest fan,
strongest supporter,
trusted confidant,
and best friend.*

*For Zach, Grace and Nathan
You are my inspiration.*

Advanced Praise for
The Relational Map

"Bob Leinberger has a deep passion to help others succeed in all of their relationships. The Relational Map is packed full of content to help you achieve high levels of relationship satisfaction. You will be inspired to be more thoughtful and intentional with those who matter most to you."

~**Ted Cunningham**, founding pastor, Woodland Hills Family Church, author, *Fun Loving You* and *Greater Joy TWOgether*

"The Relational Map is a deeply moving, personal, and freshly valuable tool for navigating the difficult world of conflict in relationships. Bob Leinberger has served as a pastor and friend to so many. His own experiences, as well as those he has walked with other people, provide a wealth of insight into the highly complex circumstances that cause us to want to flee or even attack one another. I have learned so much sitting at Bob's feet, and I highly recommend this book to anyone that wants to improve their relationships."

~**Chap Clarke,** Executive Director, Institute for Ministry Leadership and author of *Hurt 2.0: Inside the world of today's Teenagers* and *Sticky Faith*

"I have read hundreds of leadership, performance management, and relationship books. Even with the best books, I sometimes find it difficult to apply the main principles to real-life situations. Bob Leinberger is a master at taking complex relationship concepts and putting them in understandable language that can be applied to both professional and personal relationships."

~**Corey Koskie**, former Major League Baseball third baseman, Minnesota Twins, Toronto Blue Jays, and Milwaukee Brewers, elected to the Canadian Baseball Hall of Fame

"Bob Leinberger has been my friend and partner in ministry for many years. He understands people and relationships. Often, I find myself in a difficult conversation and begin thinking to myself, "What would Bob say?" I have encouraged him over and over again to share his wisdom and experience with all of us by writing a book. I am so glad he did. One of the phrases I have learned from Bob and use often is "Tell me more." This response has gotten me through some tough conversations. Let me assure you that what you will find in this book is well worth your time. Thank you, Bob!"

~**Dan Johnson**, pastor

"Relationships can be tough to navigate, but this book definitely is not! Bob Leinberger takes his readers on an engaging road trip with valuable tools to repair and sustain relationships. The best part—personal stories from his own journey and those he has helped over the last twenty-five years. Not only does Bob help diagnose the problems, he helps the reader fix them with practical principles that are both easy to understand and apply. I highly recommend this book!"

~**Molly Sanborn**—author and speaker for youth, family, and marriage

"Building healthy and fulfilling relationships is hard work, but it's good work. Whether you are navigating the realities of broken, strained, confused, or simply immature relationships, Bob Leinberger's helpful insights and actionable steps will make a big impact. This practical guide takes us on a journey to cultivate life-giving relationships. Bob reminds us of the fundamentals we've often forgotten or taken for granted. Experiencing the relationships you want will require hard work, but the people you care about are worth it! Bob is a deep well, and the tools he presents have the potential to impact all your relationships!"

~**Benjamin Woods**, Co-Founder and minister at *The Brave Way Home*

"Bob Leinberger offers invaluable insight into relationships from a biblical foundation. I am so thankful for all he has taught us. I truly believe my new marriage is set up for success. Learning these things now will help us avoid common problems and give us tools for effective communication and a marriage that thrives."

~**Brook Stensgard,** young professional, newly married

"I can't rave enough about this book. I am so excited to see how God uses it to make this world draw closer to Him! I LOVE this book!!! The Relational Map is the most practical book I've ever read. Pastor Bob Leinberger has followed Jesus' example of telling stories to teach lessons, and he uses them throughout the book to teach how we can put into practice the ways God calls us to treat one another. This book gives tangible examples of how to apply the truths found in scripture so we can exemplify Christ's love, patience, and grace, especially as we navigate challenging situations and relationships."

~**Cathy Hilary**, health care professional

"Bob is an incredibly personal pre-marriage counselor. His knowledge and experience is vast and he knows how to tailor his pre-marriage sessions to areas that need growth and knowledge. Along with that, Bob is really kind and fun to be around! There are so many things I learned from our sessions that are going to help us be ahead of the game as we prepare for our marriage. Don't miss a chance to hear Bob Leinberger speak or to read his book."

~**Dan Ostrem**, young professional newly married

Table of Contents

Introduction..viii

Part One: Choose the Best Route to Arrive At the Desired Destination..1

Chapter One: Difficult Paths, Satisfying Destination....................2

Chapter Two: Check the Oil...30

Chapter Three: Avoid Dangerous Roads.....................................55

Chapter Four: Turn Around on a Dead-End Path........................72

Part Two: Ask Clarifying Questions to Help You Stay on Course......92

Chapter Five: Stay on Course...93

Chapter Six: Create Positive Memories.....................................111

Chapter Seven: Read The Road Signs.......................................131

Part Three Decisions That Will Produce a Satisfying Adventure....148

Chapter Eight: Fill Up the Tank..149

Chapter Nine: Follow the GPS..166

Chapter Ten: Look Beyond the Biggest Obstacle......................185

Chapter Eleven: Avoid Overheating...186

Chapter Twelve: The Productive Path That Brings Resolution...............236

About the Author..254

Acknowledgements..255

Endnotes...259

Introduction

Have you ever had a discussion with an important person in your life that seemed to be going well and, without warning, it turned into an unproductive, emotionally charged ordeal that left you feeling criticized, unheard, and completely disconnected? Why is it that two reasonable people who genuinely care about each other can say such hurtful things and refuse to consider the other person's perspective? The same person can be a remarkable source of joy and break your heart so deeply that it feels like you will never recover. Our lives are much more enjoyable when we are in a connected, life-giving relationship with a friend, co-worker, parent, sibling, child, or spouse. The people we care about can bring us incredible joy and meaning, but they can also cause us unimaginable pain and suffering.

As you pick up this book, you may be filled with an expectation that you will learn some new practical tools. You may be discouraged or feel so hopeless that you are ready to give up. As a fellow traveler who has spent time on the road to misery but has found a better way, I want to open your eyes to new possibilities over the horizon. I want to give you the encouragement you need to overcome your fear of the unknown and push through uncharted territory to experience the breathtaking view on the other side. My hope is that your journey will lead to excitement, fun, closeness, and joy. I have divided the book into three sections. The first part will help you choose the best route to take to your desired destination. The second part will provide you with three clarifying questions to help you stay on course. The third part will introduce you to five seemingly insignificant choices that will ultimately turn your journey into a satisfying adventure.

Throughout this book, we will seek God's wisdom and challenge some of our most deeply held assumptions. Think of it as a guidebook to help navigate your interactions and make your relationships better. In each of the twelve chapters, we will take an in-depth look under the surface and reflect on why the people you care about act the way they do. I am praying that you will acquire understanding and clarity to turn difficult arguments into productive conversations and threatening enemies into problem-solving teammates. Throughout our lifetime, we encounter many forks in the road. Some of the decisions we face are unbelievably difficult. Often, the right path will be the more difficult route, and we need courage, humility, compassion, and wisdom to proceed in the right direction. With God's help, your journey will become an inspiring adventure.

Why should you trust me to help you navigate such an important journey? I can help you avoid the road to misery. I know what it is like to desire good relationships but be unable to build them, and I also know the satisfaction that comes from deeply connected relationships. As you read my story and see some of the chaos I've lived through, you will begin to believe your situation can get better too. If an ordinary guy like me can endure difficult circumstances and experience satisfying relationships, then there is hope for you!

I was born in Denver, Colorado, as the second of six children. I loved my parents; my dad was my hero. My life was good until I got a little older and realized my mom and dad were fighting almost every day. The fights were intense, and they would scream and yell and throw stuff. I was completely overwhelmed by my parent's arguing. I felt helpless and completely out of control. Neither one of my parents would listen to the other person's perspective. Things would escalate, and my mom would get more heightened and aggressive. My dad would get angry and eventually withdraw.

Over time, my dad refused to argue. He closed my mom out of everything. If she ever expressed her disapproval, he would end the conversation by leaving the house. The frequency and intensity of my parents' arguments only increased. When I was nine years old, my dad left permanently. I can still remember the day he took me in the backyard and told me they had stopped loving each other and they were getting divorced. I learned that people were not safe and that if you did not perform, they could leave.

After the divorce, things went from bad to worse. My mom became an angry, bitter, resentful woman. She blamed God and started drinking large quantities of Jim Beam® whiskey. I never knew what to expect with Mom. She stopped parenting and left all six of us kids to fend for ourselves. I had to change my youngest brother's diapers. The responsibility was more than I could handle. There was so much chaos in my house that I became a peacemaker out of necessity. The wounds from my father were more subtle, but probably more profound. I was never good enough. I loved my dad and tried hard to please him, but unfortunately, I was never successful.

Despite all of the chaos I grew up with, God was present, and I could feel He had a calling on my life. I sensed He wanted me to go into full-time ministry. During my freshman year of college, I met my wife, Darlene. She was beautiful, intelligent, fun to be around, and easy to talk with. She was not like any of the other girls I had dated. She was a woman of strong character and her love for God was evident. She was a great listener. Conversations were easy with Darlene, and we had so much fun. We could talk for hours about important matters of the heart. I was convinced that I had found a person who would care about my pain, accept me when I failed, forgive me when I messed up, and love me even though I was imperfect.

I was completely drawn to Darlene. I could not stop thinking about her. I proposed after dating for three months, and we were married the summer after our freshman year of college. Then I went to graduate school for the next six years to earn a Master of Divinity degree. We started a family and had two amazing kids. The Leinberger household was busy, and except for an occasional disagreement here and there, Darlene and I were happy. We were busy with our little family and a growing ministry. Life was good, but there were cracks in the foundation of our marriage.

Darlene and I were able to work through disagreements, but occasionally, fights were painful, and I did not know what to do when my wife was sad, frustrated, disappointed, or upset with me. Her feelings tapped into my insecurities and made me feel like a failure. I became exceptionally good at withdrawing, defending, and avoiding conflict. I blamed her for our arguments and let her know she was far from perfect. I was becoming bitter and resentful. I did not trust her with my heart or my fears of inadequacy. I was acting like my dad so much that it scared me, but I felt powerless to do anything about it.

My relational struggles were not limited to my marriage. I moved my family across the country for a new job. Within two months, my supervisor said he was convinced I didn't have what it took to be a pastor. Rather than find a healthy way to process my emotions and then move to address his concerns, I began to work even harder to try and please everyone. I developed work habits that were unhealthy and that had an impact not only on my relationships at work, but also my relationships at home.

We were not prepared for what was about to hit us. My wife and I refer to it as the perfect storm. In eight months and one day, four people in our immediate families unexpectedly died. It started when Darlene's dad died of heart failure. Two months later, my brother, Eric, was killed in a car accident, and a custody battle began for his eight-year-old daughter, Courtney. Three months later, Darlene's mom died after a long battle with dementia. Two months after that, my dad died of cancer. He had won custody of my niece, Courtney, a few months earlier but had kept his cancer a secret from the courts and from everyone, including us! Before we even had time to grieve, my niece had moved in with us.

The four unexpected deaths and the arrival of our niece hit us like a category 5 hurricane! When the storm hit land, it rocked us to our foundation. Darlene tried to express to me her fears about how she felt alone after the passing of both her parents. She was miserable and grieving, while trying to be a good mom and an emotional support to my niece, Courtney. I interpreted Darlene's words as an attack on my character. I defended myself and tried to prove that I would never do anything to hurt her. We had countless conversations about this without any resolution. I started withdrawing and pulling away from her emotionally. It felt like every time we talked, things got worse. My dreams of being different from my father were unraveling in front of my very own eyes.

We were at an impasse with no way to cross. I loved God and was trying to love my wife, but her words were hurting my soul. I defended myself with passion. I dismissed her feelings, denied responsibility, and complained about how painful it was to be accused by her. My bitterness continued to grow, and I blamed her for our broken relationship. In my wife's time of need, I was focused on my own pain and unable to care about her perspective. I avoided conflict at every turn. I longed to be seen as a good-hearted person, a worthy employee, and a husband who was worthy of respect. I know firsthand what it feels like to desperately want to have good relationships with the people I care about and feel completely powerless to make things better. I was helpless and inadequate and unable to improve my situation no matter how hard I tried.

God was ready to do some of his best work in my life. I was ready to make some changes, but I needed to see things from an entirely different perspective. I started going to a marriage counselor, and he encouraged me to look at my part of the breakdown in all my relationships.

At first, his request was difficult, because I had spent my entire life developing the survival skill of defending myself against pain. My defenses that once protected me from alienation and rejection ended up ensuring my own misery. I needed to learn an entirely different way of interacting with the important people in my life. I needed to learn how to hear other people's pain without justifying my position or withdrawing and blaming them. It took time, and I was awkward, but God graciously taught me to live in the tension of other people's disapproval.

I began learning to love people in a mature way. I learned how to move towards people and not withdraw...no matter what. I learned how to validate hurt feelings and be patient, present, and empathetic. I began taking responsibility for my own feelings. I learned to pay attention to my own vulnerabilities and identify which of my own buttons were being pushed. For the first time in my life, I listened to my own internal dialogue. God was teaching me how to regulate my own negative emotions. I took ownership for my part of the breakdown in my relationships. I apologized for deeply hurting the people I had wounded, including my dear wife. I was learning how to care about her and other people by considering their point of view.

I learned a lot from that storm. It is hard to imagine, but I can manage my emotions and care about other people, while receiving their feelings and not taking them personally. I now can love in a way that is not dependent on other people. I am becoming the man I have always desperately wanted to be. I have a long way to go, but I feel like I am pleasing my heavenly father and becoming a man worthy of honor and respect. My relationships are much better than I ever thought possible.

My understanding of what is taking place under the surface.

As Pastor of Adult Ministries in a large metro-area church, I do a fair amount of counseling. I have a front-row seat to people describing their unsatisfying relationships and have observed many patterns that occur in relationships. Sometimes, I've watched people tell me how much they love each other and within minutes, destroy the person they had just promised to protect in our conversation. They often argue with such intensity that you would think their very survival was at stake, just like me in my early marriage. With each conversation over the years, I gained clarity. Some things still feel elusive as I try to help people who are in the midst of intense misery and a painful inability to resolve conflict.

I've been motivated to go deeper and genuinely understand why loved ones treat the most important people in their lives in such a destructive manner. I've wrestled with more and more questions about the dynamics in my original family. I wanted to know if it was possible to deescalate an angry person and talk in a way that increased your ability to be heard. I wanted to understand why some people could connect so easlly and why others became anxious, controlling, and angry and pushed the people that mattered most further and further away. Over time, I realized the importance of emotional connection. For example, most complaints are really attempts to draw people closer. When a person is able to make sense of their arguments and know how to solve the problems they encounter, then their entire life is transformed. Most people are not aware of the negative impact they leave on other people because they are so focused on getting the other person to listen to *their* perspective and change *their* behavior.

> *When a person is able to make sense of their arguments and know how to solve the problems they encounter, then their entire life is **transformed**.*

When a person is unable to make sense of their arguments, they often become hopeless and quit trying to make things better. Their destructive spiral leads them to unhappiness and disconnection. Over the years, it has been painful to watch good people get caught in the misery of their destructive patterns. The way they argue prevents them from hearing and understanding the other perspective, and the connection they long for remains out of reach.

Such an encounter usually begins with a harmless exchange of information that taps into the other person's hurts, fears, and vulnerabilities. Once the emotions are triggered, without warning, it becomes a heated discussion with lots of intensity. The unproductive conversation morphs into a damaging argument. Before either person realizes what is happening, it is a full-fledged battle to get the other person to see their perspective. When people argue, they feel the hurt they have received very deeply and think they are completely justified in the criticism and hostility they bring to the conversation.

In an attempt to be heard, they do destructive things that cause damage to the relationship. When two people are talking, convincing, and persuading, there is no listening or receiving. There is no resolution or even the possibility of understanding. I call it the merry-go-round of misery. The more two people continue in this loop, the more unsafe they

Merry-Go-Round of Misery

When a person is overwhelmed or angry...you, or anyone, will...

..Appraise the encounter by your Relationship System

..Ask yourself questions like, "Are you listening?" "Do you care?" "Are you there for me?"

..Realize, if the answers to your subconscious questions are, "no," or "I am not sure," that your relational alarm system is sounding (with hurts, fears and vulnerabilities raised).

..Activate your emotional brain (your heart rate rises, blood pressure elevates, muscles get tense, stress hormones are released, and you become focused on danger).

..Respond with stress and fear (wanting to attack, defend, run, or freeze).

..Decide which emotions rule
Primary: sadness, fear & hurt
Secondary: anger, frustration & blame

..React by criticizing, blaming, and defending

feel and the easier it is to see the other person as the source of their pain.

It does not take long for this to become an entrenched pattern. It is a vicious cycle of unhappiness. The more they spin around the merry-go-round, the more they expect to keep spinning. The more they experience it, the more they look for it, and the more they look for it, the more they see it. Before they know it, they find themselves anticipating the attack from their enemy and blaming before they get blamed.

When they try to go back and revisit the disagreement, they get stuck arguing about the argument. Their repeated attempts to navigate the same conversation leave them with deep-seated feelings of hopelessness. The longer the argument goes unresolved, the more miserable both people become. It can impact your ability to sleep, your productivity at work, and eventually, every area of life. There is hope; you can get on a better path that leads to more happiness and greater satisfaction.

My experience helping real people.

The chaos I lived through, and my inability to make things better, drove me to help fellow travelers with practical solutions. I desperately wanted to help them experience satisfying relationships. Early on in my ministry, I found people coming to my office on a regular basis. I was faced with some extremely complex problems and challenging situations. Over the last twenty-five years, I have sat with thousands of people, listened to their stories, and cared about their pain. Each conversation has helped me gain a deeper understanding of what is fueling the negative patterns.

I have had the privilege of helping men who desperately wanted to be good fathers and husbands who wanted to eliminate the behavior that was undermining their happiness. I have listened to women express their distress about trying to get the men in their lives to hear their fears and concerns. Their repeated, unsuccessful attempts left them feeling alone, unloved, and unheard. I've often been able to help them gain clarity and give them tangible tools to communicate in a way that their husbands could hear their heart and respond to their desires. I've watched a man pour his heart out when his company callously went in another direction after he had devoted twenty years to the success of the organization. I was able to help him overcome his disappointment and connect to his purpose.

Satisfied people started encouraging their friends and family members to meet with me. I have had opportunities to help families navigate conflict and leaders rebuild trust. I've helped build a framework for entire companies to improve their communication throughout the organization. One CEO called me up and asked if I could meet with his employee whose wife kicked him out of the house. We met for ninety minutes, and the boss asked him how his time went?

This is what the employee said, "The meeting was eye opening. The first twenty minutes with him was more useful than ten sessions with my other counselor. It seems like that guy really knows his stuff. By the end of the meeting, I felt like I've finally been given the keys to my wife's heart." The young man needed to know what was causing the disconnection and how he could make things better, and by the grace of God, I was able to apply the principles I've learned and help him.

Allow me to guide you onto a path that will improve your relationships. If you want a relationship to get better, then you must choose to stop the chaos, get off the merry-go-round of misery, and get on a productive path that will bring resolution. You need to invest the time necessary to understand what is happening under the surface and what causes your conversations to get off course. You can learn how to respond in constructive ways and repair the damage that has been done.

What makes this book different?

You should find this book to be easy to understand and very practical. My prayer is that God would give you hope to see a better future and the tools you need to make your relationships better. This book is the culmination of two of my greatest passions: helping people with their relationships and teaching God's Word. I have devoted decades immersing myself in the scriptures to study God's timeless principles. God has given me a gift to teach His Word in a way that makes it understandable so people can apply it to their lives.

I want everyone who invests their time to read this book to benefit from the depth of insight. The majority of every chapter is devoted to helping the reader apply the principles to their own life. Your relationships are worth the investment. The quality of your relationships will determine the enjoyment you experience in your life.

> *Your relationships are worth the investment.*

To get the most out of the book, read each chapter and answer the questions that follow. Invite God to direct your journey and put into practice the suggestions that apply to your unique situation. Your relationships with the most important people in your life will improve in direct proportion to your willingness to change how you interact with them. You'll develop habits that will help you change your behavior. It will not be easy to see things from a completely different lens, but I am convinced that the work is worth it!

Part One:

Choose The Best Route To Arrive At The Desired Destination

Chapter One

Difficult Path, Satisfying Destination

Changing your own behavior because it is what other people see as the problem.

Have you ever wanted to have a better relationship with someone you care about and felt completely powerless to make things better? Do you ever feel misunderstood or helpless to improve a certain situation, no matter how hard you try? It is as if you are a prisoner trapped on the road to misery and there are no off ramps to get to a better destination.

On their way back from a wonderful, ten-day vacation in Missouri, Mark and Penny drove through a dangerous storm. The morning started with steady rain, then the temperature suddenly dropped twenty degrees, and in the next hour, freezing rain gave way to a rare accumulation of three inches of snow. The blowing wind and snow created a storm the Department of Transportation was not prepared to handle. Mark and Penny slowly crawled through the treacherous conditions as they passed at least a half a dozen cars and three snowplows stranded on the side of the road and in the ditch.

Nervous and very concerned, Mark looked at the weather conditions and determined if they drove straight north, they could get out of the dangerous conditions much sooner, but it was a longer route and would make them late for an important evening meeting. He asked Penny which route she thought they should take. She was confident they should veer off onto the interstate because the road crews would have a better chance of keeping the main highway clear. They were rapidly approaching the exit and Mark, who was behind the wheel, had to make an instant decision.

He knew that with the indirect route, they would avoid the heart of the storm, so he decided to drive north on the smaller state highway. He could tell Penny was frustrated, but he believed he had made the best decision. Penny folded her arms and silently looked out the window. Mark kept driving without saying a word. Thirty minutes later, they made it out of the storm.

Mark saw a road sign for Penny's favorite restaurant and wanted to connect, so he suggested they go there for lunch. She unfolded her arms and said that would be wonderful. Unfortunately, when they looked up the route for the restaurant, they would have to drive twenty-eight minutes out of the way...directly into the path of the storm.

Mark decided they had already lost enough time, and it was not worth the risk, so he kept driving. Penny was already feeling like her opinion did not matter because Mark disregarded her wishes—twice. Now she was feeling he did not care about her at all. Mark could tell that she was upset, so he asked her if everything was alright. Penny said, "Am I supposed to be? You make all the decisions, completely ignore my thoughts, and now you won't even stop for lunch. What do you expect me to feel?"

The blizzard they had just driven through was nowhere near the storm raging inside of them. Their hearts were pumping, their emotions were racing. They were both overwhelmed with a mixture of tangled thoughts and desires. They were wanting to make things better, but they felt helpless and frustrated because they were being treated unfairly. No one said a word for 200 miles! Mark reluctantly broke the deafening silence by speaking the first words. His longing to be seen in a positive light was tangled with the hurt he felt from being accused of not giving any regard to his wife's opinions. Mark asked Penny, "I don't understand how ten incredible days meant nothing to you. Why do you always see me through such a negative lens?"

Penny felt like he was ignoring her wishes and accusing her of ruining the trip by assigning him awful motives. She responded by saying, "If I made all the decisions and completely ignored someone else's wishes, I would not deceive myself by pretending to have wonderful motives. I would acknowledge my extremely selfish behavior. I can't believe you can't see it."

Mark's heart was now beating way too fast for someone who was driving a car! He could not concentrate. He reacted by defending himself and saying, "I was trying to make the best decisions for us, and you started pouting for no reason."

Penny looked at the window and mumbled, "Unbelievable."

Mark turned his head and quietly whispered, "I don't know why I try. You are impossible to please."

Penny was overwhelmed and raised her intensity by saying, "You are NOT going to blame me for your disgusting behavior."

How did ten positive days completely evaporate in one car ride? What could Mark and Penny have done to make things better? The entire trip was ruined because both people were feeling misunderstood and disrespected. They were each convinced the real problem was the hurtful behavior of the other person, and their own behavior was a justified response to the other person's unreasonable behavior.

Anyone can get along with other people when the conditions are perfect, and the other person is treating them in a manner consistent with what they believe they deserve. The only way to end up at the right destination is to hold onto what we value while under stress. That requires the ability to manage our own emotions and maintain access to our entire brain when we need it most. We need the skill to get to our heart when we feel ignored, rejected, and disrespected. We need tools to understand the other person's perspective when it is completely different than our own and the willingness to look at our part of the breakdown when all we can see is the other person's bad behavior.

What do you want to get out of your relationships? Do you want to enjoy life and have meaningful conversations? Are you interested in experiencing deeper connection and a greater level of peace and internal satisfaction? When it comes to relationships, we want to end up at the right destination, but we don't always know how to get there. Everyone would like to be treated well and get along with the important people in their life.

The easy paths rarely lead to the most satisfying destinations. If we want good relationships, we must take the path that will get us there. As you begin the journey, there is one question you may not have considered but must be answered if you want to end up at the right destination.

"Are you willing to do what it takes to get there?"

Sometimes the smallest decisions cascade into consequences we never could have seen coming. If we want to experience connected relationships and have more productive communication, we must be willing to endure the difficult conversations and the potential hurt feelings to get there. Each step in the journey will bring new challenges and opportunities. Often, the more difficult route leads to the most satisfying destination.

What do you need to improve your relationships?

We have all had a harmless conversation that quickly turned into an extremely painful encounter. We need God's help to develop humility, compassion, wisdom, and courage in order to end up at the desired destination. We need humility to gain essential information to improve our relationship and behave in ways that endear others to us. We need compassion to see the other person's perspective and demonstrate we care. We need wisdom to discover what is taking place under the surface and follow principles that will make things better. We need courage to have hard conversations that lead to course adjustments and the development of habits that produce productive behavior so we can proceed in the right direction.

Humility to gain essential information to improve the relationship.

Pride undermines relationships because prideful people behave as if they are superior to other people and entitled to use whatever means necessary to get their way. They use strategies like intimidation, ridicule, and indifference. They need to win the argument no matter what the cost to the other person.

Arrogant people are unable to grow or overcome failure because they are closed off to the information that will help them improve their relationships. They feel like they have an inalienable right to prove their point, which makes it impossible for them to change their mind or admit they are wrong. They will continue to hit a ceiling until they are willing to consider the possibility that they may have done something wrong or hurt another person. All their energy goes into protecting themselves from being seen in a negative light.

If we allow pride to lead, we will be convinced that we are the important person in the relationship and treat people like we matter and they don't. Our pride will convince us that we are always right, and they are always wrong. Conversations will be about getting the other person to see our perspective, listen to our advice, and carry out our directives. Pride will allow us to justify selfish behavior, such as manipulating them into fulfilling our desires while we dismiss their perspective. Adam Grant discusses at length in his book, *Give and Take*, that arrogant attitudes lead to destructive behaviors that undermine relationships.[1]

Are you drawn to people who think they are better than you? Do you want to be close to people who are willing to use you to meet their desires? Do you want to work for someone who acts like they possess superior knowledge and routinely dismisses and ridicules your concerns and ideas? I hope you said NO to all of these!

Humble people have a big advantage when it comes to relationships because they do not have to be right, get their way, or know everything. They can learn from anyone in any situation, and it does not matter if it is an intern or the CEO, a parent or a child. Humility allows them to gain essential information to improve their relationships. Because they are open to new ideas, helpful advice, and essential feedback, they will need to solve problems, avoid mistakes, and change their behavior. A person who can admit their mistakes can overcome failure. They don't have to spend all their energy proving they could not have done anything wrong. Instead, they learn how to do things to make the relationship better in the future.

> *A person who can **admit** their mistakes can **overcome** failure.*

Humility is endearing to others.

When we are humble, we can collaborate, share information, and make the most of the other person's talent. We can admit our limitations and share the spotlight with others. Humility is endearing to others. We can admit weaknesses, ask for support, and give credit to other people. We can schedule time to get to know someone personally and thank the people who have helped us along the way. Humble attitudes lead to productive behavior that strengthen relationships.

Compassion helps us consider the other person's perspective.

Compassion helps us in our relationships because it allows us to say things in a way that others can receive them. If we don't have compassion, then we can do significant damage to the relationship when trying to get our point across. It is compassion that allows us to open our eyes to see the impact our words and behavior leave on others. Compassion makes communication better because it speaks acceptance, safety, protection, and love. It also significantly increases the likelihood of being heard.

Hearing what the other person is saying is an act of compassion because it requires us to be fully present and consider another person's perspective, even when it is completely different than our own. If we look through the eyes of compassion, we can temporarily put aside judgment to hear what the other person is saying. We can more easily look past the other person's annoying behavior and obnoxious comments. If Mark would have been filled with compassion, he could have acknowledged his wife, Penny's, feelings and given her an opportunity to express her frustration. He could have gathered important information he did not know in order to adjust course and arrive at the desired destination. If we have the right information, we can make the best decisions.

The people we care about always have reasons for their behavior, even though the reasons might not be apparent to us when their behavior occurs. The best way to make sense of why they acted the way they did is to invest time trying to understand what happened from their perspective. Compassion allows us to give others the opportunity to share their experience and explain what it means to them. When these memories and conclusions are put on the table and given consideration, we can get access to the information we need in order to make things better and move into a better future. We can correct misunderstandings, reassure fears, apologize for the pain we have caused, and adjust the route we are taking in order to arrive at a better destination.

Compassion demonstrates we care.

We can demonstrate we care by responding to their experience with understanding and support. People feel cared for when they feel heard. Are your eyes open to see the needs of others? Do you have ears that are sympathetic for what others are going through? Compassionate people are concerned with both the feelings and general wellbeing of others. Often, when we are engaged in a painful conversation, the other person simply wants us to see their perspective and show that we care about their pain. Problems are often resolved when people talk and listen with compassion.

Wisdom helps us understand what is happening under the surface.

Let's take another look at Mark and Penny to see what was happening under the surface. We will start with Penny. When Mark made the decision to keep driving north on the smaller highway, Penny felt <u>ignored</u> and <u>disregarded</u> because she concluded her opinion did not matter to Mark. She responded by <u>withdrawing</u> and <u>silently</u> looking out the window. They both initially wanted to make things better so Mark suggested they go to her favorite restaurant, and she accepted his invitation.

When Mark made the second decision to keep driving instead of going off-course to Penny's favorite restaurant, she was already feeling ignored and disregarded. Now she felt like he did not care about her at all. Penny was feeling <u>unloved</u> and <u>alone,</u> so she started accusing Mark of ignoring her and making all their decisions. Then she blamed him for her behavior. Penny felt Mark was treating her unfairly, so she justified treating him badly.

Now let's look at Mark. He was trying to include Penny by asking her which route she wanted to take home. He considered her wishes, but leaning on his research earlier that morning, he decided there was a better way. When Penny pulled away and silently looked out the window, Mark felt <u>rejected</u> and <u>helpless</u>. He sat in silence for thirty minutes and then tried to make things better by inviting her to go to her favorite restaurant. Penny not only accepted his offer, but she even pulled out her phone and started looking for directions to get there.

When Mark heard that going to the restaurant was almost a half hour away and would bring them directly into the path of the dangerous storm, he wanted to keep them safe and also get home sooner, so he skipped the restaurant and kept driving. Mark was convinced he was doing what was best for everyone and genuinely wanted to please Penny. When she accused him of making all the decisions, he felt falsely <u>accused</u> and unfairly <u>blamed</u>. Mark felt Penny was treating him unfairly, so he justified treating her badly.

When we hear undesirable things about ourselves that paint us in a negative light and contradict what we believe about ourselves, our brain becomes overly stimulated, and we subconsciously argue the point and dismiss the content. When we lose access to our brains, our ability to listen declines rapidly, and our ability to comprehend becomes almost nonexistent.

How can two people be in the same conversation and have two completely different experiences? The simple answer is there is a gap between how we see ourselves and how other people experience us.

When we dig under the surface, we can see that the more complicated answer is connected to how people experience uncomfortable emotions. We evaluate our interactions with other people by looking at our intentions and what we hoped to accomplish. We see our emotional responses and our behavior as normal because they are connected to the circumstances.

We tend to minimize our emotional responses and factor them out of the equation. When we react intensely, we are unaware of our body language and facial expressions because we can't see them. When we say insensitive things and behave badly, we feel justified because our actions were brought about by the other person's behavior. We tell ourselves we had every right to be frustrated because of the things the other person did to irritate us and make us feel bad. We are not aware of the negative impact we have on others because we are so focused on getting the other person to listen to our perspective and change their behavior. When Penny felt ignored, she felt justified in saying harsh words to Mark and pulling away emotionally. When Mark felt rejected and unfairly labeled, he felt justified in defending himself and criticizing Penny's behavior.

The impact of heightened emotions is often invisible to the person reacting impulsively, but the intense emotion is the most important factor in the entire experience to the person witnessing the emotion. When a person is upset, they are focused on the reason they are upset, but the person on the receiving end of the overwhelming emotion is acutely aware of the threat that is posed by the intense emotion itself. We evaluate our interactions with other people by looking at how their behavior made us feel. The person witnessing the elevated emotion is focused on the danger and fear produced by the unsafe situation.

> The **intense emotion** is the most important factor in the entire experience to the person witnessing the emotion.

When that part of our brain gets activated, we react automatically and without awareness of our own destructive behavior. When we are faced with a perceived threat, our brain senses danger and considers the situation to be life threatening. As a result, our body automatically reacts to keep us safe. The increased blood flow and release of stress hormones often limits our choices and puts into motion automatic and impulsive reactions. In the heat of the moment, our emotions and desires have power over our mind and thoughts.

Some people attack the other person and assign blame, some protect their heart and defend themselves, some withdraw and run away from the source of their pain, and some freeze and do nothing. Each person is left assuming the very worst about each other and the relationship. The good news is there is a better way, but it requires an entirely different way of responding.

Wisdom helps us follow principles that work.

The best person to acquire advice from is someone who has already flourished at what we are attempting to accomplish. They have already been down a road we are traveling and successfully made it through to the other side. There is one person who was so successful relationally, that people all over the world base their entire life on the principles and insights He offered. He did not come from a wealthy or influential family, yet He has had such a profound influence, that the behaviors that were once scorned in the ancient world have become celebrated and practiced on every continent and on every day of the week.

This person lived a compelling life because He modeled the principles He taught in all his interactions with everyone. Since His death, His influence has continued to grow. This year, millions of people all over the planet will celebrate His birthday. The ideas He presented are among the most remarkable and original ideas ever presented to all of humanity. His teaching has captured the attention of so many people that He is widely considered to be the most influential person to ever live. It is in this name that hopeless people find encouragement, angry people curse, and humble people find wisdom. His name is Jesus.

*His name is **Jesus!***

The principles and insights Jesus offered work in the real world and will help you improve all your relationships. You don't have to believe that He is God to benefit from the insights Jesus offers. The principles come from the scripture and will help you experience satisfying relationships. The following verses offer you a new way of seeing your relationships and prioritizing what really matters. Let's look at the first principle.

Foundational Principle 1: Treat people the way you wish to be treated

How do you see the people in your life when they hurt you and cause you pain? When people do things to hurt us, it is hard to shake it off. It hurts when someone at work unfairly criticizes us or tarnishes our reputation. It is even worse when we are ignored and rejected. It can cause permanent damage when we are betrayed by someone we trust. What do you do when people disappoint you and fail to live up to your expectations?

The first principle is found in Luke 6:27-31 where Jesus taught his followers a better way to treat people when he said, ^{27}"But to you who are listening I say: Love your enemies, do good to those who hate you, ^{28}bless those who curse you, pray for those who mistreat you. ^{29}If someone slaps you on one cheek, turn to them the other also. If someone takes your coat, do not withhold your shirt from them. ^{30}Give to everyone who asks you, and if anyone takes what belongs to you, do not demand it back. ^{31}Do to others as you would have them do to you." (NIV)

Jesus is offering life-changing ideas that have the power to help us improve our relationships and make our lives better. He tells us to love our enemies. Most people don't think it applies to them because they don't think they have any enemies. We usually only think of enemies as someone we are at war with. But who is actually an enemy? What if an enemy is someone who let you down, someone in the office who annoys you, or a neighbor who always bothers you with a certain annoying behavior? Is it possible the enemy, as defined by scripture, could be the boss who criticizes you or the teenage daughter who breaks your heart through frequent disappointments?

Jesus was speaking to the crowd, but He was primarily addressing His disciples when He said, "but I say to you." He is speaking to people who are willing to listen with an open mind. Jesus' teaching is counterintuitive to everything that comes natural to us. He asks His disciples to love their enemies, do good to those that hate, bless those who curse, and pray for those who mistreat or abuse them. Jesus is showing His followers how to thrive even when someone is taking their clothes, stealing their property, and actively trying to harm them. Jesus knows how to grab the attention of His audience and demonstrate the seriousness of a situation. He is using amplified language to make a point and challenge our way of thinking.

I am convinced that Jesus is offering freedom and a way to flourish regardless of our circumstances. He taught His followers that they did not have to become the evil inflicted upon them. They did not have to treat people the way they were treated. The perspective that Jesus offered is different than the way most people operate. In the first century, people were completely convinced that they could only enjoy life if they were successful and being treated well. Sound familiar?

Jesus is offering a way to see people through a completely different lens. This doesn't remove the hurt and disappointment, but it also means we don't have to retaliate and seek revenge. You no longer need to see people through the lens of your unmet desires. You don't have to become a prisoner of your disappointment and unmet expectations. You are free to forgive and release the hurt others have caused, because if you are not careful, the evil done to you can grow into evil inside of you. Jesus said you can seek the best for someone trying to injure you, treat people favorably who can't stand you and are hostile towards you, speak well of people who are saying harsh things about you, and even pray for those who despise you. I grew up in a church that missed out on everything Jesus taught because they dismissed the ideas before they gave them consideration. They got caught up in the high standard Jesus requires and missed out on the freedom He offers. Jesus offers us a new way of seeing relationships and prioritizing what really matters. He understands that when your perspective changes, your actions will follow. You can shift the way you see things. Jesus taught His followers to slow down and think about what they wish others did to them. He gave us a new lens to see how to treat people. You can look at how you wish other people treated you to understand what to do.

> *You don't have to become a prisoner of your disappointment and unmet expectations.*

If someone at work takes credit for your idea, you can make it your priority to make them regret it and undermine them in front of the entire organization. But be careful. The evil inflicted upon you may become the evil inside of you. If you look at the situation through the lens of your unmet desire, you will be miserable because bitterness and resentment will grow inside of you.

We have all made mistakes. We have all done things that hurt people. We have all violated trust and wounded relationships. What do we want from others after we hurt them? When I make a mistake, I want the person I hurt to cut me some slack and give me another chance. I want them to extend me grace and treat me better than my actions deserve. When I hurt someone, I want them to forgive me. When I mess up, I want them to give me an opportunity to make it right. Do we do this when the tables are turned?

Foundational Principle 2: Treat people the way God treated you

The second principle is found in Luke 6:32-35. ³²"If you love those who love you, what credit is that to you? Even sinners love those who love them. ³³And if you do good to those who are good to you, what credit is that to you? Even sinners do that. ³⁴And if you lend to those from whom you expect repayment, what credit is that to you? Even sinners lend to sinners, expecting to be repaid in full. ³⁵But love your enemies, do good to them, and lend to them without expecting to get anything back. Then your reward will be great, and you will be children of the Most High, because he is kind to the ungrateful and wicked. ³⁶Be merciful, just as your Father is merciful."

How do you improve your relationships? Treat the people in your lives the way God treated you. You can either see the hurt and disappointment through the lens of the offense or through the lens of what God has done for you. When you understand how much God has done and how far He has gone to invite you, forgive you, accept you, and include you, then you begin to treat people differently. How do you see people? If you look at people through the lens of their offense, all you will see is the hurt they have caused you. If you allow your perspective to change, then you don't have to become the evil inflicted upon you.

You can respond in a loving way. The word Jesus chose to use for love is *agape*. According *Greek-English Lexicon of the New Testament*, the meaning of the word is "an internal commitment to act towards the best interest of the individual."[2] If you act like everyone else and treat them the way they treat you, then you will be like everyone else. Jesus asked His followers to consider these questions: What good is it? What benefit is it to you? If someone hurts you and you hurt them back, then you are stuck in an endless cycle of misery. Anger eats at you and distorts your perspective. If someone violates your trust, you will have a hard time trusting them in the future. If you don't deal with your inability to trust, it will impact every person you spend time with and distort your perspective going forward.

What benefit will it be to you and what benefit will it have on the kingdom of God? You and I are called to be an example. We can show our family, friends, and coworkers that there is a better way. God says great is our reward. It could mean we will be rewarded in heaven, but I think it has more to do with peace of mind, a soft heart, healed relationships, and change of perspective. Ultimately, it means living in peace with those around us and being full of joy instead of continued frustration and disappointment.

If someone ignores us, rejects us, or treats us like we are invisible, then the natural thing to do is to ignore them, reject them, and refuse to give them the time of day. We will change the tactic if they apologize and go out of their way to make things better. If we are going to apply this profound principle of agape love, then we don't have to see the person who hurt us through the lens of their offense. We don't have to be a prisoner to their obnoxious behavior. We can see them through the lens of what God has done for us. We can treat them the way God treated us. God notices us and pays attention to us even when we reject Him and disregard everything He says. It is because God sees us and demonstrates that we matter, we can treat people differently.

The Bible speaks often of God's face. It says God will turn his face towards us. To turn your face towards someone is to give them your wholehearted, undivided attention. It is not the casual listening of a preoccupied mind, but the kind of focus that requires awareness and attention. When we read the words of Numbers 6:22-27, we see how God encouraged His children to treat others. [22] "The Lord said to Moses, [23] 'Tell Aaron and his sons, "This is how you are to bless the Israelites. Say to them: [24] "The Lord bless you and keep you; [25]the Lord make His face shine on you and be gracious to you; [26]the Lord turn His face toward you and give you peace."' [27]'So they will put my name on the Israelites, and I will bless them.'"

To bless others is to want the best and to draw them near with your heart. To keep others is to protect them and keep them safe. But it gets better. God wants to shine his face on them. The shining face is an image of delight. It is the proud face of a beaming parent that takes delight in their children. When God's face shines on them, He gives them his favor and acceptance. Think of it as a permanent smile. We, too, can see people who treat us as if we are invisible and give them better than they deserve.

Treating our friends and loved ones the way God treats us allows us to see them with new eyes. We are free to give them our attention and say with our actions how much they matter. God sees, hears, notices, and pays attention. When you truly *see* someone, you communicate to them in a very powerful way that *they matter*. If we can see how gracious God has been and how generous His actions are towards us, then we will want to treat others the same way.

It is so easy to look at what happens through the lens of our unmet expectation. We can focus our attention on what we don't have even when something incredible is right in front of us. A dear friend of mine invited my wife, Darlene, and I to go up to his cabin to get away. We had been to the place before, and we absolutely enjoyed the entire experience. We were anticipating a very relaxing stay. The family cabin was built in the fifties and was quite rustic. It was exactly what we needed to get away and build some new memories.

The first thing we noticed when we got to the cabin is it had been updated with brand new appliances, lightning-fast Wi-Fi, and expensive furniture! The refrigerator and pantry were well stocked with food and drinks the owner had painstakingly (and lovingly) prepared for our arrival. On the way to the cabin, he texted me to make sure we eat the key lime pie he left for dessert. How considerate of him. Wait, how inconsiderate of him. He made all the decisions for us and did not even ask either of us what we enjoyed eating or drinking. And the new furniture, well, let's just say that it ruined the nostalgic feeling of the cabin.

The most difficult experience of all was sitting on the massive porch overlooking the gorgeous bay each evening to watch a bald eagle swoop in for a fish. That wasn't the bad part. The bad part was that every time the eagle entered the water to catch a fish with his talons, the cabin owner's big, incredible boat and two jet skis blocked our view. How thoughtless to give us access to such incredible toys but not do a better job finding a better place to park them.

If I were telling you this story over a cup of coffee, I bet you would challenge my attitude toward this cabin and the generous gift of using it. The truth is that Darlene and I weren't frustrated by these things. But what if we were? What if you were invited to stay in an incredible cabin and complained about the food that was provided and the partially obstructed view from the deck? It sounds ridiculous, but we all are guilty of doing this.

We sometimes focus our attention on what we don't have even when something (or someone) incredible is right in front of us. We don't have to get stuck in our unmet desires because Jesus gave us a new lens to see how to treat people. We can look at how we wish other people treated us to understand what to do. I want to emulate my friend's generous behavior and treat people the way he treated us. He treated us better than either of us deserved. And the key lime pie? It was delicious!

God has modeled the behavior that makes it possible for relationships to get better. He showers His abundant grace on us, and we don't deserve it, could never earn it, and don't ever have to repay it. We have been given an incredible invitation to experience God's abundant grace and extend it to others. We can treat people the way He treated us. What we choose to focus our attention on will determine the quality of our relationships. The important thing is that we discover how to live out these two principles in the real world with the people you interact with on a regular basis.

> *What we choose to focus our attention on will determine the quality of our relationships.*

Courage to have hard conversations.

When you picture a tunnel, what comes to your mind? Do you think of a fun trip or a terrifying ordeal? For my wife, tunnels take her back to childhood road trips when her parents and her three siblings would drive from Michigan, where they lived, to the east coast, where her mom's extended family lived. They drove through the Smoky Mountains on roads with sweet, little, picturesque tunnels. The tunnels were small enough to see all the way through with beautiful destinations on the other side. Those road trips provided fun memories as she loved scaring her younger brothers. Every time they drove through a tunnel, she would get her brothers to look in another direction and then hit the roof of the car. They would scream like little children!

After we were married, we drove from Denver, Colorado, over the Loveland Pass to go skiing. The only way to get from Denver to the ski slopes of Copper Mountain is to go through the Eisenhower Tunnel. It is 1.7 miles long, and you cannot see to the other side as you enter. Darlene felt uneasy the entire time, like she could get trapped at any moment under a mountain of rubble with no way out. Darlene was terrified and dreaded every minute of that tunnel.

Tunnels help us get to where you want to go. Conversations in important relationships can sometimes feel like tunnels. It doesn't matter how much you like or dislike tunnels, there is no other way to get to your destination except to take the tunnel. Sometimes they are short and sweet, and sometimes they can feel chaotic and never-ending. The "tunnel of chaos" is a temporary, emotionally chaotic conversation where hurts are brought into the open and revealed through tough questions and comments. This place ranges from uncomfortable to terrifying. When one person decides to leave the peace and comfort of the relationship to talk over something that is bothering them or making it difficult to draw close, it can reveal that the familiar peace and comfort the couple enjoys is, at least partially, superficial. Counterfeit peace can shatter into a level of hostility that feels downright awful.

As we begin the journey to improving our relationships, we must discover what kind of relationships we ultimately want. If all we want are surface-level relationships with people that make life fun, then we won't need to have hard conversations. We can stay in the relationship as long as we are having a good time, it is convenient to stay, and we get something from it. If it becomes too difficult, we can find someone else.

Two people can get along nicely and avoid talking about hurts, misunderstandings, or anything that could result in conflict. Even though they may function well on the surface, underneath, there are real fears and concerns waiting to be expressed. A relationship preserved through a commitment to avoid talking about important topics in order to keep the peace is neither satisfying nor sustainable.

Important relationships are not always fun, they are often inconvenient, and they require time, energy, and attention. They also define us and make life meaningful. Quality relationships with coworkers, family members, and friends help us overcome life's difficulties, and give us someone to count on. They are worth the investment, because we get to spend time with people who get us and understand who we really are. They cheer for our success, mourn our defeats, and give us the encouragement and support we need to become the best versions of ourselves.

We can settle for surface relationships, but we will miss out on the meaning that comes with connected relationships. We can describe communication in five levels. The deeper levels produce more meaningful relationships. Whether we realize it or not, many of our conversations are about insignificant topics, like the weather, mutual disdain for other people, or weariness of the drama of politics. There is nothing wrong with talking about the weather, sports, or politics, as long as our conversations are not limited to insignificant topics.

The more time you spend with someone, the more important it will be to go deeper. If you want meaningful relationships, then you will need to be able to talk about your opinions, beliefs, emotions, and values even when you disagree. When your boss says the words, "We need to talk," what comes to your mind? Are your thoughts filled with fear, anxiety, and dread, or do you anticipate a pleasant, or at worst, a neutral conversation that will produce meaningful results? Hard conversations are not easy, but believe me when I say you can make it through the tunnel to the other side!

Communication Level 1: Casual Conversation

Not much is really shared at this level. These are conversations you would have with anybody, even strangers in an elevator. You may ask questions like, "How are you?" "Weren't those Packers fans annoying after the game?" or "The meteorologists were wrong about the weather today." The person might give benign answers such as, "Fine," "Yes, they were," or "That's just our crazy weather for you." When we are communicating at this level, we don't expect anything other than a polite response. There is no depth at this level, but casual conversations can be the building blocks to meaningful conversations.

Communication Level 2: Sharing Information

In this level, you share what you know and report the facts. You tell what happened with the kids or talk about what other people said. You may inform your daughter or business partner of events that are happening or even ask them to pick up lunch, but you do not reveal anything about your own feelings. Your conversation is limited to information about essential things to operate as a family or organization. The conversation can be slightly deeper than what you would have had with a stranger, but is rarely meaningful.

Communication Level 3: Sharing Opinions

In this level, you cautiously share your opinions, your ideas, and your judgments. You begin to go underneath the surface and reveal some, but not all, of you. You take some risks and reveal what you think. As you share, you carefully watch the other person to see if they will accept your opinions or reject your ideas. Many people abandon the conversation when they feel the slightest rejection. You may bring up the fact that you'd like to spend more time with your friends, or you want to spend the next holiday with your family, or you don't know what to do on your next big vacation. Quite a few people get stuck in this level and can't get past it. They aren't willing to risk anything, because they have been hurt, so they stay in their comfort zones and miss out on the most meaningful parts of the relationship.

Communication Level 4: Sharing Emotions

In this level, you start sharing your feelings. Feelings can be hurt when you expose yourselves to this depth, but for the relationship to grow, you must do this. This is where you share things about yourself and what you feel. This could range from wanting to discipline your kids in a different way to developing a budget for handling the money differently. The other person may not agree with you, making compromise necessary. Sharing emotions is high risk and even higher reward. Be careful as this level requires extreme caution. If a friend or family member shares something with you and you use it against them, they will have difficulty sharing with you in the future. You may get hurt, but this is the only path where you can experience a meaningful friendship and a deeper connection.

Communication Level 5: Sharing Everything

In this level, you are completely open and honest with the other person. Some relationships require total transparency. Sharing "the real you" means truthfully sharing your heart, your doubts, your fears, your insecurities, your struggles, your hopes, and your dreams. In this level, you are able to share anything and everything with the other person. If they develop an annoying habit, you can share your honest feelings about it without condemnation. If you are concerned with the way a project is going, you can talk openly without fear of judgement. You trust them and believe they have your best interests at heart. This doesn't mean you won't have conflict, but it does mean that you are committed to talking through anything that comes up.

To get to the highest level of communication, you will need to be vulnerable and risk rejection. You must develop deep trust, commitment, and a willingness to have these hard conversations. It's mostly about learning how to endure the tension that comes during difficult conversations. Every time you have a successful conversation, you will gain more confidence, feel more connected, and experience greater intimacy. These meaningful conversations can have a big impact on the quality of our lives, so long as we stay humble and willing to change.

Courage to develop new habits that change behavior.

The journey to improve relationships requires courage to fight the natural drift towards the easy path that is convenient and makes the fewest demands of our time, energy, and attention. People don't see our intentions or our emotions, they only see the behavior we display on the outside. And it is usually our own behavior that needs to change. That's at least what we have control over, so it absolutely should be our focus. Our relationships will improve in direct proportion to our willingness to stop obnoxious comments and annoying behavior.

Let's look at an example of what happens when all we can see is the behavior. Tyler was sitting in his living room, staring at the clock on his cell phone, trying not to unleash his frustration on his seventeen-year-old daughter, Tia. Before she left the house, Tia agreed to be home by midnight and to fill up her dad's truck with gas because Tyler had to be at work by 5:00 a.m. to finish a project. At 2:03 a.m., Tia finally pulled into the driveway, over two hours late.

Tyler loved his daughter and wanted the best for her, but he was struggling with his anxiety because he was afraid something bad had happened to her. He had gone to bed early so he could get up at 4:00 a.m., but frightening thoughts made it impossible to sleep. He laid in bed, imagining one worst-case scenario after another. He was on edge for hours before Tia opened the door and walked into the house.

Even though he was overwhelmed, Tyler softened his intensity and calmly started the conversation by asking, "Where have you been?"

Tia nonchalantly said, "Hanging out with my friends." He asked her if she got gas in the truck. She responded by saying she did not have time.

That's when Tyler unleashed his frustration and yelled, "I am sick of your disrespectful, inconsiderate behavior. You obviously can't be trusted. Taking back the keys and his credit card, he walked into his office and slammed the door.

If we get angry and say harsh words or slam a door, then the people we care about will experience fear and begin pulling away. They will protect themselves and walk on eggshells. People we care about will avoid us because they don't feel safe. Tia was not able to see how much her dad was worried about her safety or how completely exhausted he was after not sleeping. All she could see was his behavior, which to her was harsh and seemed unfair, mean, and dangerous.

If Tyler wants to have a good relationship with Tia, he is going to have to change the only thing she can see—which is his behavior. The people we care about are often not able to see what we hope and dream for them. The people in our world do not see what we feel on the inside, they only see what we display on the outside. If it's too harsh or unclear, they will misunderstand us and likely shut down.

Our internal feelings have a big impact on what we do, but people are not always aware of what is driving our actions. They can't see the hurt we carry from the people who have treated us very badly. They were not there when we were betrayed and wounded deeply. All they can see is how we treat them. It is unfair but true. If we want people to see us differently, then we will have to change what is taking place on the outside. If our behavior is not productive, it will undermine our relationships. Perceptions are based on behavior, so to change perceptions, we must change our behavior. This alone will improve the quality of our relationships!

We often think that if we can get the other person to see what we want for them, then they will give us credit for our noble intentions, even if we botched our expression of those intentions. It makes sense until we realize they have no proof of what we are saying. Intentions motivate our attitudes which, in turn, drive our actions. People do not have the ability to read our minds. We may have the best of intentions and our motives may be genuine, but people are unable to see them. Whenever our behavior is destructive, it will undermine our relationships, regardless of our intentions.

We need courage to change our behavior, but we will have to overcome two primary obstacles to do it. We will have to overcome our existing habits and our automatic reactions. Our existing habits produce automatic reactions, which bring about destructive behavior. The destructive behavior causes disconnection and undermines our relationships.

Overcome existing habits by developing new ones.

How do we overcome our existing habits which have been so deeply entrenched? There was a time when Darlene and I were drowning in debt. We needed to spend less than we earned and get rid of the debt. Our debt was making us miserable, but we could not make any progress until we changed our behavior. We weren't living a lavish lifestyle, but we were definitely spending more than our income could support. Our existing habits were producing automatic reactions. When we wanted something, we put it on the credit card which increased our debt. We did not make any progress until we engaged in some Level 5 (Transparency) communications about this problem. We developed two habits that turned our automatic reactions into productive behavior.

The first habit Darlene and I developed was a monthly check-in. We created a budget because it was supposed to be the best tool to properly manage our finances and guarantee our success. Even though we had a budget, we did not stick to it until we set up regular check-ins to make sure we were only spending the money we had decided to spend. We started holding ourselves accountable to our budget.

The second habit we developed was to use every extra dollar to pay down the lowest balance. Using the strategies talked about in Dave Ramsey's book, *The Total Money Makeover*, we would pay the minimum balance on every bill, every month, and put the extra money towards the smallest debt. Once that debt was paid in full, then we diverted the amount we were paying for the monthly payment plus all our extra money to target the next smallest debt, and so forth.[3]

It was painful, but we started making progress and kept knocking off one debt at a time until we conquered *all* our debt. In less than five years, we were able to pay off all our credit card debt, our second mortgage, and both of our cars. Today we are debt free, except for our house, and have financial freedom we never dreamed could be possible. One of our greatest joys in all of this is that we can generously bless people whenever the Holy Spirit prompts us.

I did not know it at the time, but many years later, I was able to use the same strategy to lose forty-five pounds and have kept it off for over three years. I once heard well-known preacher, Andy Stanley, say something that motivated me to get healthy. He said, "If you eat whatever you want, then you will look like you never wanted to look." Almost all health experts say the same thing. Eat less, exercise more. But eating fewer calories than you burn is not always that simple. I did not make any progress on this until I changed my behavior by developing habits that produced better automatic reactions. I developed two habits that changed everything. I kept track of how many calories I ate, and I weighed in every morning. I am healthier now than I was twenty years ago, and I have an abundance of energy. The same strategy that helped me get out of debt and lose weight can help us improve our relationships.

Awareness, understanding, insights, principles, and habits are an important part of the change process. When it comes to changing our behavior, we need conscious awareness of what we need to change. We need a basic understanding of **why** we act the way we do. We need insights and principles to know **what** we need to do to make things better. We need habits because that is **how** we will implement the change. Genuine change requires the repetition of a new habit until it becomes so automatic that we do it without thinking.

If we want to change a behavior, we need to integrate the insights and principles we learn into our lives through the development of new habits. This means we must implement a new habit and repeat it over and over (and over) until it is so automatic that it becomes second nature. At first, the new habit will be extremely difficult, but eventually, it will be automatic. If we integrate the insights and principles deep enough, we will be able to live them out when we find ourselves in a difficult situation with heightened emotions.

Awareness   Understanding   Insights & Principles   **Habits**

This is incredibly hard work, I know. We are often unable to change our behavior because the solutions we try don't go deep enough to solve the real problem. Genuine behavioral change takes time and progress is most often gradual, measured in weeks and months, not minutes or hours. We want to read about a new insight or hear someone we respect teach us a life-changing principle and apply it to our lives immediately. Substantive change requires new habits that produce better automatic responses that bring about more productive behaviors that improve relationships! Awareness, understanding, and insights are an important part of the process, but existing habits can only be changed by developing new habits that change the behavior. The best way to change a habit is to implement a new one.

> *Existing habits can only be changed by developing new habits that change the behavior.*

Overcome existing habits by establishing new, automatic reactions.

Another obstacle we must overcome is our automatic reactions. If we want to change our behavior, then we need to pay attention to our desires and manage our emotions, because they are the main drivers of our automatic reactions. It is remarkable how often we try to separate ourselves from our emotions and pretend they are not part of the equation. We deny our feelings and ignore our desires.

Whenever we react to bad behavior with more bad behavior, we make things worse. There isn't a single one of us who hasn't been guilty of doing this! If someone is an insensitive jerk to us, and we are mean and act like a jerk back to them, then all they will see is our annoying behavior. Have you ever thought about why you react the way you do? You may be reacting to another person's behavior. If you feel someone is trying to control you, you might refuse to cooperate because you hate to be told what to do. If you feel someone is taking advantage of you,

you might set them straight because you are not going to allow anyone to walk over you.

Our desires drive so much of what we do, and our actions determine the results we experience. Our desires are often operating in the background, beneath our consciousness awareness. If we want to change our behavior, then we may have to discover the desire that drives them. The only way to prevail over automatic reactions is to hold on to what we value under stress which requires the ability to maintain access to our brain at a time when we need it the most. In chapter six, you will learn how to respond to your automatic reactions.

Overwhelming emotions make us uncomfortable and leave us feeling vulnerable and helpless. Most people either run to get away from their feelings or react immediately before the emotions dissipate. When we encounter intense emotions, we tend to either run or react. Neither is helpful. If we run, we can spend a tremendous amount of energy avoiding our feelings and eventually, they often come out sideways. If we react before the temperature comes down, we will do and say things we regret.

We can't always control the outcome, but we can respond in a productive manner that will give us the best chance to make things better. The ultimate goal is to learn how to overcome our automatic reactions and respond with productive behavior, even when our fears are activated and our emotions are heightened. We can change the way we operate when we feel like we have been treated unfairly. We must implement new habits that help us overcome our automatic reactions so we keep from reverting to our bad behavior.

This process requires changing what we want in the moment for what we ultimately value and then acting in a manner that is productive to our goal. We can choose to take the high road or the low road. Traveling down the low road is like driving downhill in an ice storm with bald tires. It is so easy to lose control and slide off the road. We feel helpless to do anything about it, so we simply follow the path where it leads without much resistance at all. If we go too fast, we end up in a ditch.

People tend to follow the familiar path formed by the habits they have developed. If they get overwhelmed emotionally and want to attack someone by pointing out all their mistakes, then they say what is on their mind without holding anything back. If they feel like withdrawing, then they walk away and hide. If they feel like blaming, then they point out how the other person is responsible.

When another person's behavior impacts our emotions, we can carry frustration, bitterness, resentment, and anger which will knock us off balance. The temperature of our emotions can go up when we are in pain emotionally, and if we don't take steps to get the temperature down, we will say harsh words and do hurtful things.

Reacting immediately before the temperature comes down is a dangerous thing. We need to learn how to take steps to regain access to our brains so we can make better decisions and treat people better. Until then, we have no business making decisions or saying what is on our mind. In chapter nine, we will learn how to manage these strong emotions.

Our destructive behavior can and will do damage to relationships. Unfortunately, when we start to feel bad for what we have done, we experience uncomfortable emotions like guilt and remorse for our own destructive behavior. This sometimes causes even more destructive behavior as we don't know what to do with these feelings of guilt and remorse. We become increasingly overwhelmed and stay focused on how bad we feel. We rarely do things to correct the situation or help the person we have hurt feel better. When we are focused on ourselves, we can only see ourselves and our limited perspective. Our existing habits and automatic reactions lead us to feel and act in such a way that things get worse.

In our important relationships, we need to take intentional steps to make things better and repair the damage we have caused with our automatic reactions. This will take work for us to develop new habits because our immediate desires will prioritize getting our way over being close. When we have access to our brain and our heart. Our intentional response will enable us to be kind, compassionate, and understanding. To get the automatic reaction under control, we will have to manage our emotions and acknowledge our desires.

Taking the high road that leads to freedom is usually much more difficult. It is like driving up a steep incline with a thin layer of snow covering a thick layer of ice. We will have to pay attention to our surroundings and work through the difficult conditions. This path is often contrary to what we are feeling.

Changing habits is a slow process that always feels awkward in the beginning. With practice, we can gradually build the skills to be able to do it consistently and in real time. Anything we do repeatedly will become automatic over time.

If we want to experience the freedom of good relationships, we need to make a conscious choice to treat people better than their actions deserve, even when we don't feel like it. One of the most crucial behaviors to relationship success must be implemented at moments when it feels like the other person is making our life difficult. The ability to respond effectively when we are feeling rejected, criticized, ignored, and disrespected will determine the quality of our relationship. It is precisely at these moments when we feel strong emotions that we will need to take the high road. Over time, we can train our brain to choose what we value. The low road is easier, but the high road will end up at a much better destination. The more we choose the high road, the easier it will be to go down it again. The more we experience the benefits of the high road, the more motivation we will have to repeat high-road behavior.

If we want to improve our relationships, we will need courage—courage to have difficult conversations, courage to make course corrections, and courage to develop new habits.

Completing This Leg of the Journey

As we begin an important journey, we have a remarkable opportunity to learn how to experience more connected relationships and have more productive conversations. If we want our relationships to get better, we will have to invest the time necessary to understand what is happening under the surface and what causes our conversations to get off course.

We need humility to behave in ways that endear others to us and help us gain essential information to improve our relationship. We need compassion to see the other person's perspective and the chance to demonstrate we care. We need wisdom to discover what is taking place under the surface and the commitment to follow principles that will make things better. We need courage to have hard conversations that allow us to make course adjustments and develop habits that produce productive behavior so we can proceed in the right direction.

We can see things from a completely different lens. We don't have to see people through the lens of our unmet desire. We can treat people the way we want to be treated and don't have to see people through the lens of their offense. Then we are free to treat them the way God treated us. Remember, the people we care about are unable to see what we want for them or what we hope happens to them. Because they only see what we do and how we treat them, if our behavior is not productive, it will undermine our relationships. Our behavior will determine the quality of our relationships.

Significant change is possible, but it requires more than profound insights and practical solutions. Remember, we must develop new habits that produce better automatic responses that bring about productive behavior which improve relationships—and in that order! Our relationships will improve in direct proportion to our willingness to change our annoying behavior with the important people in our life. My hope is that your journey will produce remarkable results which will allow you arrive at your desired destination.

Questions for Discussion

- Which person, Mark or Penny, could you relate to more? Why?

- Think of a time when someone demonstrated compassion by attempting to understand your perspective? How did you feel?

- How do you respond to an arrogant person who dismisses your ideas, thoughts, or opinions?

- Why do people settle for surface conversations?

- What comes to your mind when you think about having a hard conversation?

- What behavior do you need to change to improve your current relationships?

- How often do you look through the lens of your unmet desire?

- Why is it so difficult to overcome our automatic reactions?

- How do you respond to the idea that people can't see our intentions, they can only see our behavior?

- Do you agree that if we want to improve our relationships, we will need to stop our obnoxious comments and annoying behavior?

- Can you commit to focusing on your own thought patterns and habits in order to bring about change in your relationships? What is something you can start doing right away that will help bring about change?

Chapter Two

Check the Oil

Building meaningful connection with the people your care about.

I was twenty-two years old when my friend, Tony, invited me to meet a group of our friends in Colorado Springs for a fun evening. I was looking forward to the adventure, but what I really wanted was to spend time with the beautiful girl I had a crush on. Her name was Darlene. She was easy to talk with and fun to be around. Tony mentioned that Darlene wanted to join us in the Springs, but she would need a ride. I volunteered to pick her up, but I pretended like it would be a little inconvenient and said I would do it if she absolutely needed a ride. I was not willing to admit that I really liked her. The night before the adventure, Tony called me and said I didn't have to worry about picking up Darlene because his friend, Norman, was willing to pick her up, but he can't get there until 5:00 p.m. Without even thinking, I said I could pick Darlene up at 4:00 p.m., because I suspected Norman liked Darlene as much as I did. I looked forward to the ninety-minute ride. I went to bed early because I had a big job to complete. I was so excited that I barely slept in eager anticipation of the fun I was going to experience.

    I hopped in my truck and headed down the freeway, wishing I had taken the time to check the oil. I figured it would be okay until I got to Colorado Springs. I was in a hurry to get to Darlene's place, after all. As I was speeding down the freeway, I heard an ear-piercing noise that sounded like thirty hammers violently smashing the engine. Just as soon as the noise started, it stopped. The engine seized. In an instant, the engine was destroyed, the truck totally useless. I missed out on a wonderful time with my friends, and Norman got to spend ninety minutes with Darlene.

I learned an important lesson that day. I was so focused on getting to my destination that I missed a real problem. Let's just say that bad things happen to engines that do not have enough oil to lubricate the metal. If the level of oil goes below a certain threshold, the engine will come to a violent end and stop working all together. If I had taken two minutes to check the oil, I would have added two quarts and been on my way.

The good news is I eventually connected with Darlene, and as you know by now, we were married! Over the last twenty-five years in my life as a pastor, I have watched many relationships lacking meaningful connection come to an end. The destruction is devastating, and the people involved are traumatized. Bad things happen to friendships, business partnerships, and marriages that do not have enough connection. When relationships end, everyone suffers. Our relationships may not always end when running low on connection, but they will surely suffer. If we do not prioritize connection, we will find ourselves facing unproductive conversations and profoundly painful circumstances. It is impossible to overstate how critical connection is to *all* of our relationships.

Friction is what happens when people rub each other the wrong way and things get heated, just like the engine in my truck that day I was supposed to pick up Darlene. A combination of conflict, discord, tension, and disagreement cause us all kinds of problems. But what causes this friction in our relationships? Everyone is unique, but the differences are often infuriating. When you put two people who have strongly held opinions, unique personalities, annoying habits, and weird personal preferences in close proximity with each other, and add the fact that they grew up in completely different types of families, not to mention they are sinful, selfish, and broken people, it can get unmanageable pretty quickly!

Friction is inevitable in every relationship, so let's just start with that fact! As I share examples of things that cause friction, take a moment to think about the things that are causing friction in your relationships. It could be demands on your time, too much responsibility, disappointment, financial hardship, children, employees, or personal or business competition. The metal hitting metal can cause damage to the relationship. Connection is the oil that lubricates the relationship and makes it possible to navigate friction.

What does connection look like? When we are connected, we have an internal feeling that the person we care about is present, available, and receptive. We are convinced the other person cares and wants to understand us. This person is there for us, and we can trust them with our heart. Some people have developed an extraordinarily strong connection, and they are able to talk about anything. Others have a dangerously low connection, and their relationship is hanging on by a thread. There was a time in my relationship with my wife when we could not even talk about our schedule for the day without the conversation becoming a huge argument. I had no idea what was wrong with our relationship. Our problem was not our inability to put words into sentences; the real issue was a lack of connection.

Let me give a couple examples of difficulties caused by lack of connection. Heather and her business partner, Kim, had developed a very profitable company that successfully navigated numerous obstacles. They complemented each other in so many ways, but recently had resorted to days of silence and many lost business opportunities. Kim blamed Heather and accused her of destroying the company. Heather passionately defended herself and ignored Kim's phone calls. When Heather did answer the phone, the only topic she was willing to speak about was Kim's critical attitude and harsh comments. The more Kim tried to address Heather's immature behavior, the more Heather withdrew and the more unavailable she became. The more Heather refused to talk, the more Kim's intensity increased and her desperation grew.

Another example is about a forty-year-old father, Dan, who was experiencing increased conflict with his thirteen-year-old daughter, Nicole. They used to play catch and watch movies together, but as Nicole grew, her interests changed, and Dan stopped reaching out. They constantly argued about friends, homework, clothes, and music. Nicole wanted freedom, and her dad wanted to see her act responsibly. As far as fathers and teenage daughters go, they had a good relationship. But more recently, they experienced a lot of friction. They both were saying hurtful things and refusing to consider the other person's perspective. Their anger grew daily, and every conversation ended with one of them either raising their voice or walking away in disgust. Tension was rising.

The business partners and the father and daughter were unable to resolve their differences. Each was convinced the other person was the problem. Sometimes, people think the real problem has to do with their family of origin, while others are convinced it's about power and control or even communication skills. All of those things are almost always contributing factors, but the arguments are actually unsuccessful protests over failed attempts to connect and the emotional disconnection that results. In order to solve the problem, we must address the central need for connection and our desperate fear of losing it. We all long for companionship and comfort from people we care about, and it is very painful when they remain elusive. Disconnection is the real problem.

> *Disconnection is the real problem.*

Whenever people communicate, there are always two conversations taking place simultaneously. One conversation is about the words that are being used and the other is about the longings and desires of the people who are in the conversation. Everyone has emotional baggage that can activate the emotional part of the brain. Whenever this happens, the argument shifts from ordinary events to big issues with deep meaning. Every time a person is hurt, the soft spots in their heart are vulnerable. These sensitive places in our hearts result from hurts, fears, and vulnerabilities.

Hurts are injuries we have sustained over the years. They are painful, emotional wounds that we have personally experienced. They can come from painful words like, "You will never amount to anything." Hurts can also come from times when we received little or no emotional nurturing, security, affection, or discipline. They can come from unpredictable behavior, from unbridled anger, and from having no voice to express our sadness, disappointment, or ideas.

Fears are the things we are afraid may happen to us. We might be afraid of being abandoned when someone expresses disappointment. Instead of the disappointment, we may hear them saying, "I am going to leave." We can be afraid our boss will think we are a failure when she criticizes our ideas, behavior, or words. Disappointing our spouse may activate our fear that we are not good enough or that we don't measure up.

Vulnerabilities are the things we are sensitive to because of the hurts we have received. When our daughter questions our idea, we might hear criticism and withdraw. When our boss blames us for disrespecting him, even if it wasn't true, his words might tap into an inner vulnerability and produce intense emotions that are overpowering. Sometimes we are not able to hear a word our boss, child, friend, or spouse is saying because the conversation becomes heated or emotionally intense.

We need to know what is happening under the surface, so we can better understand why the people we care about act the way they do when they are disconnected. Whenever we are in a conversation with a person that matters to us, our internal alarm sounds an alert and warns us the other person is not available, receptive, or willing to be influenced. We subconsciously access the connection we have with the other person. Our relationship threat indicator appraises the encounter and subconsciously asks a series of questions. Are you listening? Do I matter to you? Are you available and responsive? Do you care? Do you understand? If the answer is yes and the connection is strong, then our alarm does not sound. We can have a conversation about the topic, no problem. If the answer to any of the questions is no, or I don't know, then our relational threat indicator sounds the alarm and our hurts, fears, and vulnerabilities are raised and become part of the conversation. Our heart rate goes up, our blood pressure rises, and our stress hormones are released. Our muscles become tense, and our brain begins focusing on danger as we react to our fear of disconnection. To read more about this phenomenon, read Sharon Morris May's book, *How to Argue So Your Spouse Will Listen*.[1]

Whenever our hurts, fears, and vulnerabilities are triggered, we do not even have access to the part of our brain that can solve problems or see solutions. When our identity is at stake, we feel the desire to argue our worth as a person. For some of us, losing connection becomes a matter of life and death and our entire wellbeing is in danger. Our fear makes complete sense when we realize that it stems from our deepest fear, which is losing the people we care about the most. The more we care about the person, the more painful the disconnection becomes. The longer the disconnection remains, the more destructive our interactions become and the more insecure we feel.

What we want is to have the people in our lives available and receptive to us. We want the people that matter to celebrate our victories and comfort us in our defeats. We want to be known, loved, valued, and respected. We want to be encouraged, challenged, and comforted. When we sense the connection slipping away and the person no longer available or receptive to us, we become emotionally overwhelmed.

Unfortunately, most of us do not know how to handle the stress we feel, so we react subconsciously. Whenever we experience a similar feeling to what we have experienced in the past, we automatically react because our emotional brain is triggered. The increased blood flow and release of stress hormones often limit our choices and put into motion automatic responses. In the heat of the moment, emotions, not logic, have more power over our mind, thoughts, and reactions. Some people attack the other person and assign blame, some protect their heart and defend themselves, some withdraw and run away from the source of their pain, and some freeze and do nothing.

Most people are unable to process their negative emotions and identify their primary emotions of sadness, fear, and hurt. They tend to express their secondary emotions of anger, frustration, and blame by attacking and criticizing the other person or protecting themselves and defending their actions. Most people are unaware of what is really going on and have no idea how to address the problem. Disconnection is the real problem. Maintaining connection is just as important as keeping oil in your engine; it prevents destructive reactions and keeps the relationship healthy. Connection is the oil that lubricates the relationship and makes it possible to navigate the friction.

How do we establish a strong connection, and what do we need to do to repair the connection once it is damaged? People communicate well when they are connected and poorly when they are not. The apostle Paul gives us a template for the attitude

> *People communicate well when they are connected and poorly when they are not.*

and actions that will be helpful. His advice will be worthwhile for anyone, but he tells followers of Christ, "Do nothing out of selfish ambition or vain conceit. Rather, in humility value others above yourselves, not looking to your own interests but each of you to the interest of others" (Philippians 2:3-4). Peter repeatedly tells people that all kinds of relationships work when people seek peace and pursue it with compassion and humility. Read 1 Peter 2:11-3:12 and reflect on his words and ways to connect. What is relevant today? We are encouraged to submit and give priority to the needs and desires of the people in our lives.

We desperately need wisdom, compassion, humility, and courage to establish the connection that will allow us to experience successful relationships. If disconnection is the problem and connection is the solution, then how do we establish a strong connection, and what do we need to do to repair the connection once it is damaged? The rest of the chapter will be devoted to giving six ways to create connection and mend it when it becomes broken. We can establish or repair a connection by enjoying playful interactions, thinking positive thoughts, and creating a safe environment. We can repair a connection by completing conversations, mending hurts, and receiving attempts to connect.

Playful interactions build connection.

Laughter, fun, and playful interactions will increase the satisfaction of our relationship. Have you noticed how easy it is to connect with others when you are having fun? How often do you laugh? Proverbs 17:12 says, "Laughter is good medicine, but a crushed spirit dries up the bones." Connection is the one thing you will need to complete the journey. If you don't take time to build connection, the entire journey will be miserable. Set aside time to do things you enjoy doing together. It's especially important for married couples to set aside time for something fun they both enjoy. If you live near your parents, invite them to do something you will enjoy together. Almost everyone enjoys spending time with someone who is interested and engaged. Need some starter ideas? Try camping, fishing, hiking, biking, watching a movie, listening to an audio book on a road trip, playing a sport, painting, solving puzzles or riddles, going to a concert or sporting event, volunteering, or cooking and eating a meal together.

Shared experience builds connection, especially in marriage. Jim Burns, author of *Creating and Intimate Marriage*, talks about how to build physical, relational, and emotional intimacy.[2] Playful banter, smiles, and laughter can be powerful ways to connect. Appropriate teasing and silly moments are priceless. There are times to be serious and there are times to have fun, so go ahead and relax, do a goofy dance, or sing off key. Life requires a balance of it all!

Building connection at work.

We have all experienced the disconnect of big businesses treating customers and employees as numbers. Every company should pay attention to the connection of their employees. Set aside time for some sort of team building that includes playful interactions, laughter, fun, and food. Stressful environments can be overcome with solid friendships. People need a relaxed atmosphere where topics are about more than projects and deadlines. Connection is the glue that holds everything else together.

As a boss or manager, how did you feel when you were not appreciated for your contribution or acknowledged for your sacrifices? As an employee, have you ever felt undervalued or experienced stress due to poor relationships with your colleagues, manager, or boss? The way we interact with each other in a business setting greatly influences our mood, motivation, and productivity, both in the office and at home. Great teams are ones that support each member, adapt to change, and create strong connections. Each person is valued, appreciated, and supported.

Building connection with your kids.

Parents, it's so important to find ways to let your kids know that you enjoy spending time with them. One creative father who could not get time off to take a vacation, but knew how important it was for his family, put months into planning every intricate detail of his family's vacation. Even though he wouldn't get to participate, he helped them schedule what they would do every day of the two-week road trip. He even planned the precise route they would take. He then said goodbye to the family and wished them a great trip as they drove off without him. On the third day of their trip, the family was driving down the freeway when the youngest boy spotted a man who he said "looked like Dad." They were a thousand miles from home at this point so it couldn't be true, everyone agreed. The youngest boy insisted it was their dad, so the family turned the car around, and sure enough, it was their father with a smile beaming from ear to ear! Everyone was surprised and filled with so much excitement. Later that evening, the family sat around a campfire, retelling the story of seeing their dad looking like a hitchhiker. The oldest daughter asked her dad what he would have done if they had driven past him. He replied, "I don't know, but I am glad someone recognized me!" Twenty years later, his kids still talk about how shocked they were to see their dad on the side of the road.

A wonderful lesson you can teach your kids is to not take yourself too seriously and to enjoy a laugh at your own expense now and then. I am known by my family for not paying attention to details. My daughter still laughs whenever she thinks about the time we stopped at a gas station to get some food. I set the microwave timer for three minutes to warm up a frozen burrito. We were standing around waiting for my burrito to finish heating up when, without warning, there was an explosion. It was my burrito! The burrito exploded so violently, it knocked open the door of the microwave and splattered beans, cheese, and tortilla shell ten feet in every direction! After the initial shock and realization of what just happened, we saw a sign close by that said this was a "high-powered microwave" and a list of how much time to cook each food item. My daughter had to leave. Not only did she not want anything to do with me or the mess I had to clean up, but she was laughing so hard that she couldn't contain herself. We both sat in the parking lot laughing hysterically at the incredible mess I made because I failed to pay attention to something so obvious. To this day, I can make my daughter laugh by asking her if she wants to stop and get a burrito.

Thinking positive thoughts builds connection.

Most people think there is no link between what they think and how they feel. When we choose to think good things about the people we care about, then we will naturally feel more optimistic about them and our relationship. Learn to give other people the benefit of the doubt and do not take things personally. It is not productive to ruminate over the negative things our friends, classmates, colleagues, and family members do. Learn to replace destructive thoughts with honoring thoughts. *Get Out of Your Head* by Jennie Allen is a great resource on this.[3] Try this experiment the next time you are upset with your children, coworker, parents, or spouse. Go into a different room, make a list of ten of their positive attributes, and think about how much you appreciate those attributes. Keep a list for every significant person in your life, work on building the list, and look at it often. This simple exercise can make a huge difference!

Be sure to understand that I'm not suggesting you ignore what other people do to hurt you. Instead, find a way to voice a constructive complaint and then fill in the gaps by focusing on their strengths and positive characteristics. Even though you might have something that needs to be addressed, you can still choose what you focus your attention upon. You can either focus on the problems the other person creates or the joy they offer. A positive perspective acts as a buffer against the kind of negativity that will destroy a relationship. There is a point in relationships when negativity takes over and dominates all positive stories, memories, and feelings. Taking a minute to remind yourself of the good things you share and the qualities that bonded you to the person in the beginning will help you build connection. When we assume positive things and learn to give other people the benefit of the doubt, we are protecting the relationship from becoming adversarial and taking significant steps backwards. Look through the lens of how you want to be treated and give this a try.

Creating a safe environment builds connection.

Human beings are hard wired with the desire to feel safe. Our subconscious brains are constantly scanning our environment to determine if a person or a situation is safe or dangerous. Whenever we conclude that something or someone is dangerous, then we protect ourselves from the perceived harm. On the other hand, if we determine someone is safe, then we can relax, open our heart, and be present in the moment. In those cases, we can let our guard down and be completely ourselves. When safety is not present, we are guarded, fearful, suspicious, and defensive. We walk on eggshells and withhold our true feelings, because we are concerned about how the other person will react. We aren't as pleasant to be around either, because we can't be ourselves when we are uptight. We do not feel free to share our opinions, dreams, or desires. A safe environment is critical to connection.

> *A safe environment is critical to connection.*

The two essential ingredients for a safe environment are **trust** and **vulnerability**. Trust is the deep conviction that the other person has genuine concern for our well-being. The more we believe they have our best interest at heart, the more we trust them and the stronger our connection becomes. Trust is essential to any healthy relationship; we need to be able to rely on the people closest to us. There will be times in our lives when a relationship with someone we care about will be tested. We need to know that someone is reliable, and that they will be there for us no matter what.

The core components of trust.

So how do you build trust and store up that precious relationship capital? People tend to trust people when they believe they are interacting with a person who will do the right thing even when no one is looking (depth of character), when they have confidence in their judgment and competence (ability to execute), and when they feel they care about them and have their best interest at heart (capacity to care). When trust is lost, it can almost always be traced back to a breakdown in one of these three components.

Core Components of Trust

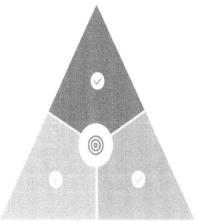

Capacity to Care
People must believe that you care about them and have their best interest at heart.

Depth of Character
People must have faith that you will do what is right even when no one is looking, and that they will get to experience the genuine person.

Ability to Execute
People must have confidence in your judgement to analyze the situation and your ability to deliver on what you are supposed to, or going to, do.

Behaviors that undermine trust.

The three primary components of trust: depth of character, ability to execute, and capacity to care, are key in nearly any relationship. To build trust as a spouse, parent, friend, leader, teammate, or employee, you first need to figure out which component you are lacking and invest energy making changes.

Selfishness, secrecy, and arrogance can all undermine trust in our character. Sometimes highly driven people lose trust in this arena because they prioritize outcomes over relationships. Arrogance communicates a strong message to the people around us that we think we are more important than they are, especially when we constantly make them give in and concede to our desires. Secrecy sends the message that we are hiding something, while selfishness leaves them wondering how often we are going to prioritize our best interests over theirs.

Unclear communication, poor decision making, and lack of follow through can all undermine trust. Sometimes compassionate people lose trust in this arena because they prioritize relationships over tasks. If the message is unclear or we fail to give the information others need, we are withholding critical information that makes it possible for a person to trust us. How we follow through leads people to question our judgement and our ability to deliver on what we are supposed to do. Trust is lost in the little things. If we act irresponsibly and make bad decisions in one area, they will question if they want us in the driver's seat in other areas. If they don't trust our judgment, why would they want us at the wheel? People do not feel safe when our competency and judgement are in question.

Hurtful behavior, failure to notice, and unwillingness to listen can all undermine trust in our capacity to care. Sometimes task-oriented people lose trust in this arena because they prioritize tasks over relationships. Any time we hurt a person with judgment, rejection, shame, threats, condemnation, and harsh criticism, we break trust and create an unsafe environment. Some ways of creating an unsafe environment are subtle and difficult to detect. Each time we overlook someone or fail to notice them or their concerns, we lose a little more trust. When we respond with silence, withdrawal, defensiveness, or an unwillingness to listen, we are not receiving critical information that makes it possible for a person to trust us. Our unwillingness to be vulnerable and share our concerns, fears, hopes, dreams, and opinions are also destructive and cause immeasurable damage to connection or to the possibility of building connection.

Behaviors that build trust.

Humility, transparency, and self-sacrifice convey the message that we can be trusted. If we want to build trust in the depths of our character, we must put other people first or at least learn to recognize when we should do this. Humble people do not feel they have to be right to always get their way or know everything. They allow other people to get the credit. It is understandable to keep some information to yourself, just as it is human nature to want to be recognized for your hard work, but we must all learn to give essential information, share the spotlight, and recognize the contributions of others for a job well done. People must have faith that we will pay attention to the needs and desires of others and help foster confidence in them. We build trust when we are willing to sacrifice our time, energy, and the need to be right.

We demonstrate we can be trusted in our capacity to care when we listen empathetically, treat people in a caring manner, and take the time to get to know them and understand their heart. People must believe we care about them and have their best interests in mind. Taking the time to ask questions and listen communicates you care enough to understand what they are saying and what truly matters to them. If they share that their sister Susie is facing cancer, then remember what they said and ask them how Susie is doing the next time you see them. People trust people who care about their concerns. People feel safe when they can count on us to be honest and kind. When we take the time to find out who they are and what matters to them, we communicate we care and misunderstandings and other relationship woes are minimized or prevented altogether.

Clear communication, sound decision making, and consistent follow-through are critical to creating trust in our ability to execute. Clarity, discernment, and dependability convey the message we can be trusted. There are multiple ways to increase the safety in our relationships, but let's start with communication.

There are generally two ways to communicate complex thoughts. The first takes the audience on a journey with interesting twists and turns along the way. If we take time to give context and build dramatic tension, we eventually arrive at the destination. Many of the world's best storytellers use this technique. The storyteller takes a meandering route until they eventually get to the point. This path is often fascinating but can cause confusion. With all the meandering, detours, and interesting side roads, we can lose our audience along the way rather than build trust in our judgment. To avoid confusion, it's better start with the main point and then build with reinforcing evidence after that. This approach brings clarity and makes it possible for everyone to follow. We build trust when we clearly communicate our ideas by giving people the information they need.

To build trust, people must have confidence in our ability to make sound decisions and to consider how our decisions impact others. Every good decision we make allows others who are watching to trust our judgement in the future. One of the fastest ways to erode trust is to disregard the needs and desires of those affected by the choices we make. *Rebuilding Trust in the Workplace* by Dennis and Michelle Reina, talks in depth about the effects of our choices at work. [4] Of course, it applies to all of our relationships. People need to feel confident that we know where we are going before they will feel willing to follow us.

Sometimes we know what is right, but the execution is the problem. People with good decision-making skills can sometimes not exercise those great skills with the people who are closest to them. How does this happen? Sometimes we need to follow through and other times we need to communicate that we have followed through. You see, communication is *part* of the follow-through. When other people know what to expect, then they can relax. We need to work on becoming dependable and reliable, even in the small things. We need to avoid saying one thing, then doing another. Trust is built through a million experiences. If we act responsibly and do what we say, then the people that depend on us will be able to trust us. We need to keep our promises even when it is inconvenient.

> *Keep your promises, even when it's inconvenient.*

To identify the most important trust component that needs your attention, think of a recent incident when you were not given as much trust as you would like. Then give the person the benefit of the doubt and assume that their inability to trust you is valid because you are the one responsible for the breakdown of trust. What behavior did you exhibit? What words did you say that contributed to them feeling uncomfortable? If you are genuinely wanting to build trust, then look at the pattern of distrust across multiple incidents and hone in on *your* part in the situation. Go ahead, pick two or three events and do a quick trust diagnosis for each one. Then ask yourself: Was I transparent? Did I act with humility? Was I self-sacrificing?

The core components of vulnerability.

Vulnerability is the doorway to connection and has three primary components: openness, risk, and engagement. When vulnerability is absent, it can almost always be traced back to retreating in one of the three areas. We start out early in life, we are open and free to share ourselves and fully engage with other people. Vulnerability can look different, but it always includes opening our heart, risking hurt, and engaging with real people. Without vulnerability, relationships struggle. It builds trust, closeness, and a sense of belonging. Relationships won't thrive without it. Vulnerability is openness to people and experiences and often comes with uncertainty. It's terrifying at times, and always requires courage. We are being vulnerable when we open our heart to reveal personal information that we instinctively want to keep secret. We risk being hurt when we take chances that could lead to rejection and when we admit mistakes that might make others see us as a failure. We engage when we are vulnerable enough to say, "I love you" and "I miss you" to the people we care about. We engage when we ask for help, listen with empathy, and reach out for emotional connection or physical intimacy.

What are the behaviors that eliminate vulnerability?

Building walls around our hearts.

When we get hurt or feel unsafe, we build walls around our heart to protect ourselves from harm. The wall is strengthened and reinforced whenever we experience more pain. Every time someone treats us badly, or we feel rejected, the wall gets bigger, and our defense grows stronger. If someone we trust abandons us or betrays us, then we build the biggest, most impenetrable fortress emotions can buy! We no longer trust that others will respond to our vulnerable hearts in caring and supportive ways, so we shut down and protect our hearts.

Closing ourselves off to people and difficult emotions.

We often close ourselves off to people and difficult emotions because we want to avoid feeling uncomfortable or exposed. We do not want to feel uncertain. We don't want to feel fear. Unpleasant emotions like shame, grief, and disappointment leave us feeling at risk. We armor up because we do not want to feel incredibly painful emotions and get stuck in a dark place. When we are vulnerable, we will experience difficult emotions because it is the place where we are open, at risk, and engaged, but it is also a prerequisite for every meaningful connection that our hearts long for. There is no way to have a good relationship without risk.

> *There is no way to have a good relationship without risk.*

Vulnerability is the doorway to connection. When we close the door, we have placed a barrier to protect us from hurt and uncomfortable emotions, but we have also placed a barrier that will prevent us from experiencing love, joy, and connection. Our defenses are supposed to protect us from alienation and rejection, but they can also ensure our own misery. Both pain and enjoyment come to us through the same entrance. When we close the door to one, we close it to the other. We may get hurt, but the benefits of trusting outweigh the potential pain of not trusting. C.S. Lewis talked about the danger of becoming vulnerable in his book, *The Four Loves*. He said, "Love anything and your heart will be wrung and possibly broken. If you want to make sure of keeping it intact, you must give it to no one, not even an animal. Wrap it carefully round with hobbies and little luxuries; avoid all entanglements. Lock it up safely in the casket or coffin of your selfishness. But in that casket, safe, dark, motionless, airless, it will change. It will not be broken; it will become unbreakable, impenetrable, and irredeemable."[5]

What are the behaviors that demonstrate vulnerability?

Take intentional risks.

There is no way to have a good relationship without risk. Walls are not always bad. They help us navigate painful experiences and give us a safe place to retreat, but they become problematic when they are applied too frequently and for too long. To love another person is to accept that they may let us down, fail to live up to our expectations, or even reject us. Patrick Lencioni says I his business fable, *Getting Naked*, "Without the willingness to be vulnerable, we will not build deep and lasting relationships in life. That's because there is no better way to earn a person's trust than by putting ourselves in a position of unprotected weakness and demonstrating that we believe they will support us."[6] We can take intentional risks for the sake of our most important relationships.

Occasionally, when we take a risk, people hurt us. In my son's backyard, he has a wall around the perimeter. Maybe you do too. His gate is meant to keep bad people out and allow his family members and close friends in. He keeps it closed most of the time. Whenever my son wants to allow people in his yard, he can open it and let them in. Similarly, the gate to our heart can remain closed to strangers and dangerous people, but we must intentionally choose to allow our inner circle to enter the gate to our hearts. What do we do if someone hurts us and makes us feel unsafe? The simple answer is to close the gate and only open it when the person is willing to protect your heart. It is much more difficult if a family member or someone who is supposed to protect us is the source of our pain.

How do we determine if a person is safe? If a person who hurt us has compassion for how deeply they hurt us, has been making changes, and is presently treating us well, then we can consider opening the gate a little bit at a time. If they protect us, then we can risk giving them an opportunity to experience more of us and continue to demonstrate that they are trustworthy. Vulnerability requires risk, but there is a difference between reckless risks and intentional risk. It is reckless to completely open up to someone who continues to be unsafe. It is reasonable to keep our protective wall up and our gate closed as long as we open the gate for our most important relationships. It's important to remember that when trying anything new, it will feel awkward for a while and the temptation will be to run back to what's familiar. If we pay attention, we can retreat behind our protective wall if we need to, as long as the wall is a temporary refuge and not a permanent hiding place. That is the difficult part. Keep the gate open to the people you determine are worthy of taking a risk for and close the gate to the people who continue to hurt you.

Open your heart.

There are no guarantees we won't experience rejection and disappointment, but we can learn skills to handle it when it happens. If we are having trouble opening our heart to people, it may be helpful to think about what we will miss if our heart remains closed. The people we want to be close to will feel our distance and they will miss out on knowing how important they are to us. We will also be unavailable to the people who need us, since the walls we put up make us less effective in reaching others as well.

Jessica was a mom who loved her children but was carrying residual hurt from a past relationship. To protect her heart, she closed off part of it. Unfortunately, her children didn't get much empathy from her because a closed heart is unavailable to show such complex emotions. When Jessica's nine-year-old son did not make the travel basketball team, she responded to his sadness by telling him it was nothing but his own fault for not practicing more. Her son was reaching out for his mom to show him understanding and support, and her closed heart was not available to him when he needed it. If her heart was open, she could have cared about his disappointment and comforted his sadness. She could have encouraged him to focus on some things he could do to become a better basketball player.

What would happen if you opened your heart and let yourself be vulnerable? Will you tell someone who currently doesn't know or never hears it from you that you love them? Jessica should have told her son that she was so sad he did not make the team and asked him what he needed from her at the time. Don't live disconnected from the people you care about. Open your heart and drop your guard to the extent that you can. Your wounds don't need to wound you anymore. Connection will only happen when you are vulnerable. Take down the walls, open your heart, and allow people to give you what you need—true connection.

Fully engage.

We can learn to be fully engaged and emotionally responsive as we allow the people we care about to experience the real us in a deep and meaningful way. This doesn't mean we can attack, criticize, and blame others in the name of honesty. The phrase, "I'm just being honest" is often an unfair excuse to be cruel and hurt people. Friendship requires engagement, which can be difficult when you have been hurt.

We need to move towards the person and engage. It is unlikely that you will ever drift your way into a meaningful connection. We know there is a substantial difference between a routine interaction where we are going through the motions and a meaningful experience where we are connecting. We must intentionally choose to be present in the moment and fully engaged with the person.

We are present when we give the other person our attention, so we need to stop watching the game, checking our phone, or attempting to accomplish other things *while* we are listening. A dedicated presence requires us to ignore the many things that are competing for our attention and focus on being with the other person. When we are fully engaged, we are moving towards the person, initiating conversations, and expressing appreciation. The important people in our lives need to know that we are available, receptive, and willing to share parts of our innermost being. We need to be open enough to reveal some of our internal thoughts, feelings, and dreams, before another person can feel close to us. To love another person is to accept that they may let us down, fail to live up to our expectations, and even reject or hurt us.

Vulnerability is essential for business success because people withhold critical information when they don't feel safe. When a person feels safe to completely show up and share essential information, then the entire organization benefits. People make better decisions when everyone has access to accurate information. Full engagement and good communication will bring another dimension to the productivity of an organization. Creating a safe environment increases connection and makes it possible to enjoy the people you work with. Collaboration and creativity flow when safety is present. When you dismiss all close, trusting relationships, you are also closing the door to great joy and a fullness of the life God intends for you.

What if someone you care about is not vulnerable with you?

If someone is closed off and not fully engaging, it will be painfully hard to experience connection. You can point out their unwillingness to be vulnerable and demand that they open their heart and allow you unhindered access, but that can make things worse. If they have built a wall to protect themselves, that means they feel unsafe. The more we try and knock someone's wall down, the more they will be convinced they need the wall and will reinforce the barrier to keep themselves safe. The best strategy to convince someone to tear down a wall is to acknowledge its existence and show you care about why the wall was built.

Vulnerability is a two-way street. Our loved ones and friends need to know that they have access to our time and attention. They need to know we will receive their thoughts, feelings, and emotions without judgment. When someone shares their heart and discloses information about themselves to us, we must be careful and protect

> *Vulnerability is a two-way street.*

the information they shared with us. If we mishandle the valuable information, they are not likely to be vulnerable with us again in the future.

If you have created an unsafe environment, then you will need to gain awareness of the devastating impact of your behavior and the fear they carry when contemplating trusting you again. You need to become cognizant of what is happening internally during a traumatic encounter, and the lasting after-effects that make them reluctant to trust you. Take ownership of the specific actions that have created the unsafe environment, which includes an understanding that you did something wrong and a willingness to change direction. The genuine article includes regret, remorse, and a genuine concern for the damage you caused. Accepting responsibility for your own thoughts, feelings, actions, and choices is a powerful step. I've found that it needs to be specific and detailed, though. Stop making excuses, stop blaming others, and start taking steps to restore trust and heal the hurt you have caused.

Completing conversations repairs connection.

Every time we have a conversation that brings up an issue that does not get resolved, we are left with an open loop. The unresolved conflict destroys hope and leaves us with an unsettling feeling that we will never be able to solve problems. The more open loops, the more hopelessness we feel. One of the most powerful things we can do is close loops by making sure to complete conversations. A loop is closed when both people are working together to solve the actual problem. There are sequential steps that will make it possible to complete a real conversation, and I will introduce you to the four steps now and unfold them much deeper as we move through the book.

    Step 1: Work together to identify the issue
    Step 2: Determine who gets to talk first
    Step 3: Say things from your heart
    Step 4: Work together to solve the real problem

Every closed loop builds a deeper connection and leaves us with hope, knowing that we will be able to navigate disagreements and become problem-solving teammates. When we can work together to defeat a common enemy and accomplish a shared purpose, we thoroughly enjoy spending time in each other's presence, and we develop a connection that goes beyond words.

Mending hurts repairs connection.

It is impossible to avoid arguments and keep from hurting the people we care about, but we can learn how to heal the hurts we have caused and repair the damage we have done. We can repair the relationship and reconnect with the person we care about. Apologizing, forgiving, and restoring the connection are all essential to maintaining good relationships. The key to not allowing arguments to destroy your relationships is to heal the hurts and reestablish the connection. Unresolved hurts cause damage to your connection. The longer the hurts remain unresolved, the more damage is caused to the connection. Wise people repair a broken connection as soon as possible.

I have watched couples stay mad for months over minor offenses. One time, a wife stayed mad at her husband for two months because he forgot how she liked her burger. The more important the relationship, the higher our expectations become for the other person to meet our needs and fulfill our desires. If she would have met a friend for lunch and the friend forgot to order her burger without mayonnaise, would she tell her friend she is selfish and inconsiderate for not remembering the way she liked her burger? Of course not! She would scrape off the mayonnaise and eat the burger. People experience greater satisfaction in life when they let small offenses go and choose to not let the little things make them miserable.

> *The more important the relationship, the higher our expectations become for the other person to meet our needs and fulfill our desires.*

When you hurt someone else, be quick to apologize for the hurt you caused and do what you can to restore the connection. Everyone is occasionally insensitive, inconsiderate, and selfish. What gets us in trouble is if we apologize and then go on to make excuses for the things we did. Sometimes, we completely undermine an apology by minimizing their pain and telling them they misunderstood our intentions or made a mountain out of a mole hill.

Some offenses are more painful and cause greater damage than others. When someone betrays your trust, their actions often injure you deeply, causing a great deal of pain and sometimes even an attachment injury of the heart. Often, you are left with a confusing mix of jumbled emotions like fear, love, sadness, grief, disgust, and anger. Those feelings are real and reasonable and should not be ignored. Unresolved hurt builds walls between people and changes the way you see the person that hurt you, your relationship, and the future of the relationship. The person you were once close to is not only no longer safe, but also the source of your pain. A breach of trust causes disconnection because the bond that holds you together has been damaged.

When you do not trust a person you care about, it is extremely difficult to experience a close and satisfying relationship with them. It is natural to protect yourself from them, and it is extremely difficult to risk being hurt in the future. Some hurts can be released with relative ease and others require an apology and intentional choice to forgive the person. Other offenses require a change of behavior and repairs for the damage that has been inflicted. Some injuries are so deep that they require outside help to navigate the process. God requires His followers to forgive everyone, but He encourages us to reconcile with only those who are willing to take ownership for the hurt they caused and make the necessary changes to become safe and no longer cause you pain. Please don't ignore the hurt and do what you can to repair the connection. Two important things that impact your relationship are how you argue and how you turn towards each other when attempting to repair the connection after the argument.

Receiving attempts to connect builds connection.

One of my greatest joys as a father has been the privilege of coaching my kids when they played sports. One year, when our son was seventeen, he played baseball. We practiced on a holiday weekend, so all the assistant coaches were gone. One of the boys' dads volunteered to help me run the practice. I was hitting fly balls to the outfield, and the boys were throwing the ball back towards home plate. Unexpectedly, a baseball whizzed about six inches over my head, and soon after, another ball came right towards me. I had to maneuver to block the ball with the bat I was holding. I looked at the dad who was supposed to be catching the baseballs. At that moment, he was ducking away from another ball that was flying in towards us. I finally realized he did not know how to catch a baseball! Seventeen-year-old boys can throw the baseballs very hard, so I had to have an awkward conversation and asked the dad to go back to the stands where he would be safe. I did not want him to get hurt, but I was also terrified of getting hit in the head with a baseball.

When you are playing baseball, you need someone who can catch the ball. When someone misses the ball, it is dangerous.

In relationships, people make attempts to connect all the time, but most of us are preoccupied with other things, so we miss them. They fly right over our heads. When a person tries to connect and someone misses the signal, they experience disappointment, frustration, anger, and eventually they feel the sting of rejection and quit trying. Wise people pay attention to the people around them so they will recognize when they are attempting to connect. There are a variety of good strategies we can use to connect. I want to highlight a few so we can identify them when we see them.

The first connection strategy is to attempt to make things better. When someone you care about hurts you, the bond between you is damaged and needs to be repaired. When a person apologizes or acknowledges their mistakes, they are attempting to repair the relationship and make things better. Unless we receive their attempt, they will assume we did not see it and likely feel like we rejected them. Things get complicated because we judge ourselves by our intentions and what we were trying to accomplish, and we judge others by their actions and what we experienced during the offense.

How to receive attempts at connection:

- Acknowledge it
- Appreciate it
- Accept it

The second connection strategy is to attempt to draw close. There are numerous ways people attempt to do this. People might reach out to grab your hand, smile and try to make you laugh, do something nice, begin a casual conversation, invite you to spend time, give you a thoughtful gift, move in for a hug, or speak affirming words. Things get complicated because we almost always are looking for an expression of love in a way that is different from what they are offering. In order to receive an attempt to draw close, we must either acknowledge their attempt, thank them for it, or accept it. We can learn to acknowledge when people reach out to draw close, even when they do it in a different way than we were hoping to receive. We can learn how to recognize attempts to draw close and accept them. We can say, "Thank you for the thoughtful gift," "I really appreciate your affirming words," "I want to be close to you," or "I would love to spend time with you."

The third connection strategy is to attempt to reach out for support or connection. Mature people make reasonable requests and ask for what they want or need. For instance, "I'd really like to spend time with you doing something fun. Can we put a date on the calendar?" Things get complicated because most people don't even know what they want or how to ask for it in a specific way. Asking for specific help requires vulnerability and comes with the risk of rejection, which is terrifying and incomprehensible. It is much easier to mask our requests in complaints and accusations such as "You never spend time with me." Instead of asking for help with homework, a kid may say, "I have to figure everything out myself" or" There is no way you could even do my homework." Parents have no idea what their child wants and leave the encounter feeling stupid and inadequate. We often are looking for an expression of love in a way that is different from what other people are offering. In order to receive an attempt to draw close, we must either acknowledge their attempt, thank them for it, or accept it. We can learn to acknowledge when people reach out for support even when it comes in the form of a complaint or accusation.

Completing This Leg of the Journey

We almost always minimize our behavior and elevate the actions of others. The result is that most people have no idea how badly we have been hurt by their actions, so they give themselves the benefit of the doubt and assume their good intentions were noted. As a result, they rarely take ownership for the level of pain they have caused, or at least the level of pain we *feel* they have caused. In order to receive an attempt to make things better, we must do one of three things. We can either acknowledge their attempt, thank them for it, or accept it. We can learn to acknowledge when people make a step in the right direction even when they only take small steps. We can learn how to recognize attempts to make things better and receive them kindly. We can say, "I don't feel better right now, but I really do appreciate your apology."

Questions for Discussion

- Think of a challenging relationship you are navigating. What are some of the things that cause friction in that relationship?

- In a current important relationship, what do you do when you feel disconnected?

- Why should you prioritize connection in that relationship now?

- Where do you need to strengthen your connection the most at work, with friends, or at home?

- In what ways do you make the important people in your life feel unsafe?

- What could you do to create a safe environment?

- How can you set aside time for fun, team building, or playful interactions?

- Which person should you make a top ten list for so you can begin thinking positive thoughts about them?

- What happens to you emotionally when you are unable to complete conversations?

- For whom do you need to invest time in repairing hurts that you have caused?

- What would you need to learn or do in order to better receive attempts at connection?

Chapter Three

Avoid Dangerous Roads

Blaming others and making excuses will destroy your relationships.

There is one thing that will complicate all our relationships with our friends, coworkers, and family members. It is far too easy to do and usually brings devastating results. If we do this one thing, we will leave the people closest to us feeling fearful, inadequate, and stressed. If we do it often, it will destroy their trust and wound them to the core of their being. This activity will cause damage to the relationship and ensure our own misery. It will turn us into a helpless and extremely unhappy person. If we allow ourselves to participate in this activity, it will steal our joy and undermine our connection with the people we care about. It will rob us of everything we are looking for in our relationships, alienate the people we care about, and ensure our own misery. If we want to relinquish control of our life, then we can point our finger and blame someone else for everything wrong in our life. Blame is the road to destruction and ownership is the path to freedom.

> *Blame is the road to destruction and ownership is the path to freedom.*

On the other hand, there is another activity that will simplify all our relationships and will improve the quality of our lives. This behavior is hard to do but will leave the people closest to us feeling, safe, important, and relaxed. If we do it often, it will build trust and heal the hurts we have caused. It will empower us to become the best version of ourselves. This action comes with many positive benefits. If we push ourselves to participate in this activity, we will earn the abiding respect of our family members, coworkers, and friends. It will also help us accomplish our goals, improve our health, reduce our stress, and increase our confidence. This one thing will bring us everything we are looking for in our relationships, endear us to the important people in our lives, and ensure peace of mind. The solution is simple, but the application is difficult. We make our relationships better when we take responsibility and focus on ourselves as the person that needs to make changes.

If things are going to be different, then we will have to reflect on what we do wrong and what we can change. Every person will experience disappointment and heartache. We can refuse to take responsibility for our actions and assign blame to someone else, or we can look inward to see what we can change and control. Damaged relationships or more connection...What will you do?

We all make mistakes. We all can think of times in our lives when we would like to have a chance to start over. We overspend when we are already in debt, or we say harsh words to someone we care about. We wish we had a big red "do-over" button that we could push whenever we mess up. I know I do. As a matter of fact, I would wear out the button! If we were given a second chance, would we do better? If we could get a fresh start, would we do something with it? Unfortunately, it has been my experience that, even when people are given a second chance, they usually end up doing the same thing they did the first time. Just because you have an experience does not necessarily mean you will learn from the experience or act any differently.

The only thing more discouraging than hurting the people you care about is making the same mistake over and over again. If you blame someone else, then you will set yourself up for a repeat performance, because if it was not your fault, there is no need to change anything. If we do not make any changes, we will repeat the same behavior another time. Pastor Andy Stanley said in his sermon series called, "Starting Over," that the only way we can make sure that next time does not end up like last time is to take ownership for our own actions.[1] If we refuse to learn from our mistakes, we will repeat them in the future. This applies to business partners, close friends, brothers and sisters, and husbands and wives.

Why do we have such a hard time admitting we make mistakes? Our culture is addicted to blame.

There are three major reasons we struggle to take ownership for our mistakes. First, we live in a culture that is addicted to blame. People distance themselves from failure. Lawyers caution their clients to never admit to any blame. Politicians make a living demonstrating the inadequacy and finding fault in the opposing party. Most complex problems are the result of multiple contributing factors, but it is difficult to focus on all of them, so we generally blame one. When a public person makes a mistake, the media places a target on their back, and everyone joins in on the attack. People are not satisfied until they find a scapegoat and punish them for the mistakes. Blaming has become more than just a process of allocating fault; it often ends in shaming the person and labeling them as worthless. People often conclude that it is unacceptable to make mistakes. We think, "If I make mistakes, people will not accept me. If I get anything wrong, I will be punished."

Blame has an immediate payoff.

Blaming other people has an immediate pay off. It is so easy to blame other people. In doing so, we get to avoid the immediate consequences for our actions, stay angry, and continue our bad behavior. When we blame other people, we receive sympathy from the people we care about, we feel better, and we get rewarded. When we tell our sad story, other people feel sorry for us and give us stuff. If the reason we tell people we lost our job is because we worked for a callous employer that laid off their employees to increase their profit margins, then we get sympathy for our pain. And if you live in Minnesota like I do, you might even get a tator-tot hot dish dropped off at your door! When we blame someone else, we can avoid disappointing the people we care about as well as the embarrassment that comes when we admit we were wrong.

So why is it so hard for us to take ownership? As we all know, it can cause immediate pain to be held accountable for our actions. When we tell the truth of what we did, we experience the uncomfortable emotions of shame and regret, and people sometimes get angry and say harsh words about our character. What if we admitted we got laid off because we showed up twenty minutes late ten times in the last month and did not let anyone know when we were going to be there? When we take ownership and admit fault, no one feels sorry for us, we feel pain, and we are left with the consequences of our irresponsible behavior. We experience deep sadness from disappointing the people we care about.

Our inability to admit mistakes.

We have such a hard time admitting our mistakes because we have a fragile self-image and can't always handle the emotional trauma of taking ownership. Carol Tavris and Elliot Aronson offer a reason in their fascinating book called, Mistakes Were Made (but Not By Me): Why We Justify Foolish Beliefs, Bad Decisions, and Hurtful Acts. "When our behavior threatens our self-concept, our ego automatically goes into hyper-defense mode, circles the wagons, and begins issuing self-justifications designed to protect itself. The higher the moral, financial, and emotional stakes, the more our self-concept and our very identity is threatened, the greater the dissonance that arises, the harder it is to admit a mistake, and the more we seek to justify ourselves to preserve our self-image."2 There are different kinds of mistakes. Some mistakes are insignificant and minor, others are more serious and cause pain. What are you going to do about it?

What can we do to make our relationships better?

We can admit our mistakes, take responsibility for our actions, and make the necessary adjustments. The solution is simple, but the application is difficult. We make our relationships better when we take responsibility and focus on ourselves as the person who needs to make changes.

> *Take responsibility for **yourself**.*

Jesus had an uncanny ability to ask profound questions that cut right to the heart of the matter. In Matthew 7:3-5, He asked two questions that can make a profound difference in our relationships if we are willing to answer them for ourselves. The first question, "Why do you look at the speck of sawdust in your brother's eye and pay no attention to the plank in your own eye?" Notice the comparison between the size of the speck and the plank. A speck is insignificant, and a plank is massive! This question asks us to consider why we look at the insignificant speck and fail to notice the massive plank. It's easy to see the mistakes of others.

After all, the problem is literally staring us in the face. Our coworker is the reason we missed the deadline. Our spouse started the argument. Our neighbor planted the tree on our property. Our child is unwilling to listen to our advice. Our boss or sibling has unrealistic expectations. It's always much easier to identify someone else as the source of the problem. It's more difficult to see our own role in the problem, partially because we are unable to see it ourselves, and even more likely because we don't want to accept responsibility. It's so much easier to blame others and ask them to change instead of doing the hard work to change ourselves. We naturally want to place the emphasis on the changes other people need to make.

The second question in Matthew 7:3-5 is, "How can you say to your brother, 'Let me take the speck out of your eye,' when all the time there is a plank in your own eye?" This question asks how. The picture Jesus uses to illustrate His point is a humorous exaggeration. How would you ever examine another person's eye closely enough to notice a mere speck while you have a tree trunk in your own eye? Jesus' questions can give us clarity if we are willing to look at ourselves as the person that needs to make the changes.

In verse 5, Jesus makes a statement to help us clarify our priorities, "You hypocrite, first take the plank out of your own eye, and then you will see clearly to remove the speck from your brother's eye." Jesus made it abundantly clear where to place our focus. He said we need a major overhaul. Our focus needs to be placed entirely on ourselves. If we take responsibility for our own actions and deal with our own major issues, then we will be able to assist in the minor adjustments of other people. Have you ever had someone attempt to help you remove something from your eye? If so, you can readily understand the amount of gentleness and tenderness that's required. The eye is very sensitive. It takes a compassionate hand and a delicate touch to remove something from the eye.

See ourselves through a different lens.

When we take ownership of our part, we will become a better person, parent, boss, and co-worker. If we want to experience better relationships, we must develop a stronger identity and learn to see ourselves through a different lens. Our identity is the story we define about ourselves.

There are at least three parts of our internal narrative that determine who we are:

1. Values (what we stand for)
2. Competencies (what we are good at and capable of accomplishing)
3. Priorities (what we hold as important and are trying to live up to)

We want to be honest and tell others the truth, but when we are caught telling a lie, we have two choices. We can either make excuses and blame someone else or own up to the lie and admit we did something wrong. When we admit we deceived someone, then we come to the conclusion that we are not a good person because we did not live out our deepest values. We naturally want to find something wrong with the accusation so our internal narrative does not completely unravel. But what if there is another choice? What if we don't have to see everything through such a black-and-white, all-or-nothing lens? The real world is much more complicated than we make it out to be, and we can make mistakes without having to become a bad person. We often hide mistakes because we are convinced others will think less of us if they know the things we have done and the hurt we have caused. We must develop an identity that tells a more accurate story.

> *We must develop an identity that tells a more accurate story.*

The truth is we all want to be a good person, but we don't always make the best choices. We have noble intentions but occasionally, our selfishness breaks through and our less-than-ideal desires are lived out in the form of ugly behavior. If we are going to learn from our experiences and make the necessary adjustments, then we must see the whole picture and tell an internal narrative that includes our mistakes. Is it possible that the definition of a good person is not a person who never makes mistakes, but rather someone who takes ownership for their mistakes and makes the necessary adjustments?

In the first three chapters of Genesis, God shows us why we hide from others and blame them for our mistakes. The problem is shame and guilt. We feel shame when others see who we really are, and we blame others for our destructive behavior. Our shame makes us want to hide; our guilt drives us to blame someone else. Our worst fear has come true when someone else discovers we are an imposter and a fraud. We find ourselves completely vulnerable and go to great lengths to hide our true condition. Guilt reveals we have violated His commands and have done what was forbidden. We find ourselves not worthy of being trusted and terrified of being held accountable. We know that we are not innocent, and our actions are worthy of punishment.

When Adam and Eve sinned, God covered their shame with a garment and promised a solution for their guilt. We can allow our guilt and shame to move us toward God and receive what He has done for us. God graciously provided a solution and made it available for anyone willing to receive it. He wants to cover our shame, remove our guilt, restore our honor with the righteousness of Christ, and declare us innocent because of what Jesus did on the cross. God paid the penalty for our guilt through the sacrificial death of Jesus Christ. He has made it possible for you and me to experience forgiveness and reconciliation!

When we allow God to speak into our identity, we discover that He wants to restore our innocence and give us honor. God is more than a righteous judge waiting to hold us accountable. He is also a loving father who wants a relationship with His dearly loved children. God is just and holy and willing to bring punishment, but He is also gracious and merciful and passionately wants people to come to repentance and enjoy the relationship. Only people who know they are dearly loved can admit their mistakes and take ownership for their irresponsible behavior. When you learn to see yourself through a different lens, the voice of the world isn't quite as loud, and you are able to respond properly to your shame and guilt. *I am not worthless or beyond repair. I am valuable and worthy of honor.*

> *Only people who know they are dearly loved can admit their mistakes and take ownership for their irresponsible behavior.*

God's grace makes it possible for us to admit our mistake and take responsibility for our part in the chaos of our relationships. God's glory is neither enhanced by our success nor tarnished by our failure. When we see ourselves accurately, we will realize that it is okay to make mistakes, and we do not have to be perfect. Before I understood my true identity, I longed to be seen as a good-hearted person who was worthy of respect but unwilling to do the hard work of treating people the way God wanted me to treat them. My shame and guilt no longer have the power to define me. We must learn to see God for who He is, so we can accurately see who He says we are. People who

> *We must learn to see God for who He is, so we can accurately see who He says we are.*

have a strong sense of who they are can admit mistakes without it affecting their self-worth.

Sit with uncomfortable emotions.

If we want to gain the respect our heart longs for, we must learn to sit with uncomfortable emotions and give ourselves an opportunity to change. This is *extremely hard* to do, especially if you have never done it. To be comfortable in the tension of the dissonance our brain feels takes self-control and practice. When we hear the phrase "sit with," what does that even mean, and how do we do it? It means we must notice the emotion, give it attention, and then do something about it. You can no longer ignore it, dismiss it, distract yourself from it, or throw yourself into something else.

Why would anyone want to get comfortable with uncomfortable emotions? Uncomfortable emotions are terrifying to most people. Running from emotions or pushing them away might work temporarily, but they must go somewhere. The feelings that we ignore don't disappear, they just go under the surface. When we stuff our uncomfortable feelings into a box, all of the other feelings get shoved away as well. Silencing one emotion often turns down the volume of other emotions, have you noticed? If we don't allow ourselves to feel grief and sadness, then it will be hard to feel joy and excitement. Stuffed emotions often work their way to the surface and can cause damage to the people we care about.

When we are asked to sit with difficult emotions, we feel like we are supposed to learn to sit next to a scorpion and not move. That does not make sense. The idea of welcoming a dangerous creature with deadly venom to stay a while seems ridiculous. What if emotions themselves are not dangerous? What if the dangerous activity is ignoring or silencing the emotions?

A potentially more helpful way to think of emotions is to see them like we would a friend who cares about us and is trying to get our attention. When the friend approaches us with something important, they want us to pay attention. If we ignore them or dismiss them, then the friend (or in this case, the emotions) will increase their volume and intensity until we notice them and address their concern. The longer we ignore an emotion, the more pain we will experience and the longer it will take us to recover from the pain. Each emotion is pleading for your attention and the longer it goes unnoticed, the louder it becomes.

When we hurt people with our mistakes, we are embarrassed. We failed to live up to our values. We disappoint the people we care about by not meeting their expectations. Our mistakes are in the spotlight. We can either give into the uncomfortable feelings and succumb to the tension by denying we did anything wrong, making excuses for our behavior and justifying our actions, or we can sit with the tension of embarrassment and make the necessary corrections. The next time you experience an uncomfortable emotion from a mistake you made, would you be willing to consider sitting with it? Go against your instincts and give the emotion your attention. Let it sit until you can determine the best course of action. Your emotion is a friend trying to get your attention to put you in touch with what you should do. Before you ignore the emotion, explore it and determine the appropriate response.

If we choose to deny responsibility, make excuses, and assign blame to someone else, then we will temporarily feel better, but we will break the trust of the people we care about and lose their respect. We will be guaranteed to repeat the same mistakes in the future and disappoint the God we serve. We will miss out on a wonderful opportunity to change for the better. An important step in stopping the things we used to do is to gain awareness that we are doing them. We will have tension either way—short-term discomfort or long-term agony. I would much rather feel slight discomfort for a few minutes than misery for several months or years.

The more important the person, the more difficult it becomes to sit with the tension. It is easier to have someone we just met be frustrated with us than a close colleague or family member. It can be extremely uncomfortable when someone particularly important sees us in a bad light. How do we manage the tension? We will feel bad whenever we act unlovingly or bring harm to another person, and we will feel good, in direct proportion, to how we live out who God has made us to be.

Would you be willing to try an experiment the next time you have an argument with your boss, coworker, friend, parent, or spouse? Pay attention to how you feel. If you said something mean, denied their feelings, or were unloving, notice if your feelings are bad or good. If you were kind, generous, or loving, pay attention to how you feel. When a person points out our negative behavior or characteristics, their words should only have power when there is truth to what they are saying. If the words are only partially true, only keep and manage the part that will bring about productive and lasting improvements.

If we are compassionate and kind, and our friend tells us that we are unloving, then their accusations will roll right off our back. When we receive feedback with humility and take responsibility for our actions, we release the tension and begin feeling better. Blame can lead both people down a path of psychological ruin. Taking ownership can mitigate the risk of this happening and will lead us to a place of emotional freedom and peace.

Blame is always hurtful and will cause damage to the relationship no matter how it is expressed. It has devastating consequences in the workplace because when people work in an atmosphere of blame, they cover up their mistakes and hide their real concerns. Emotionally mature individuals can respond with an open mind and consider the possibility that they may be at fault. The best gift we can give the people we care about is to manage our emotions in constructive and honoring ways. We can learn to sit with the tension and respond based on our long-term best interest.

Admit your part.

Before we embark on a journey toward improved relationships, it's important that we've considered the importance of both humility and courage in all of this. Humility and courage are critical in taking our relationships to the next level. It takes courage to admit our part in the breakdown of a relationship. It takes humility to stay with the responsibility long enough to make the necessary adjustments. In James 3:13-4:10, James talks about the kind of wisdom that honors God and works in the real world. The genuine article pursues peace and is fueled by humility. The counterfeit produces conflict because it comes from selfish desires and is fueled by selfish ambition.

When pride takes over, we become focused on our own interests, and we are convinced we are right. Pride and selfishness are a nauseating combination that produce devastating results and ensure our own misery. When pride is leading the way, we are unable to admit fault or take responsibility. When pride is in charge, we treat people badly and tell ourselves they had it coming. The book of Proverbs warns of the painful consequences of pride. "When pride comes, then comes disgrace" (Proverbs 11:2). "Pride goes before destruction, and a haughty spirit before a fall" (Proverbs 16:18). "One's pride will bring him low" (Proverbs 29:23). People who are humble not only get to experience longer lasting and more satisfying relationships, but they also can move on from their moments of misery because they can identify the behavior that needs to be changed and work on it.

Early on in my marriage to Darlene, I was absolutely convinced that she was, at a minimum, at least 90 percent of the problem. My pride would not let me see my part in the chaos of our relationship. God gave me a marriage counselor with wisdom to help me see my part. I'm so grateful for that because we were not on a good path. The marriage counselor patiently listened to me complain and then asked me to consider taking on a very difficult assignment. He said for the next two weeks, I want you to only look at yourself. He said, "It may be absolutely true that your wife is ninety percent of the problem, but for two weeks, I want you to focus only on the ten percent that is your part. Any time you experience chaos in your mind, as soon as you can, record your part." He knew I was a slow learner, so he gave me specific instructions to help me complete the assignment. He said, "Bob, this means that if you have an argument with Darlene or feel tension and know that you did something dumb, leave the room, get out a piece of paper, and write down everything you did to contribute to the tension or misunderstanding. No matter how small of a part you think you played in the chaos, do this for two weeks."

I promised I would remain open and would take note of the part I was playing in the tension in our marriage. I prayed an extremely dangerous prayer. I asked God to reveal to me my part of the breakdown in our relationship. Over the next two weeks, through my attempts at doing the assignment, I discovered that I did three things that caused chaos in our relationship. I actually did more, but at that time, my level of humility was not deep enough to handle more than three things. I was defensive, I withdrew, and when I became really upset, I would say hurtful things and blame Darlene. Thankfully, I was able to admit my part. And I realized very quickly that I was much more than 10 percent of the problem!

Humility gives you the ability to consider the other person's point of view, to look at different alternatives, and to put others' needs before your own. Humility allows you to consider your part and to work on changing it. The next time you have an argument, do you have the courage to ask yourself two difficult questions? Only courageous people admit their part in the breakdown of their relationship, and only humble people sit with both of these questions long enough to get an answer.

Ask yourself these two dangerous questions:

> What was my part of the problem?
> What role did I play?

It's very freeing for us to realize that we can admit our part without appearing weak or believing everything is our fault. There will be times when the majority of the responsibility rests with the other person. Even if the other person is 90 percent to blame, while only 10 percent of the problem is our fault. Think of it this way. Our role is to own 100 percent of our 10 percent! We can do our part, however insignificant (or monumental) it may be. Don't use the other person's awful behavior as an excuse to behave poorly in return. The pathway to peace, freedom, and better relationships is to admit our part.

> *The pathway to peace is to admit your part.*

Stop playing the role of the victim.

If we want to improve our relationships, we need to stop dwelling on how we were wronged and allow God to empower us to become part of the solution. There are three fictional stories I tell myself to keep from taking responsibility.

I tell myself, "I am the victim. It is not my fault." I tell other people only the parts of the story that makes me out to be innocent. I tell my story in a way that strategically avoids telling the things I did wrong or the things I failed to do. I tell about my good motives, which are sometimes a revised version of my true motives. I exaggerate my own innocence and ignore the role I played.

I tell myself, "The other person is the villain. It is all their fault." I place the emphasis on the other person's obvious guilt. I assign them bad motives and give them negative labels, such as control freak or insensitive jerk. I'll say to anyone who will listen, "I had no choice, but to defend myself. Their stubborn unwillingness left me with no other alternative."

I tell myself, "I am helpless. There is nothing else I can do." I convince myself that there is no healthy alternative for dealing with the predicament, so it's best to not try anymore. I say things like, "If I didn't yell at my son, then he wouldn't do the right thing." It's not helpful to focus on the reasons why I am helpless to change my situation. If I want to make things better, then I must allow God to help me determine my part in the breakdown, stop justifying my behavior, and take ownership for my mistakes.

We tell ourselves these fictional stories when we feel inadequate, helpless, or too weary to make things better. We often feel powerless and want to gain control, so we attempt to get the weight of the responsibility off us. Any time we make excuses or blame someone else, we feel like we have gained control, but we have actually rendered ourselves impotent by giving away our power to someone we have no control over.

On Sunday evenings, I get the privilege of working in a marriage ministry with my wife, Darlene, called, "Re-engage," put out by Watermark Resources. The foundational principle in the material is called "The Circle."[3] Individuals are encouraged to draw a circle around themselves and promise to work on changing everyone inside the circle. In other words, we should focus on correcting ourselves first and foremost. That means any relationship in which we are experiencing problems, the person we should work on is ourselves. If a person can grasp that single principle, it literally changes everything. Every bit of energy we spend trying to change someone else is useless, and every bit of energy we spend working on ourselves is productive. If we change ourselves, then we change the entire relationship system and give the other person hope and the ability to let down their guard and engage in healing.

God gave us power to make our relationship better, but the power is found in working on ourselves, responding differently, and treating people the way God treats us. Refusing to participate in a narrative that allows us to be a victim, label others as a villain, or claim helplessness will help us in every relationship, whether it is with a coworker, boss, friend, or child. We will make progress when we learn to focus on ourselves as the only person we can change.

What if the other person is abusive?

I want to be sensitive to the fact that there will be some people reading this book who are in an abusive relationship, or you may know someone who is. If you are a victim of abuse, past or present, listen to what I have to say. The problem isn't the relationship but rather the person who is abusive. The Bible views all forms of abuse as completely unacceptable (Malachi 2:16-17, Psalm 11:5, Colossians 3:19). This includes verbal abuse (Proverbs 12:18, Proverbs 18:21, Colossians 3:8).

Scripture is often used to try to convince a married person to stay in an abusive relationship. God loves marriage! He highly values a committed relationship, but He also hates abuse and passionately cares about the wellbeing of His people. Do not stay in an abusive relationship and do everything you can to protect yourself from dangerous people (Proverbs 27:12; Proverbs 11:9). If you are in danger, it is not in your best interest, or God's intention for you, to remain in an unsafe situation where you are being exploited or abused.

You may need to establish personal boundaries and protect yourself and/or your children. You may need to get support to help you make a safe plan to separate from the person who is hurting you. The abusive person needs to be held accountable and seek the help they need to change their destructive behavior. If there is a truly repentant heart, followed by evidence over time of a drastic change in behavior, then you could choose to seek reconciliation.

In 1 Corinthians 13:4-7, Paul describes what true love looks like in a relationship. The passage says, [4]"Love is patient, love is kind. It does not envy, it does not boast, it is not proud. [5]It does not dishonor others, it is not self-seeking, it is not easily angered, it keeps no record of wrongs. [6]Love does not delight in evil but rejoices with the truth. [7]It always protects, always trusts, always hopes, always perseveres." True love desires the spiritual, mental, physical, and emotional wellbeing of the other person. Staying in a relationship where you allow someone to abuse or exploit you is not helping you or them. Pastor Tim Keller said it well, "Abusers may be so dangerous that to have anything to do with them is to invite them to sin. In that case, the 'good' you can do them is to stay away from them."[4]

Any form of abuse goes against God's desire for how He wants His followers to relate to each other in love. Abuse can take many forms, mental, verbal, emotional, and/or physical. The complexity of the many possible difficult situations is impossible for me to address, but if you or anyone you know is in this situation, please seek professional help. The Bible makes it abundantly clear that all forms of abuse are wrong. When we know what love looks like, we will be able to recognize the counterfeit. When we know how love is displayed, we know how to love others, and we know how to treat others.

Make the necessary adjustments.

Let's go back to the request of my marriage counselor when he encouraged me look at my part of the breakdown in my relationship with Darlene. At first, his request was difficult, because I had spent my entire life developing the survival skill of defending myself against pain. My defenses were supposed to protect me from alienation and rejection, and they did, but in our marriage, they were making us miserable. I needed to learn an entirely different way of interacting with my wife.

At first, I felt completely powerless to make things better. I felt helpless, inadequate, and unable to improve my situation, no matter how hard I tried. It was as if I was a prisoner trapped on the road to misery and there were no off ramps to get to a better destination. God was ready to do some of his best work in my life, but I needed to make the necessary adjustments.

I began a journey that has led to very fruitful, personal discovery. Being defensive creates an environment where the other person does not have a voice to express their hurts, sadness, fear, or disappointment. I have devoted an entire chapter on how to overcome being defensive, because my defensiveness almost cost me my most important human relationship.

In Proverbs 25:28, I read a verse that deeply connected with my situation. A person without self-control is like a city without walls. I felt like a turtle without a shell, vulnerable with no way to protect myself. I needed to learn how to be comfortable with my wife's disappointment and surrender my need to be seen as good, innocent, and loving. I needed to learn how to hear her pain without justifying my position or withdrawing and blaming her. It took time, and I was awkward, but God graciously taught me to live in the tension of her unhappiness long enough to find resolution.

I began learning to love my wife in a mature way. I learned how to move towards her and not withdraw—no matter what. I learned how to acknowledge and validate her feelings and be patient, present, and empathetic. I began taking responsibility for my own feelings, actions, and choices. I learned to pay attention to my own vulnerabilities and identify which of my own buttons were being pushed. For the first time in my life, I listened to my own internal dialogue. God was teaching me how to regulate my own negative emotions. I took ownership for my part of the breakdown in our relationship. I apologized for deeply wounding Darlene and learned how to consider her point of view.

As you keep reading, I will show you how to make each of the necessary adjustments and move into a better future. The blame game is a destructive spiral that leads to unhappiness and disconnection. It starts when one person accuses the other of doing or saying something harmful to the relationship. Instead of giving it consideration, the accused person sends it back with even more intensity. Before we realize what is happening, it is a full-fledged battle to shift responsibility away from ourselves. When two people are blaming each other, there is no listening or receiving going on, only labeling. As long as it continues, there is no resolution or even the possibility of understanding.

Completing This Leg of the Journey

The blame game is an endless loop of destruction and a slightly different version of the merry-go-round of misery. The more we continue in the loop, the more unsafe we feel and the easier it is to see the other person as the source of our pain. It doesn't take long to become an entrenched and vicious pattern. It is a chaotic cycle of unhappiness. The more we take laps around the circle, the more we expect it to end in more destruction. The more we look for it, the more we see it. Before we know it, we find ourselves anticipating the attack and blame them before they blame us.

If we want our relationships to get better, then we need to choose to stop this chaos and get off the merry-go-round of misery. We must stop blaming, labeling, claiming helplessness, and seeing ourselves as an innocent victim. When we take ownership for our behavior and stop making excuses, then we become a vessel for God and can be part of the solution. If we learn to see ourselves as our biggest relationship problem and focus our attention on changing ourselves, we will have the power to change—ourselves.

Questions for Discussion

- What is going on inside of me that makes me want to get out of responsibility?
- In what ways did my habit of not taking responsibility pay off when I was a child?
- How do I dodge responsibility or deflect the blame away from myself?
- Who do I know who wants to be in a relationship with a selfish, arrogant, and know-it-all person?
- What is my first response after I make a mistake?
- Why does pride make it hard to take ownership for my part in the chaos of my relationships?
- What does humility look like in relationships and why is it so important?
- What would you need in order to be able to rest in the tension of difficult emotions?
- What do I need to do in response to the material in this chapter?
- Some people deny that they ever made a mistake. Some people blame other people. Is this my tendency? If so, what can I do to improve?

Chapter Four

Turn Around on a Dead-End Path

Avoiding behaviors that look promising but don't lead anywhere productive.

Darlene and I were headed to dinner to meet our daughter and her fiancé. There were a few factors that complicated the situation. I was hungry, I hate being late, and I am stubborn. I had been to the steak house before, and I knew it was less than five blocks from our hotel. We were supposed to meet them at 5:30 p.m. and it was already 5:40 p.m. by the time we left the hotel. The GPS told us to take a left out of the parking lot and go way out of the way. Darlene also told me to turn left, but I was positive I could save time, so I did what made complete sense to me. I turned right out of the parking lot and proceeded to the nearby service road. When I was able to turn onto the service road; I smiled and told her that I knew this route would get us where we wanted to go.

Unfortunately, the path went two blocks and came to a dead end. I was not easily dissuaded, so I continued in the fruitless endeavor. I pulled into an adjacent parking lot and continued to look for a way to the restaurant. I refused to admit I was wrong until I exhausted every possibility and literally came to a concrete wall which finally convinced me that I could not get there on the path I had chosen. I had to turn around and go back to the hotel parking lot where we originally started twenty-five minutes previous. This time, I turned left out of the parking lot and made it with no issues. I told you I was stubborn!

By the time I admitted the road was a dead end, I was left with some painful consequences. We lost our reservation which added twenty more minutes to our wait at the restaurant. Darlene was rightfully frustrated because I did not listen to her. I had to admit I was wrong and apologize to my wife, my daughter, and my future son-in-law for my immature behavior.

Sometimes we go down a path we are absolutely convinced will lead us exactly where we want to go, but no matter how convinced we are that the path will lead us to our destination, or how much effort we give to it, the road leads to a dead end. Most of the time, we act the way we do because we are convinced our way is best. Wise people are willing to choose the best route to ensure that they arrive at the desired destination. They learn to avoid roads that do not lead anywhere and turn around as soon as they discover it is the wrong route.

Why do we resist change?
We are afraid.

It is part of human nature to refuse change. Most people will not change until their level of pain exceeds their fear of change. Some people are afraid of the unknown, others are afraid of the amount of work they will have to do, and others are afraid they will not be able to change or will not have the motivation to sustain it. Some people are afraid they will make the relationship worse, and others are terrified they will be rejected. What are you afraid of? We act the way we do because we are convinced our way is best and it comes natural to us.

There is one word that can set us on a completely different path that can bring us the fulfillment, meaning, and purpose we are looking for. If we embrace it, the word can change everything. The word is RISK. Moving into uncharted territory requires risk. We are going to have to step outside the familiar and try something different. We need the courage to identify what we need to do and how we need to do it. The first step on a productive journey is to name our fear so we know what we are up against and then take steps to overcome our fear of the unknown and take the risk to embrace change.

We are stubborn.

Most of us have good habits that make us valued teammates, partners, and coworkers, but we also have some bad habits that those closest to us would probably rather do without. One obnoxious behavior, which by now you know I have to work hard to keep under wraps, is stubbornness. It can cause our relationships considerable harm, especially if it becomes a pattern we repeat often. Stubbornness can sabotage our relationships and make us refuse to see the other person's point of view. Refusing to give in can make it difficult to work or overcome obstacles together and can cause fights and eventual break-ups.

We can learn to avoid fruitless pursuits. Michele Weiner-Davis in her book, *The Divorce Remedy: The Proven 7-Step Program for Saving Your Marriage*, educates her clients with a principle she calls, "Stop going down cheeseless tunnels."[1] Before Michele was a marriage counselor, she worked in a lab where they did experiments with rats. In the lab, the maze had five tunnels. The scientist would start the experiment by placing cheese in tunnel number three. As soon as the rat entered the maze, it started going down different tunnels until it found the cheese. After the initial time in the maze, the rat knew to start by going down tunnel number three. If there wasn't cheese there like last time, the rat would try other tunnels until it found the cheese. Michele and her research group discovered that rats stop fruitless pursuits in a relatively short period of time, but she has contrasted this with the human being's tendency to settle into their misery. We are often willing to try something we are convinced will work again and again even if it never produces the desired outcome. If it doesn't work, we will pull out a lawn chair, set up a tent, and keep trying.

How do I recognize when I am on a dead-end path?
Look at the outcome.

I recognize that sometimes we need to persist, hang on, and continue until we have a breakthrough, and other times, we need to recognize we are on a dead-end path and change direction. There are objective criteria to help us see clearly, so we can discern if we are on the right path. There is a powerful question we can ask that will shine a light on the right path. We need the courage to ask ourselves this crucial question: *Are my words and actions allowing me to arrive at the desired destination?* There are two kinds of paths in relationships. We need to pay attention to the end of the road because one path has positive outcomes, deeper connections, a more enjoyable life, a greater level of peace, and an internal satisfaction, while the other path doesn't have an outlet and will not lead us anywhere productive. It will waste our time, increase our frustration, decrease our joy, weaken our connection, steal our peace, and reduce our satisfaction. If the path we are on is producing the desired outcomes, then it makes sense to stay on the productive path. If the activity we are doing or the words we are speaking do not bring us closer to the person we care about or increase our ability to enjoy the time we spend together, then the path is probably not worth doing.

Pay attention to your internal dialogue.

It is important to evaluate our own experience and be honest about our own wellbeing. It can also be helpful to listen to our own internal dialogue. Some of us are not good at determining how we are feeling and assessing how our relationships are going. We need to pay attention to what we say to ourselves. If we are constantly making excuses, blaming others, and having to reassure ourselves that things are going to be alright, we are almost certainly on a dead-end path. We need to pay attention to our thoughts and catch ourselves when we try and sell ourselves on behavior that will undermine our own wellbeing. When we detect we are trying to convince ourselves that we are right, it's time to get completely honest.

Let's look at how Jeffery could have recognized he was on a dead-end path if he only would have paid attention to the outcome his behavior was producing. He was constantly defending himself from his girlfriend, Kimberly's, comments and it was not working. They argued every day for ten days straight. If Jeffrey could have paid attention to his internal dialogue, he would have noticed that he was telling himself two things: *I'm defending myself because she is attacking me*, and *I am unhappy because she is trying to control me*. If Jeffrey's strategy was working, he wouldn't need to make these excuses. When it comes to relationships, some paths are dead ends and do not produce anything meaningful. We need the humility to admit our strategy is not working and stop doing it. That sounds simple. It is simple...but it is far from easy. We, like the example of Jeffrey and Kimberly, are convinced that our strategy should be working, but until we stop doing it, we will continue to experience negative consequences.

Admit your strategy is not working.

Have you ever thought about why a person will try the same destructive thing repeatedly even when they never experience favorable results? Most people act the way they do for one of three reasons. First, they believe that what they are doing is the best way to do things. Second, what they are doing comes natural to them. Third, an important person in their life has modeled the same behavior. Everyone is convinced that their way is the best way, or they would not be doing it that way. The most painful part about turning onto a different path is having to concede we were headed in the wrong direction The further we go down a path in the wrong direction, the more difficult it will be to acknowledge we need to turn around.

> *The most painful part about turning onto a different path is having to concede we were headed in the wrong direction.*

Over the years, I have tried many seemingly innocent things and spoken many seemingly harmless words, but only after I recognized they were destructive and stopped the behavior, did the frustration stop. Whenever we repeat the same mistake and suffer similar consequences, we can ask ourselves a key question: *When will I stop doing what is not working?*

Let me give you an example from a real person. Angela was a single mom with four children. She had to work two jobs to be able to make ends meet. She was often cranky when she finally got home from her long day of work. Angela was exhausted and emotionally drained when she interacted with her children, so she demanded obedience and silenced their complaining. She simply couldn't handle it. Angela felt guilty and knew that being overly critical and emotionally unavailable was not working. She knew in her heart that she needed to swallow her pride and go through the pain of stopping the ineffective parenting. Her friend said, "Angela, you've got to build a connection with each child before they will feel loved. The progress couldn't start until Angela recognized and stopped her unproductive behavior.

In Portia Nelson's poem, "Autobiography in Five Short Chapters," she describes the same remarkable principle.

I.

I walk down the street. There is a deep hole in the sidewalk.
I fall in. I am lost. I am helpless. It isn't my fault. It takes forever to find a way out.

II.

I walk down the same street. There is a deep hole in the sidewalk. I still don't see it. I fall in again.
I can't believe I am in the same place. It isn't my fault. It still takes a long time to get out.

III.

I walk down the same street. There is a deep hole in the sidewalk. I see it there, I still fall in. It's habit. It's my fault. I know where I am. I get out immediately.

IV.

I walk down the same street. There is a deep hole in the sidewalk. I walk around it.

V.

I walk down a different street.[2]

Change our definition of a good person.

When I grew up, I was taught that a good person does not make mistakes and intelligent people do not do dumb things. To make matters worse, both my parents and the most important peers in my life would ridicule, make fun of, label, and isolate themselves from me whenever I was wrong. To admit I was wrong and make a mistake was synonymous to admitting that I was stupid and a miserable failure. Before I could grow out of this, and admit I made a mistake, I needed to learn how to see my mistakes through a different lens. I needed to learn how to distinguish between my thoughts, choices, beliefs, and behavior from my identity as a good person. There is a difference between what we do and who we are. We can do bad things without being a bad person, and we can do dumb things without being dumb.

> *There is a difference between what we do and who we are.*

Humility gives us the ability to see things through a different lens. I had two formidable obstacles that made it almost impossible to admit I was wrong. I did not know how to acknowledge my mistakes and maintain my dignity, especially when I hurt people I loved. I grew up thinking that my beliefs were an essential part of my identity. I thought that what I believed was connected to who I am, and my actions, opinions, and choices were an absolute reflection of my character. I learned that ideas, choices, strategies, and beliefs should be in the process of changing and are not necessarily connected to my intelligence or my character. Changing our belief on "what makes a good person" can have a powerful impact on the way we see ourselves. What if we were to develop and accept the definition that intelligent people are open to new information and believe that their character, intelligence, and abilities can be developed through hard work, concentrated learning, and perseverance?

This new definition can allow us to develop a passion for learning and a desire to be a better person. We can stop wasting our time proving to ourselves and other people that we are intelligent. We can spend our time become a better person and gathering information to improve our situation. If we change our definition, then we can acknowledge we made the best choice given what we knew at the time, but when more information becomes available, it makes sense to change our mind and our behavior. Wise people are open to new information, and good people work on getting better. We can keep our dignity because we do not have to admit we are a personal failure over and over again. It's time to notice when we are operating on false assumptions or trying to use a strategy that is ineffective.

> *Wise people are open to new information.*

Evaluate our experience and learn from it.

It is one thing to stop doing destructive things, it is altogether different to understand why the behavior is destructive and what we could do instead. As I have gotten older, I passionately want to be known as a wise person. The book of Proverbs has profoundly impacted the way I think about change and what is required for it to be lasting. According to Solomon, wisdom is our most prized possession! In Proverbs 8:10-11, he says, "Choose my instruction instead of silver, knowledge rather than choice gold, for wisdom is more precious than rubies and nothing you desire can compare with her." The way you respond to your experiences determines the stories you get to tell, what you can do differently in the future, and how great of an impact you can have on others. Your decision to trust God in life's difficulties may yield some incredible fruit.

We have all watched people we care about make the same dumb mistakes over and over and over without learning anything from them. Experience does not make you wiser or more prepared to navigate difficulties in your relationships. Experience only means you have been through something. But "evaluated experience" prepares you for the future and sets you up for success. Evaluated experience sets you up to make better decisions. We must take the time to understand what we did poorly and why it did not work. We need to put in the time to reflect on what produced a desired outcome and what should probably never be attempted again. You will not learn from an argument until you record the words you used and the responses they produced. Evaluating an experience creates wisdom.

Another verse that has profoundly affected me is Proverbs 24:32. "I applied my heart to what I observed and learned a lesson from what I saw." Solomon understood an important principle. To learn from your experience, you must reflect on what you observed. You must think about what you see and learn from it. When I was in my thirties, I had received a job evaluation that was not very favorable. I heard words I never wanted to hear. I was hurting and willing to ask for help. A wise counselor, William France, taught me that the only way to change your behavior is to "add life experience with your eyes open." When he first introduced me to the concept, I had no idea what he was talking about. He said most people do the same things subconsciously over and over because it brings a familiar and predictable result.

William explained why some women will stay in an abusive relationship; they will choose the known over the unknown every time. The unknown is terrifying because we do not know what to expect. He said if I want to change, then I have to pay attention to what is happening inside me—my feelings. He said to watch and see how the other person reacts. I did not know at the time that he was teaching me the same principle that Solomon understood. Yogi Berra described the same idea with fewer words: "You can see a lot just by looking."[3] Wise people live with their eyes open and learn from what they see.

Evaluated experience is a top-tier and very productive skill! With this mindset, we can add life experience with our eyes open. Anytime we experience something difficult, we must take time to learn from it. We can learn from bad decisions, senseless arguments, thoughtless words, and bad attitudes. The same principle applies to positive experiences, by the way. We can learn from good decisions, productive arguments, considerate words, and good attitudes. When we gain clarity from our reflection, then we will make better decisions (or more good decisions). There are some important things that we need to get right in order to experience satisfying relationships.

Imagine how much pain we would avoid if we could learn from our mistakes and allow God to use our heartache to benefit other people. God works all things together for the good of those who love Him. God can provide purpose in our embarrassing moments and meaning in our pain if we are willing to invite Him in and ask Him to help us learn from our experience. God will bring healing and hope to the people who are willing to surrender their experiences to their Father who loves them.

Make the appropriate changes to our actions and behavior.

There is good news if you are currently suffering from the consequences of a dead-end path. Our actions, not our intentions, will determine our destination. Some paths initially look promising but are essentially dead-end routes which do not allow us to make progress towards our desired destination. Let me give you an example from two real-life strangers who have two things in common but have never met. One person was willing to make changes and the other one was not. Jimmy and Laney were both in long-term relationships that came to an end. They were both devastated and deeply wounded by their breakups.

Jimmy was accused by his girlfriend, Corrin, of unleashing his criticism and saying shaming words when she did not live up to his expectations. Jimmy was disappointed and felt unfairly accused. He was willing to admit that his criticism played a role in the breakdown, but he was unwilling to acknowledge his words were harsh or shaming. He also refused to see how painful his words were to his girlfriend. When he felt rejected and unfairly accused, he did not give Corrin's concerns any consideration. He focused on the unfairness of the accusation and tried to convince her that his criticism was really loving because it would help her grow into a better person. After the breakup, he remained confident he was not the problem. Jimmy did not evaluate his behavior, nor did he make any changes. He determined he did not do anything wrong and blamed Corrin for falsely accusing him and refusing to see how much he loved her through all the wonderful things he did to demonstrate his affection.

In the other example, Laney was accused of withdrawing and staying distant whenever she felt emotionally overwhelmed. Laney was equally disappointed when her boyfriend, John, ended the relationship. In his words, he said, "Laney is impossible to connect with because she shuts down, runs away, and closes me out."

Laney felt unfairly accused, but after two months of recovering from the painful rejection, she wondered what she could learn from the experience. She gave some consideration to the possibility that shutting down, pulling away, and remaining unavailable could be difficult and painful for her boyfriend or to anyone in her life for that matter.

Laney had an entirely different response than Jimmy. They both felt rejected and unfairly accused, but she began asking questions and reading everything she could about the negative impact of running away. Laney took ownership for her part of the breakdown and started making changes. She even started looking into *why* she ran away. It was difficult and at times overwhelming, but her discoveries were fruitful and helped her move into a better future. It's easy to blame a breakup on your circumstances or your partner, but if you do that, you will likely bring the same destructive behavior into your next relationship.

So much of what we do to try and make things better ends up alienating the other person and making things worse. One thoughtless word or selfish action can evaporate hours of positive momentum. Everyone wants to enjoy time spent with their friends, get along with their parents, experience great relationships, and/or earn the respect of their adult children.

> *Intentions do not change your relationships—choices, words, and actions do.*

Intentions do not change your relationships—choices, words, and actions do. We can move into a better future if we have the courage to identify what we need to do and do it. There are many paths that do not lead anywhere productive. There are thirteen behaviors that are so damaging, they are addressed at length in this book.

Anyone can talk about being willing to change, but very few identify the specific behavior they need to change, and even fewer actually do anything about it. If you want to change but you're not willing to change, then even the greatest idea, process, or method will not help you achieve want you want. You could hear the most innovative idea from the most prominent expert, and it won't make any difference or do you any good, at least not until you are ready to change.

Take a moment and read the following list of thirteen dead-end paths and identify one thing you need to stop doing. Then read through the thirteen paths that will lead to your desired destination. Each of the positive behaviors will improve your relationships. If you need help identifying the specific behavior, then stop and ask God to help you see which one needs your attention. If you are courageous, then ask three people you trust to point you in the right direction. See what patterns emerge in their answers and consider what they have to say.

Dead-End Behaviors	Desired Destination Behaviors
1. Assigning blame to another person for the chaos in your relationship	1. Taking responsibility for your part of the chaos in your relationship
2. Invalidating another person's feelings by denying, disregarding, or dismissing their experience	2. Validating and acknowledging the other person's experience
3. Unleashing your negative emotions	3. Managing your emotions in constructive and honoring ways
4. Defending yourself, taking things personally, or protecting yourself	4. Receiving what they say by seeking to understand before you respond to what they are saying
5. Telling another person what to think or feel	5. Asking another person what they and feel and listening carefully
6. Saying shaming or overly critical things	6. Speaking life-giving and encouraging words over them
7. Withdrawing and remaining emotionally unavailable	7. Moving towards them and remaining emotionally available
8. Refusing to apologize for the hurt you have caused	8. Apologizing for the hurt you have caused, taking steps to repair the relationship
9. Starting a conversation harshly	9. Starting a conversation gently from the heart
10. Threatening to leave or abandon a person	10. Finding ways to affirm your commitment to the other person

Dead-End Behaviors	Desired Destination Behaviors
11. Using another person's vulnerabilities against them	11. Understanding the other person's vulnerabilities and protecting them by treading softly with care
12. Forgetting the things that are important to another person	12. Remembering the things that are important to the other person
13. Pushing through boundaries to get your way	13. Respecting boundaries and patiently waiting until the other person is ready

Now that you have identified what you need to do, you can start making the necessary adjustments and do something about it. Any time we try to change, we will face obstacles. Some will come from other people, but most will come from within.

There are three essential ingredients to make lasting change. I dare say you will not change if any of them are missing:

1. a compelling vision of where you want to go

2. a realistic strategy to help you get from where you are to where you want to end up

3. a willingness to change

You can get a compelling vision and a realistic strategy from other people, but the willingness to change must come from yourself. Anyone who's ever had to lose weight understands this firsthand. If you want to change, but you're not willing to change, then any idea, process, or method will not help you achieve want you want. Without a willingness to change, all the expert advice in the world is useless.

We will need perseverance, commitment, and focused attention to overcome the obstacles. To increase our chances of success, we need to surround ourselves with two kinds of people. Look for people who have made the change we want to make and learn from them. Next, look for people with empathy who can give us the emotional support we will need. You can find help in an individual such as a trusted friend, pastor, mentor, coach, or counselor, or in a small group made up of friends or neighbors or people from your church.

A genuine act of love or appreciation is giving another person something that is important to them, whether we understand it, like it, agree with it, or not. We will not get to reap any of the positive benefits until we make some personal changes and do things differently. We can learn how to demonstrate love and appreciation to our friends, parents, business partners, children, and spouses the way they want to be loved and appreciated. If our present strategy is not working, then we might want to consider trying a different strategy. What we need is the courage to identify what we need to do and to do it.

> *Identify what we need to do and to do it.*

Three dead-end paths and what to do about them.

Let's look at three of the dead-end paths from the chart in this chapter that are sure to cause damage and observe why they don't work. After we see why they are fruitless, we will see a productive path that will produce much better results.

Dead-end path #1: Harsh Start Up.

Starting a conversation harshly by attacking another person is almost never a good idea. The first minute of an argument sets the tone and is extremely important. Jake was having a great day when he noticed that one of his employees returned the truck to the shop without any gas. He ran into the warehouse and started yelling at Mark. He said, "You selfish [*bleep*], you never give any consideration to anyone but yourself." Mark immediately responded by moving towards Jake and giving him a piece of his mind, he could not afford to lose. Jake got in Mark's face and started screaming, "I think I'm going to fire you today. You are a useless employee!" How did the encounter get so bad so quickly? Jake actually liked Mark and thought he was a very good employee.

A harsh start up puts the other person on the defensive and can escalate very quickly, even when the person who started it didn't intend to go far. When a legitimate complaint, concern, or point is brought up in a harsh manner, things will almost always go sideways. Starting a conversation harshly is a dead-end path because it combines emotional intensity with anger, assumptions, and accusations. The person on the receiving end must overcome so many obstacles before they can hear anything that is said. The higher the intensity, the lower the understanding. When you combine intensity with harsh comments, that is a perilous combination.

A harsh start up can be more subtle but just as ineffective. Julie was looking forward to her son, Trevor, getting home. He had gone on his first date with a new girl he met online. Julie was wanting to find out how they interacted. She was hoping to connect with her son, and she was excited, anxious, and concerned. When he came home, she met him at the door and said, "We need to talk." Trevor turned around and walked right back to his car without saying a word. Julie only said four words and the conversation was over. Most people do not know what to do with an intense start to the conversation, because the fast start can trigger feelings of inadequacy or make them fear the conversation before it even starts.

Start a conversation gently from the heart.

When a conversation is started gently from the heart, it will often produce a better outcome. Julie could have waited a few minutes after her son arrived home and said more gently, "When you have time to talk, I would love to have the privilege of hearing about your date." Start conversations slowly and pay attention to how you talk. Take time to build rapport and establish common ground by having casual conversations about ordinary things. Be friendly, pleasant, playful, and available. A simple change can affect the entire outcome.

If your mood is relaxed, calm, and peaceful, then it will make a difference. Pay attention to body language, eye contact, and facial expressions. Try smiling and entering the conversation slowly. Share details about yourself and ask the other person nicely if you need their help or want them to do something for you. The first five words can improve all your conversations, not just the ones that you think will be difficult. If the only time someone starts a conversation is when there is criticism, then the other person may not want to have any more conversations with that individual. We all are significantly more likely to listen if the other person is responsive, cooperative, and kind. Remain open and be willing to generate options, consider alternatives, and propose solutions. Stay calm, flexible, curious, and relaxed.

Dead-end path #2: Threatening to leave.

Threatening to leave or abandon a person you care about is a dead-end path. This path will lead you to destruction. Usually, people resort to threats when they are desperate and have a particularly important longing/desire they want to communicate and have no way of expressing it. What they really want is to have the other person hear their concerns, change their behavior, reassure them, and/or demonstrate how important the relationship is to them. Unless the other person is extremely mature emotionally, they will not be able to hear your longing and address your concerns and needs.

Karla worked for Jenny in a rapidly growing organization. As the company continued to expand, the demands upon the employees continued to increase. As the orders increased, more deadlines were missed, and more customers were dissatisfied. Karla approached Jenny, asking her to add more staff to keep up with the demands. Jenny wasn't opposed to hiring more people, but she was unsure if the growth would be sustainable. Mostly, she didn't want to hire people and then have to let them go. On Friday afternoon, another order came that was impossible to fill. Karla was overwhelmed and frustrated by constant stress and relentless pace, so she walked into Jenny's office and said to her, "If you don't address this issue and get some new people hired by the end of the month, I will be turning in my resignation and finding another job."

A threat to leave puts people on the defensive and sets them up to protect themselves from you. It is easy to hear threats as blame. When you say, "I have no choice but to leave," you are basically saying the other person is the problem. They will resist you because they will feel forced to give into your demands against their will. Threats of abandonment do not solve relational problems and will create a much bigger problem. The person you threatened will subconsciously begin thinking of life without you and pull away from you emotionally. It's an instinctive protective measure. The more important the relationship, the more dangerous the threat is. If you have ever threatened to leave, please pay attention to how painful it can be for the other person. Hearing that a person you depend upon is threatening to leave can be very traumatic.

Some people say to threaten abandonment is manipulative, others take it a step further and say, it is abuse, while others call it emotional terrorism. I cannot argue that some threats are extreme. Threats of abandonment are the equivalent of pulling out a hand grenade because that's the kind of damage it causes. Threatening to leave undermines trust by creating an unsafe environment for connection. For some, it communicates that the relationship is fragile, unable to stand under any pressure or stress. For other people, usually people who have been wounded in this way in the past, it triggers a pain that goes to the core of their being. Once their fear of abandonment is triggered, it is almost impossible to undo. They will walk on eggshells and live in constant fear.

Affirm your commitment.

There is a more productive way to address the underlying issues and make things better. When we feel like we are not able to communicate the importance of our concerns, we jump directly to the ultimate weapon, which is to threaten to end the relationship altogether.

Here are a few ways Karla could have expressed her concerns to Jenny more effectively:

1. My frustration is growing because the problem is increasing, and I feel like you are not listening. Could we take a few minutes to talk about how significant the problem is becoming?

2. I am afraid our employees are experiencing a toxic environment that will cause some of them to leave. When can we set a time to work on solving this problem?

3. I can understand your concern about adding employees at this time. Your loyalty and commitment to your employees is the very reason why people want to work for this company. Could we talk about the specific metrics we would need to hit to be able to add staff?

If you have ever gone down this dead-end path of threatening to leave, I would strongly encourage you to avoid it before you do permanent damage. Affirm your commitment to the other person. Take some time and learn constructive ways to communicate your important longings, apologize for instilling fear in the people you care about, and repair the wounds you have caused. Be careful not to use threatening language, because it can trigger fear of abandonment and can undermine the security in the relationship. There are more effective ways to express an important concern, such as identifying the longing and expressing it. For those of you who are married, divorce threats often stem from an inability to directly communicate the underlying problem. The longer you go without addressing the problem, the longer it will take you to unravel it all in the future.

You will be significantly more effective in getting people to give your concerns consideration if you learn to speak words that affirm your commitment and build safety with people. I'm talking about words like, "I am committed to you no matter what" or "We can accomplish this together." Commitment is essential to building security in a relationship. If a person knows they can rely on you, then they will have more emotional freedom to work through issues, endure difficult seasons, and move into new levels of intimacy.

Dead-end path #3: Telling another person what they need to think or feel.

How do you get people at work to follow your lead? How do you get them energized and committed in such a way that they not only support your initiatives but carry them out? How do you get your family members to see you in a positive light? Most people are convinced that if they can just get the other person to see the logic in their position, then the other person will come to the same conclusion and see them in a positive light. Each person thinks, "If I can only get this person to listen to what I intended, then they will see the rationale behind my actions." This approach does not work and usually makes things worse.

I call it the "convince-and-tell strategy." It is fundamentally based on the flawed premise that other people have the same thought processes we do. If we tell them what they are missing and convince them what they should feel, then they will come to the same conclusion and accept what we are saying as fact. Not only do they not have the same thought process, but they have completely different motivational drivers. Everyone is unique and motivated by a different combination of factors, and we have different ideas about what is reasonable. Every person has a unique profile of motivational drivers, values, and biases. This frequent mismatch of perceptions leads to unsuccessful attempts at motivation.

Ask what they think or feel and then listen.

Is there a better way to discover what is going on inside a person? Rafael spent three months trying to convince his son, José to participate in a three-week, elite pitchers boot camp during his summer break. José was a very talented baseball player who made the varsity as a freshman in high school. The head coach pulled the father and son aside and told them he had never seen such natural pitching talent in his lifetime. Rafael tried to convince his son to go to the camp by telling him he could improve his pitching and earn the opening day starter position as a sophomore. He told him the camp would increase his velocity and give him quality secondary pitches to get strike outs. He told him he could use it to take his game to the next level and command the strike zone, and if he could do that, he'd get an NCAA Division I scholarship and a totally free education.

The more Rafael tried to convince his son, the more José resisted, and the more disconnected he became. Rafael was convinced if he could tell José what to think and what to feel, that he would motivate him to want to fully participate. Instead of using the flawed strategy of showing and convincing, he could have employed the effective strategy of listening to discover his son's thought process and personal motivational drivers.

If Rafael would have taken the time to discover what José was feeling and what he was thinking, he would have understood why he was resisting. José was not opposed to going to the pitching camp or improving as a player, but what his dad didn't know is that he was looking forward to going to a different camp to meet a girl that he met at that camp the previous year. Her name was Ashley and she had captured José's attention. They had been texting and learned that both camps were happening at the same time. Rafael would have had a significantly better chance of motivating José if he took the time to understand what motivated him. You will make progress when you stop looking at the situation as a problem to solve but rather, a person to understand. This is such an important idea that I have devoted two entire chapters to give you the skills to become proficient at increasing your influence with others.

> *You will make progress when you stop looking at the situation as a problem to solve but rather, a person to understand.*

Completing This Leg of the Journey

Are you willing to choose the best route to ensure that you arrive at the desired destination? We need to pay attention to the end of the road. How much pain will it take for you to learn to avoid roads that do not lead anywhere? When it comes to relationships, some paths are dead ends and do not produce anything meaningful. Turn around as soon as possible when you discover the road is a dead end.

Questions for Discussion

- Why do your friends have such a difficult time changing?

- How often do you dig your heels in and refuse to change?

- Do you agree that people will not change until their level of pain exceeds their fear of change? What does that mean in your own words?

- Share a time when you watched someone endure a considerable level of pain because they were afraid to change.

- There are three reasons most people act the way they do. 1) They believe what they are doing is the best way to do things. 2) What they are doing comes naturally to them. 3) An important person in their life has modeled the behavior. Which of the three reasons most often determines why you act the way you do?

- Why should you evaluate positive experiences that are working and producing the desired outcome?

- Have you ever watched a friend or loved one make the same mistakes over and over and over without learning anything from their past? If yes, what kind of emotions did you experience? What do you wish they would have been willing to change?

- Which damaging behavior are you likely to implement? What could you do differently?

- Which conversation topics are the most likely to prompt an argument from you?

- Why do you think sincerity and commitment are not enough to make lasting changes?

Part Two:
Ask Clarifying Questions to Help You Stay on Course

Chapter Five

Stay on Course

*Paying attention to the mode you are in and
moving toward the productive mode.*

Is it possible to respond in a productive manner to the people we care about when our fears are activated and our emotions are heightened? Can we change the way we operate when we feel like we have been treated unfairly?

It started with an innocent comment. For six months, Victor worked long hours while his wife, Trish, felt disconnected from him. Both exhausted and in need of some rest, Victor rented a beautiful cabin overlooking a magnificent lake. Trish was feeling cared for, snuggled up to Victor, and said in a soft voice, "I appreciate you so much, thank you for bringing me to this amazing place. Everything would be absolutely perfect if you would have left the laptop at home."

Victor reacted to her comment by saying, "Why do you have to ruin every moment?"

Trish's disappointment was all over her face. By this time, they were both sitting up, fully awake, and looking at one another. She asked, "What exactly did I ruin? I thanked you for getting us an amazing place. Is it a crime to show appreciation?"

Victor rolled his eyes and said, "You had to comment on the laptop. Didn't I warn you I would need to spend at least two hours finishing the project?"

Trish was indignant and said, "Why did we even come up here if you were going to spend an entire day working?"

Victor was frustrated and replied, "I haven't even touched the computer yet. The only reason I work so hard is for us, you know. And it's my work that makes it possible for us to even come to this cabin."

Trish retorted, "Your work is the only thing you care about. I can't believe I fell for this. I knew you were not going to spend time with me. You don't actually care about my feelings, and you are selfish."

Victor's heart was pumping, his hands were sweating, and his shoulders were getting so tight he could no longer concentrate. He was feeling unfairly attacked. He was defending his character as if his life was at stake. He said with heightened emotion, "How could you say I am selfish? You get upset over the mere presence of a computer and are willing to ruin our entire weekend over it." He continued sarcastically, "You are correct that I am selfish. I have had it with your ridiculous accusations."

Trish stood up and shouted, "If this is how you are going to treat me, I am going for a drive." She got in the car, slammed the door, and drove away. Victor sat in complete silence wondering how things got so bad so quickly, feeling helpless to make things better.

How did that conversation get off track so quickly? What could Trish or Victor have done to make that encounter more productive and less hurtful? All of us get caught up in these negative interactions at some point in our relationships. Sometimes they can be brief and insignificant, and other times, they are habitual responses that cause distress. Sometimes, all it takes is a hint of negativity to set off a firestorm of destructive behavior. Eventually, the toxic patterns can become so engrained and permanent that they undermine the entire relationship.

When people are frustrated or under stress, they tend to either attack another person, defend themselves, withdraw from the source of pain, or freeze and do nothing at all. The mode or automatic reaction is the way a person operates on autopilot when under stress.

Fighting is Trish's automatic reaction. She reacted strongly because she was convinced a softer response would not get through to her husband. She felt she needed to make him understand how wrong he was and how hurt she felt, and her job was not done until both were accomplished. After all, she had told him what she needs before, and he had ignored it. Trish felt completely justified for feeling angry and reacting the way she did.

Defending is Victor's automatic reaction. Feeling misunderstood makes him angry, and he can hardly form the words fast enough in order to defend himself against the accusations. In interactions like the one he and Trish had at the cabin, his mind is filled with thoughts like, *I am not even sure I want to be in a relationship with someone who is completely irrational and sees me in such an unreasonable and unfavorable light.*

The more Trish attacks Victor, the more he defends himself, and the more he defends, the more cutting the attack becomes. The stronger her attack, the more he is convinced that a vigorous defense is the only reasonable response.

That night at the cabin, Victor and Trish were both on edge. Their senses were heightened and keenly aware of what was going on around them. Trish's physiological response prepared her to move into the fight and leave the scene. The unconscious threat prepared him to armor up, stand his ground, and when Trish left, he completely shut down.

Like Victor, when that part of our brain gets activated, we react instinctively without awareness of our own destive behavior. When we are faced with a perceived threat, our brain senses danger and considers the situation to be life threatening. As a result, our body automatically reacts to keep us safe.

Most subconscious reactions to overwhelming, emotional situations are unproductive. The more distressed people are, the more they resort to automatic, habitual reactions, and the more they open themselves up to vicious spirals of unhappiness that push people further and further apart. As more and more painful encounters take place, each person is left feeling unsafe and will resort to unproductive behavior. Each person is left assuming the very worst about each other and the relationship. The good news is there is a better way, but it requires an entirely different way of responding.

If we want to enjoy satisfying relationships, then we need to pay attention to the way we react when our fears are activated and our emotions are heightened. When we are emotionally overwhelmed, we need to be willing to make the necessary changes to our own behavior. Some people attack, some defend, some withdraw, and some become paralyzed. If you can identify the behavior pattern, I call them modes, then you can take appropriate action and stop the destructive behavior.

As you read through the four destructive modes below—Attack Mode, Defend Mode, Withdraw Mode, and Freeze Mode—do your best to identify which one of the four negative modes is your go-to mode and which one is your secondary mode. Some of us have the special ability to react badly in all four destructive modes!

ATTACK MODE

When this group is overwhelmed, they assign blame, make accusations, and point out the other person's flaws and shortcomings. They criticize the other person's motives, feelings, actions, intentions, and even character. Sometimes an attack can be subtle and other times, it can be outright hostile.

Insight into their thinking: Attackers secretly want the other person to recognize and receive their attempt for connection, hear their heart, and move closer to them. They desperately want their perspective to be understood. The reason they blame and get aggressive is to get a response. They might even feel their aggression is going to be helpful.

Likely Result: The people attacked will almost always leave the encounter feeling blamed, vulnerable, and unsafe.

DEFEND MODE

When this group is overwhelmed, they protect themselves by denying responsibility and trying to prove they are not to blame. Feeling like their entire well-being is at stake, they desperately defend their motives, feelings, actions, intentions, and even character.

Insight into their thinking: Defenders secretly want the other person that is hurt, frustrated, or in pain to hear their excuses as proof that they are kind, loving, and worthy of connection. It feels to them like a matter of life and death. The reason they defend is to prove their innocence.

Likely result: The people pushed away from this rigorous defense will almost always feel alone, unheard, unimportant, and unloved.

WITHDRAW MODE

When this group feels overwhelmed, they run from the source of the pain, pull away emotionally, and hide—for as *long* as it takes. Often, the rejection and disapproval they feel causes so much pain, they feel their only option is to close off the conversation and shut out the other person.

Insight into their thinking: Withdrawers secretly want the other person to notice they are pulling away, stop hurting them, and respond with kindness. They feel their actions are honorable and have no idea how destructive disconnection and silence can be to a relationship. The reason they run is to create space between them and the person who is causing them pain.

Likely result: The people left alone will almost always feel isolated—as if their partner or friend is neither available nor receptive to their needs.

FREEZE MODE

When this group is overwhelmed, they panic, get emotionally overpowered, and do...NOTHING. Paralyzed, they go numb inside and look for ways to escape and distract themselves. They watch T.V., go shopping, play video games, and immerse themselves in anything but what they need to be accomplishing, such as talking things out with the person who is harming them.

Insight into their thinking: Freezers secretly want the other person to see their pain and reach out to comfort them. The reason they freeze is they are either terrified they will do something wrong or can't decide how best to respond. They feel helpless to please the person they care about and fail to recognize that hiding out and escaping rarely makes things better.

Likely result: The people who are "frozen out" will feel frustrated because they can't get freezers to move towards them, so they leave the encounter feeling distance, disapproval, rejection, and disgust.

All four destructive modes can escalate the situation, make things worse, and increase the length of the disconnection. Whenever we attack, defend, withdraw, or freeze and do nothing, we increase the disconnection and heighten the emotional distress. The person who is reaching out and looking for a response is asking the questions, *Are you available? Do I matter? Can I count on you to be there for me?* When the answer to any of these extremely important questions is *No*, then the person's internal chaos intensifies and makes all their hurts, fears, and vulnerabilities part of the conversation.

To make matters worse, Attack Mode, Defend Mode, Withdraw Mode, and Freeze Mode all create an additional problem. Not only are you unavailable and not receptive to the other person's deepest longings, but now you are subconsciously communicating that you don't care, that they are not important to you, and that you do not value the relationship enough to try. They originally felt disconnected, isolated, and alone and those feelings are confirmed and compounded by the feeling that they are unloved, disrespected, and unworthy of connection. Fortunately, there is a better way! God has given us a way to respond that will not make things worse or create additional problems.

Whenever we are hurt or emotionally overwhelmed, there is a better way. We can choose the Productive Mode—an approach where we intentionally move toward the other person. If we ask ourselves, *What response mode am I in?* and give an honest answer, we can take appropriate action and choose the mode that will make things better.

PRODUCTIVE MODE

Fortunately, there is one mode that will lead us to better results—Productive Mode. When this group is overwhelmed, they respond by moving towards people with gentleness and receptivity. Take appropriate action and choose the **only** mode that will make things better. When you are overwhelmed emotionally, attack, defend, withdraw, and freeze are not your only options. First, move towards them by showing interest, concern, care, and enjoyment—show a desire to connect with them. Second, receive their words by trying to understand their perspective—it is critical that you are willing to be influenced. Third, pay attention to the impact your words and actions have on them—you must be friendly, patient, and kind and avoid being harsh, mean, or critical.

Insight into their thinking: This is the only mode that will make things better. Using this mode, you will not escalate an existing problem or create another one.

Likely result: The people you care about will experience your respect, approval, and appreciation. They will feel safe, heard, valued, and important.

We can learn a better way.

God has given us a way to successfully navigate difficult situations if we are humble enough to listen. Jesus gave us a road map in Luke 6:32-34. He helps us identify a pattern most people live by but does not work. He said, [32] "If you love those who love you, what credit is that to you? Even sinners love those who love them. [33]And if you do good to those who are good to you, what credit is that to you? Even sinners do that. [34]And if you lend to those from whom you expect repayment, what credit is that to you? Even sinners lend to sinners, expecting to be repaid in full." (NIV) Jesus asks the same question three times to see if we treat people the same way they treat us.

Henry Cloud, bestselling co-author of the book, *Changes That Heal*, says the same thing with different words. He says, "If you play fair, you will ruin all of your relationships."[1] By playing fair, he means that people are required to treat other people the way they are treated. They are nice as long as they are being treated nicely. They are loving as long as they are being loved. If someone gives us less than we desire, then we can give them less than they desire right back. If we play fair, then we give others exactly what they deserve.

Treat people better than their actions deserve.

We must stop reacting to the way other people treat us and instead, respond in ways that are more productive. Most people try to play fair and react to people the way they are treated. This pattern works well when people treat each other well and act maturely. It is very easy to be kind when we are treated kindly, but what happens when people are mean, or we perceive their actions to be mean? As soon as one person feels like they are being treated badly, then everything breaks down. The only way to move the needle in our relationships is to treat people with more kindness and patience than their actions deserve.

When we are treated unfairly, and our sense of justice is violated, we want to respond in the same way so they will know how it feels. If they hurt us and we hurt them back, then we are nothing but stuck in an endless cycle of misery. Trish and Victor were good people who came from great families, but they were caught in a destructive cycle. They were treating each other the way they were treated, or worse. When Trish attacked, Victor defended. When Victor defended, Trish increased the intensity. Victor reacted with sarcasm and blame, which was hurtful to Trish. This couple learned the hard way that these actions are a fruitless pursuit!

Jesus encourages His followers to respond in a better way. In Luke 6:35-36, He said, [35]"But love your enemies, do good to them, and lend to them without expecting to get anything back. Then your reward will be great, and you will be children of the Most High, because he is kind to the ungrateful and wicked. [36]Be merciful, just as your Father is merciful." God calls us to a mature love that is not dependent on how we are treated. Jesus encourages us to love, do good, and invest without expecting to get anything in return. He promises that if we respond this way, then our reward will "be great" and we will be acting like "His children." It is possible to respond in a productive mode that will make things better, but it requires a response that is not dependent upon the other person.

> God calls us to a mature love that is not dependent on how we are treated.

In Romans 12:17-19, Paul says, [17]"Do not repay anyone evil for evil. Be careful to do what is right in the eyes of everyone. [18]If it is possible, as far as it depends on you, live at peace with everyone. [19]Do not take revenge, my dear friends, but leave room for God's wrath, for it is written: 'It is mine to avenge; I will repay,' says the Lord." Paul encourages us to treat people significantly better than we are treated. He is offering a better way to respond when we are treated poorly. We are required to do everything in our power to make things better and not just resist but refuse to retaliate or seek revenge.

In Romans 12:20-21 he says, [20]"On the contrary: 'If your enemy is hungry, feed him; if he is thirsty, give him something to drink. In doing this, you will heap burning coals on his head.' [21]Do not be overcome by evil, but overcome evil with good." Anyone can return bad behavior with more bad behavior. That's easy! Instead of continuing the unproductive cycle by retaliating and inflicting pain, God's Word says we can overcome evil with good. Contrary to what the world tells us, we do not have to become the evil inflicted upon us. We can give hungry people food and thirsty people something to drink, even if they are our enemy. We can be kind to people even if they look down on us and mock the very things we hold dear. We can care about them even when they are doing things to make our lives difficult.

What does it mean to heap burning coals on their heads? In the ancient world, people needed fire to survive. They needed it to cook food and to stay warm. If their fire went out, it was a massive problem. In certain seasons of the year, having a fire was a matter of life or death. People who ran out of coals would carry an empty container on their heads and ask people for coals. The person sharing the coals would be meeting a desperate need and showing kindness. If the person shared their coals with an adversary, that would be *remarkable* kindness, much more than they deserved.

When people injure or insult us, we have a choice to make. We can bless them through an act of mercy or curse them through an act of revenge. Heaping burning coals upon the head is a metaphor, like having egg on one's face. It means instead of returning evil for evil and taking revenge, we can return good for evil and offer mercy.

In addition to giving us a way to break the cycle of misery, treating people better than they deserve helps them access the parts of their brain that house regret and remorse. If we react to bad behavior with more bad behavior, the only thing the other person will remember is our bad behavior. We can be blamed as part of the problem. If we respond with humility and compassion, the stark contrast between their harsh words and our gentle response will give them the space to consider their part in the breakdown of the relationship. We will rarely receive an apology from someone who treats us badly when we react with equally destructive behavior, but we will often receive an apology (and a path forward) when we respond gently and with kindness.

In 1 Peter 3:8-11, Peter, builds on the words of Jesus by saying, [8]"Finally, all of you, be like-minded, be sympathetic, love one another, be compassionate and humble. [9]Do not repay evil with evil or insult with insult. On the contrary, repay evil with blessing, because to this you were called so that you may inherit a blessing. [10]For, "Whoever would love life and see good days must keep their tongue from evil and their lips from deceitful speech. [11]They must turn from evil and do good; they must seek peace and pursue it." Peter says that compassion and humility can help us respond to an insult with a blessing. He also says that responding to an insult with an insult is evil. We can keep our tongue from evil by not by reacting in destructive ways. He offers the possibility that we can "enjoy life" and "see good days," but we must turn from evil and seek and pursue peace.

Peter adds a remarkable promise that God sees our actions and is willing to reward us when we treat others better than their actions deserve. Peter continues by saying in chapter 3, verse 12, "For the eyes of the Lord are on the righteous and His ears are attentive to their prayer, but the face of the Lord is against those who do evil." In this verse, Peter reminds us that God sees all of our interactions. He is watching and paying attention. It is the kind of focus that requires awareness and attention. When we read these words, we can be assured that God knows, He cares about us, and He looks at us with pleasure when we act in a manner that honors Him. His ears are open to our prayers. He is ready and willing to hear us as we refuse to react outwardly to being emotionally overwhelmed. Let this truth sink in. God actively works on our behalf when we are seeking and pursuing peace.

You may be resisting this idea because you are afraid other people will take advantage of your open heart and generous behavior. When selfish people are involved, it's only a matter of time before that open heart can become a broken one, right? I cannot claim this is not a possibility. It's true there are people who will use your generosity against you. The cost of learning to extend mercy and treat people better than they deserve will likely lead to insults, uncomfortable feelings, and painful tears.

Take heart. God also notices those who do evil. Peter's words are meant as a comfort: God does not simply ignore the hurtful actions of those who bring suffering to His people. Remember, "His face is against those who do evil." We don't have to retaliate, punish, or get even. Justice will come because God promises to take care of His people and protect them from harm.

The benefits of treating people better than their actions deserve will far exceed the costs. It's no accident that people who are open-hearted, kind, and willing to do hard things experience significantly better relationships. You will be rewarded with peace of mind and the ability to enjoy life and see good days. As you protect the people you care about, you may even receive an apology and elevate other people to better behavior. You will miss out on hundreds of needless arguments, and you won't have to carry the regret of destructive behavior. You will experience the honor and abiding respect from living out your values and acting like the person you want to be. The God of the universe will protect you from harm, see your behavior from heaven, look at you with great pleasure, and actively work on your behalf.

When it comes to relationships, most people don't realize that the little things that nobody sees produce the big things that everyone wants. When you take a step toward Productive Mode you will improve all of your relationships. Over time, the people you care about will eventually notice. Let's dig a little deeper into what productive interactions look like.

> *The little things that nobody sees produce the big things that everyone wants.*

Understand what genuine love and productive behavior look like.

We need to know what the genuine article looks like before we can spot the counterfeit. We need to slow down and take an in-depth look at genuine love and productive behavior, so we know when we are hitting the target. It is important to think about how we would want others to treat us so we can evaluate when our actions are loving, and our behaviors are productive. There are three dimensions of our productive interactions, and all three must be simultaneously present for our actions to be seen as loving. They are Direction, Receptivity, and Impact. Productive interactions with these three qualities will produce the desired results. If any one of them is missing, the entire encounter will be painful and unproductive.

3 Dimensions of productive interactions

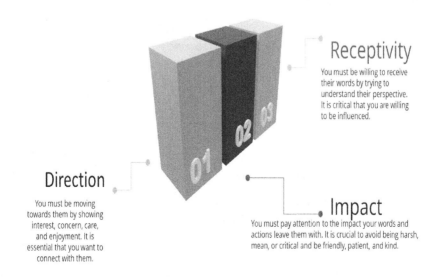

Receptivity
You must be willing to receive their words by trying to understand their perspective. It is critical that you are willing to be influenced.

Direction
You must be moving towards them by showing interest, concern, care, and enjoyment. It is essential that you want to connect with them.

Impact
You must pay attention to the impact your words and actions leave them with. It is crucial to avoid being harsh, mean, or critical and be friendly, patient, and kind.

First dimension of productive interactions: Direction

When we are acting in a productive manner, we are choosing to move in the right direction. We must approach and move towards people by showing interest, concern, care, and enjoyment. It is essential that we show we want to connect with them by moving towards the person, engaging in their concern, and trying to make things better. Something important is missing whenever we withdraw, create emotional distance, or avoid them. We should intentionally take steps to engage with the other person.

We need to be physically and emotionally present. Moving in the right direction includes internal motivation, external actions, and physical proximity. We should resist the desire to pull away, withdraw emotionally, or flee. When we are headed in the right direction, we initiate contact and pursue them with invitations to spend time together.

Helpful insight: It takes more than good intentions to leave another person feeling connected. We need to take steps to move in the right direction, engage emotionally, and do tangible things to help make things better.

Positive result: If you approach them and do something concrete or tangible to help make things better, then you will leave them feeling more connected because of your acceptance and approval.

Second dimension of productive interactions: Receptivity

When we respond in a productive manner, we must be willing to receive people's words by first trying to understand their perspective. The critical part to this process is that we are willing to be influenced. Something important is missing when we are unavailable or unwilling to give their perspective consideration. It takes discipline and vulnerability, but we need to remain accessible to them and open to hearing what they are saying from their perspective. People feel heard and understood when we listen with empathy, consider their perspective, and acknowledge and validate their feelings or experience.

We must be open to changing our mind and our behavior because that person matters to us. It is completely essential that we learn to listen in a way that makes our friend or spouse feel heard. James says, "My dear brothers and sisters, take note of this: Everyone should be quick to listen and slow to speak and slow to become angry" (James 1:19). If you remain available, then you can care about their isolation and disconnection rather than making excuses or giving advice. The more distressed a person is, the more difficult it will be to recognize their signal for connection and receive it.

Helpful insight: When a person feels emotionally distant or disconnected, they send out a signal for connection and closeness. We can learn to recognize and receive their signal for connection and give them verbal or non-verbal confirmation that we have received their message.

Positive result: If we receive their cry for connection, then they will feel heard and valued. We can make things better by comforting their distress.

Third dimension of productive interactions: Impact

When we respond in a productive manner, we pay attention to the impact our words and actions leave on people. It is crucial to avoid being harsh, mean, or critical, and equally crucial to be friendly, patient, and kind. What kind of impact are you having with your words? The words we speak *will* have an impact on our relationships. Our words will either bring hope or cause damage. We are surrounded with countless examples of how harsh words destroy our relationships. Critical words impact an employee's confidence. Thoughtless words impact the way our children see themselves when they look in the mirror. Sometimes the injury comes not only from the words, but also from the manner in which they are said. We need to pay attention to what we say and how we say it.

What kind of words are coming out of our mouth? Your life-giving words of encouragement will communicate, in a powerful way, an abiding sense of worth, importance, and value to the people in your life. A productive manner requires us to pay attention to the impact we make on others and the weight the other person takes on after a negative encounter with us.

We want to be seen as an endearing puppy, not a dangerous porcupine! We must avoid any behavior that leaves people feeling miserable or causes wounds. We want them to feel safe enough to become vulnerable and share their heart with us now and in the future.

We should focus on being helpful, kind, supportive, and encouraging and eliminate selfish, inconsiderate, and critical behavior.

Helpful insight: When we become aware of the impact our actions have on other people, then we can act in a manner that creates a hunger in them to draw near and spend time with us.

Positive result: If we pay close attention to the impact of our words and behavior, then we can create a safe environment where trust and vulnerability flourish and people want to move closer to us.

Choose to respond when your instinct is to react.

The automatic reactions of attacking, defending, withdrawing, and freezing are not effective solutions for solving relationship issues, but these are the things we almost always reach for first. When we feel helpless, we believe there is nothing we can do to make things better. We lack the confidence or desire to keep trying. When we feel powerless to do anything, we tell ourselves we don't really care. When our futile attempts make things worse, we keep repeating our automatic reactions, trying to repair the relationship the wrong way, which pushes the people we care about further and further away.

The next time your friend, boss, teammate, child, or spouse does something that irritates you and overwhelms you emotionally, what will you do? Will you react in a way that might escalate the situation into a full-scale, contentious confrontation, or will you just sit there and take it? Will you defend yourself from your attacker, or will you run to get away from an uncomfortable situation? Will you choose the better way? Reacting and responding are significantly different actions, and one is the much better choice for your precious relationships.

When we react, it is automatic, impulsive, and often negative. It may occasionally produce a favorable outcome, but often escalates situations and produces less-than-ideal results. When we respond, it is thoughtful, purposeful, and often positive. If you are willing to prepare your response in advance, then you increase the likelihood of producing the outcome you desire. A similar concept is further described in *The Anger Workbook* by Les Carter and Frank Minerth.[2]

Let's review the main points from the last two chapters so we can apply them to this situation. Blaming others and making excuses is a dead-end road that leaves us feeling helpless. Taking responsibility is the path that produces positive outcomes. We are not responsible for anyone else's actions, but we can move into Productive Mode, regardless of what anyone else does. This means, no matter who started the argument and no matter who is more to blame, we can look at our part and take steps to make things better. When we are in Productive Mode, we repair the relationship by taking ownership for our part in the breakdown and also receive the other person's attempts at repairing the relationship.

Would you be willing to take on an assignment? For the next ten days, choose to get in Productive Mode and stay there, regardless of what anyone else does. Do not allow yourself to operate in any of the four destructive modes for ten days. When you are overwhelmed emotionally, move into Productive Mode and try doing three things. First, move towards the other person by showing interest, concern, care, and enjoyment—show a desire to connect with them. Second, receive their words by trying to understand their perspective—it is critical that you remain willing to be influenced. Third, pay attention to the impact your words and actions have on them—you must be friendly, patient, kind, and avoid being harsh, mean, or critical.

Do everything you can to stay in Productive Mode, no matter what gets thrown your way. If for any reason you are unable to remain in this mode, ask yourself why and sit with it until you get an answer. You will not make the situation worse, and you will not create an additional problem, but you will put yourself in the best place to make things better. When I started learning to ask myself this question, I discovered two things about myself. First, I was so conditioned to defending myself that it was a well-worn, natural response. I had to learn how to stop protecting myself. Second, I learned I did not know how to manage my emotions. If you keep reading, I will devote an entire chapter to help you stop defending yourself and another one to help you manage your own emotions. When you learn to operate with direction, receptivity, and impact, you will be able to enjoy significantly better relationships.

My response to the other person's mode.

When you are in a heated conversation, it can also be helpful to figure out which mode the other person is operating in, so you can know the best way to respond to them and make things better. Pay attention to their mode for the sole purpose of understanding how to respond in the most productive manner possible.

Start by changing your mode from one of the four destructive modes to Productive Mode. Try to discover the other person's mode so that you can know the best way for you to respond to them and make things better. **Warning:** Do not criticize the other person, tell them what they need to change, or tell them what mode they are in. This is for you in order to increase your effectiveness and personal growth.

Ask yourself two questions:

    1) What is it like to be on the other side of me?

    2) How am I coming across?

Then respond instead of reacting by asking the following questions:

If a person is in Attack Mode, then ask yourself, "Am I invalidating, defending, or not taking ownership for my actions?" You can also try and pay attention to what they secretly want. They are likely hoping for you to give their concern consideration and move towards them to connect.

If a person is in Defense Mode, then ask yourself, "What is it about me that makes it hard for them to stay in the conversation with me? Am I attacking, criticizing, or blaming them?" You can also try and have compassion for their inability to handle the perceived threat and try a softer approach.

If a person is in Withdraw Mode, then ask yourself, "Do I ever push through boundaries, demand action, or start the conversation in a harsh manner? What could I do to make them feel safe?" You might not have hurt them, but someone did. Notice they are hurting and choose to respond with an extra dose of kindness and patience.

If a person is in Freeze Mode, then ask yourself, "Am I aware of their hurts, fears, and vulnerabilities? Do I harshly criticize, point out their mistakes, or give them unwanted advice? What could I do to make them feel safe and experience my approval?" You could also see their pain and reach out to comfort them or reassure them.

Let's go back to the cabin with Victor and Trish. You were likely annoyed with both of them by the end of the story! What could either one of them have done to make the encounter more productive? If Victor was in Productive Mode, he would not have defended himself and the argument may have never happened. He could have approached Trish and let her know that he cared about how much his busy schedule negatively impacted the relationship. He could have acknowledged her concerns or communicated how important she is to him.

Trish could have realized Victor was feeling defensive and either acknowledged the comment or reiterated her appreciation for his attempts to connect. She could have protected him from her critical comments by stopping with, "I appreciate you so much, thank you for bringing me to this amazing place." They both could have apologized for escalating the conversation to near destruction. Neither one was helpless. They both could have chosen a better way.

Completing This Leg of the Journey

We can't control the outcome, but we can choose what mode we operate in. We can respond in a manner that will leave us without regrets or missed opportunities. We can do something profound to make things better by refusing to react in our automatic pattern and responding in a productive manner to the people we care about, even when our fears are activated and our emotions are heightened.

We can receive the words of our friends, loved ones, and coworkers by seeking to understand their perspective and pay attention to the impact their words and actions have on the other person. It is one thing to wish, want, and desire something, but it is something altogether different to respond in a productive, healthy way when you are overwhelmed, discouraged, or frustrated.

We can ask a single question that will bring clarity and help us get back on course. This question will change everything. The sooner we ask it the better off we will be. We need to ask ourselves what mode am I in? If I am in any of the four destructive modes, then I can move into Productive Mode.

Questions for Discussion

- Which Destructive Mode is your go-to mode? (Attack, Defend, Withdraw, or Freeze)
- How does your mode impact the important people in your life?
- When we feel like we are being treated unfairly we feel completely justified reacting the way we do. How do we learn to act in a way that will make things better?
- What is the goal of communication?
- What is the reason you want to be right, get your point across, and win the argument?
- What would you have to change to stay in Productive Mode?
- How are each of the four destructive modes negatively impacting your relationships?
- Which one of the three dimensions of Productive Mode is the most difficult for you to stay in? (Direction, Receptivity, and Impact) Why?
- How can paying more attention to your Reaction Modes improve your relationship?
- What stands out to you in Luke 6:31-36?
- How can you bless people who curse you according to Romans 12:17-21?
- Read 1 Peter 3:8-11. Why would you want to treat people better well who insult you?
- Are you up for the ten-day challenge described in this chapter?

Chapter Six

Create Positive Memories

Figuring out the most important message and communicating it in every conversation.

Growing up, I loved my dad and I wanted to spend time with him, but he was impossible to please. He was distant, withdrawn, harsh, and angry. Every once in a while, he actually said the words, "I love you," but I had a hard time believing him because his harsh words were difficult to forget. One particular Saturday, when I was eleven years old, I asked my dad if I could go to work with him. He reluctantly said, "yes." When we arrived on site for his next house painting job, he was immediately focused on getting the task done so he could get to the next job. After two hours of staying silent, I asked if I could help. He handed me a paint brush and said it will ruin the brush if you don't get it completely clean. I spent extra time scrubbing and rinsing the brush so he would see me as a good worker. I got the brush completely clean! Unfortunately, I got paint and water all over the side of the house.

My dad was not happy. He communicated his displeasure with his silence. He told me to sit in the lawn chair until he cleaned up the mess. I sat in silence for over an hour until it was time to go. He told me to pick up the drop cloths and take them to the car. I wanted to carry them all in one trip so my dad could see I was a good worker. Unfortunately, I did not see the open can of oil-based paint on the brand-new deck. I tripped over it and got paint everywhere. It was a disaster. My dad was livid, and he unleashed his anger on me. His words cut like a knife. Two of the things he said were so painful I can remember them over four decades later, "You are useless! I am never bringing you to work with me again, Bob!"

How would you feel in that moment? Who do you relate with the most? You may have had harsh words spoken over you, or you may be the one who spoke the critical comments to someone you care about. It is easy to get focused on what is happening in the moment and fail to pay attention to the impact of our words. At the end of every conversation, people are left with the weight of our words. The other person will be left with an overriding message that may be entirely different than the one we were trying to send.

It is so easy to focus on what we want to say in the moment or on what is wrong with the people we care about. We can see so clearly what they need to hear or what is wrong with their behavior, their thinking, or their attitude. What we choose to focus our attention on determines the quality of our relationships. We can significantly increase the likelihood of being heard if we learn to ask ourselves a powerful question before we begin a conversation. What is the most important message I want to leave with the person I care about?

> *What we choose to focus our attention on determines the quality of our relationships.*

We can develop the advanced relationship skill of seeing beyond what we immediately want to what we ultimately want. When we focus on what we want immediately, we will tell people what they need to do, how they need to change, what is wrong with them, and how they are not enough, but all those words will do damage to the relationship and prevent us from experiencing the connection our heart longs to experience.

When I became a dad, I promised myself I would be different. I wanted to be a good father. When my son, Zach, was seven years old, I took him swimming at the local health club. When getting back in the truck to go home, my son wanted to get a toy out of the back of the truck. He eventually found the toy, but in the process, he somehow lost the truck keys. It was ten degrees *below* zero, and I could not find the keys. We were cold and wet. I was exhausted and frustrated. I started yelling. I started yelling at my son. I saw his face looking back at me, and it scared me. I remembered the weight of my father's words and instantly felt horrible. I wanted to be different, but I did not know how to be different.

About one month later, it was twenty degrees below zero, and my son was in a wrestling tournament in Wisconsin. Darlene, was busy at a weekend retreat, so I took the two kids to a hotel. My two-year-old daughter, Grace, was sleeping in the car seat when I pulled up and parked the car right in front of the hotel's main entrance so I could check in. I left the car running so she could stay warm since it was dangerously cold outside. I gave Zach (who was seven) specific instructions. I told him to make sure his sister was safe by staying with her until I returned. I walked ten feet into the lobby and started checking into the hotel. Two minutes later, Zach walked into the lobby with a big-boy smile on his face. When I asked what he was doing, he looked at me and confidently said, "Don't worry dad, Grace is safe. I locked the door."

When I got to the car, my daughter was definitely safe, but the car was running, and the keys were inside, and this was not at all a safe situation! I tried for a half hour to get the door open, but I could no longer feel my fingers. Unfortunately, the locksmith who came to help me retrieve my precious daughter cost more than the one-night's stay at the hotel. I was just as frustrated as I was in the last scenario, but this time I responded differently. I didn't yell, and I did not do anything I would regret. While I didn't yell or do anything I regret, I stopped short of using my words for good by asking the most important question.

How do we stop leaving people with the weight of our destructive words?
Gain awareness that we say destructive words.

In between the first encounter after Zach's swimming lesson and the second encounter after Grace getting locked in the car at the hotel, I was able to recognize that my words carried weight and I needed to learn techniques to help me respond better. I did not know how to leave a positive message, but I knew I could stop the destructive message. I learned to slow down and take a few deep breaths. I learned to allow my heart rate to settle down a little. This gives me some time to calm down and regroup. I also learned to call a time out and say, "I don't want to say anything that will hurt you, so I am going to take a few minutes to calm down. I will be back in thirty minutes." Then leave the room. The last thing I learned has proven to be the most effective for me, personally. I learned to recognize the damage that can be done and refuse to allow myself to say destructive things. When I took away the possibility of tossing hand grenades or other explosives at my loved ones, then I was forced to figure out a different plan.

When we are aware that we sometimes respond poorly and say destructive words, we can either get discouraged, or we can use the experience to learn a better way. We can use the situation to our advantage if we are willing to prepare ahead of time and think through our responses. Being prepared will enable us to manage these encounters with increased confidence and set us up to respond productively. We must prepare in advance, practice our responses, and execute when the inevitable happens.

The next time someone does something that disappoints us or says something that does not live up to our expectations, we can choose our response carefully. We can place our emphasis on what they need to improve or on how much we value the relationship. This powerful question will bring clarity to what we need to say and how we need to say it. It will prevent us from doing significant damage to the relationship and increase our ability to influence the person we care about in the future. The question to ask ourselves when the stakes are high is, "What is the most important message I want to leave this person I care about with after this conversation?"

Understand the devastating impact.

Understand the devastating impact of focusing on what people are doing wrong. It is much easier to criticize what a person is doing wrong than it is to compliment them on what they are doing right. Whenever you criticize people, you do damage to your relationship and destroy the connection you have with the person. Negative words can go deep into a person's heart and have a long-lasting impact. The more important the person, the more devastating the impact. Criticism hurts regardless of the person, but when a person that should love you and protect you does not appear to think very much of you, it is extremely difficult to overcome.

If we do not pay attention to the weight of our words, we will leave people we care about with a heavy burden to carry, even if we have no intention of doing so. *How to Improve Your Marriage Without Talking About It* is a good read on this subject.[1] The more authority the person is entrusted with, the more devastating the impact. Whenever we have authority or hold some kind of power, our words weigh more, whether we want them to or not. If we are a parent, leader, boss, or coach, then our words weigh more. We can wish it wasn't true. We can pretend it isn't true. But it is true.

If you do not believe me, then how do you see the coach who criticized you when you were younger? Take a moment and say their name and write down the thoughts that come to your mind. Most people see the coach as a mean person who unfairly criticized them and sabotaged their ability to succeed both then and now. How do you see the mentor who encouraged you? Most people see the mentor in a positive light and view him/her as a remarkable person who was "on your side." She was a wonderful ally that paved the way for you to reach your potential, for example. At the end of the conversation, we want the person we care about to see us as their ally not their enemy.

We can have multiple different kinds of intentions when we say negative things. Sometimes we want to express our frustration, and other times we just want them to feel rotten. We may want to motivate the person we care about to become a better person or change a behavior that is irritating us. Unfortunately, our attempts to motivate them to become the best version of themselves could come with a heavy price tag.

As human beings, we are not only affected by what happens to us, but also by the filter through which we view what happens to us. Negative comments color the way we see ourselves and the person who pointed out our inadequacies. Criticism often has a very predictable outcome. The person being criticized thinks less of themselves and questions their own lovability. They subconsciously protect themselves from the person criticizing them and resist their ideas, advice, influence, and even love.

When I was seventeen, I wanted to move out of the house, but my mom wanted me to stay home because she valued the contribution I made to the family. I would usually start the conversation by talking about moving out of the house. My mom would respond by saying, "You are not ready to move out." I would respond by arguing with her and trying to make a point. I was defensive and tried to prove her wrong. I would tell her about all the things I did on my own and passionately list all the things I did without any help.

The more I argued my position, and the more passionately I delivered my conclusion, the more my mom felt like I did not need her, and she was not a good mom. The conversation would escalate until she would say, "You will never amount to anything" and "You will never be successful." I would get angry, slam the door, and walk away, avoiding her for as long as I could. I was left with the overriding message that I did not have what it takes, I was not capable, and something was wrong with me. Years later, my mom expressed what she really felt and wished she would have been able to communicate. She was going to miss me and genuinely respected me. She was frightened to do life at home with me not there, but the overriding message she got from me was she was unloved, unimportant, and alone. I wish I would have been able to communicate how much I loved her and appreciated all the things she did for me and my brothers and sisters.

Pay special attention to rejection, fear, or anxiety.

There are times to avoid being critical and to be careful with your words. Using optimistic language creates connection and hope; these are life-giving words. One crucial time to pay attention is when people are feeling rejected. Constructive criticism delivered at the right time can be helpful, but be especially careful not to attack them when they are most vulnerable. Your critical voice will cause damage, while your hopeful voice will bring life. A critical voice would say, "See? I told you it would not work out." It is understandable because you can see how they were not ready. A hopeful voice would say, "I am so sorry to hear it did not work out, but I can see better days ahead for you."

A second crucial time to pay attention is when they are afraid. Your crucial voice may say, "No one will ever really like you if you continue to act that way." You can see how destructive their behavior is and how it needs to change. Your hopeful voice may say, "I can't wait until the day when somebody sees how amazing you are."

A third crucial time to pay attention is when they are anxious or worried. Your critical voice may say, "You will never find the job you want until you complete your education." What you want for them is for them to finish that last semester. Your hopeful voice may say, "The perfect job is going to be out there waiting for you."

We must gain awareness of the damaging impact our words are having on the people we care about and eliminate those harsh words from all our conversations. Our negative words will leave the people we care about feeling anxious, depressed, angry, and hopeless. Whenever we criticize someone, it does damage to the relationship and puts us in a negative

> *We must eliminate harsh words from all our conversations.*

light as well. Pay attention to the devastating impact of focusing on what they are doing wrong so you can eliminate destructive words.

You may want to ask yourself the following questions in preparation for an important conversation. Do my words communicate my dissatisfaction, disapproval, and rejection, or do I leave the person feeling important, valued, and respected? Do I want to injure them and assign blame, or do I want to create a safe environment to solve problems and work toward solutions? We need to move beyond our hurt, frustration, and disappointment to say what is most important to us. We can learn to say encouraging, life-giving words if we are willing to slow down and ask a profound question. What is the most important message I want to leave the person I care about with after the conversation?

If you choose to focus on what they need to improve, then we will leave them with our disapproval. If we choose to focus on how they are not measuring up to our expectations, then we will leave them with our disgust. The good news is there is a healthier and better way to interact with the important people in our lives. Let's find out how to communicate the most important message. Before entering a tough conversation, remember the most important message you are trying to communicate and allow that message to guide the entire conversation.

How do we start leaving people with the weight of our lifegiving words?
Focus on the inherent value.

As we focus our attention on how much we value the person and the relationship, we can choose to highlight the information our brain concentrates upon. We must do two things simultaneously. We need to highlight their inherent value and notice the things they do wrong. You see, we do not have to ignore negative behavior or refuse to see the many improvements other people need to make, but we do need to prioritize the most important thing. There will always be negative behavior and improvement that needs to happen. If we don't pay attention to the right thing, we will come to the wrong conclusions, answer the wrong questions, perform the wrong tasks, and say the wrong words.

We notice what we are looking for. If we are looking for bad behavior, it will be there, and we will find it. We do not have to be perfect. In fact, if we have rarely done it, then people will not expect it and the encouraging words will have a bigger impact. We do not have to change our fundamental hardwiring to enjoy more satisfying relationships, but we must start seeing some of the positive things that are present in the people we care about and start speaking life-giving words out loud.

A remarkable way to communicate value is through appreciation. Our friends will feel accepted when we offer genuine thanks. The more specific we make it, the more effective it will be. We focus by slowing down enough to notice when people go out of their way to do something nice or helpful. Seek to make a conscientious and deliberate effort to thank people. Do not assume the important people in your life know you care and appreciate them.

John was a small business owner who had not learned that what you choose to focus your attention on determines the quality of your relationships. In the span of about six months, several of his key employees quit working for him and started working for one of his competitors for less money. John was dumbfounded and believed that the paycheck was all the thanks his employees needed to feel satisfied with working for him.

Very few people experience satisfaction from money alone, even when the paycheck is substantial. One of the main reasons people leave jobs is they want to do something meaningful for someone who appreciates their contributions. Wise employers compliment their employees for their good ideas and give them plenty of recognition for their efforts. People will remain loyal to us and receptive to our ideas when we take the time to encourage them and appreciate their contributions. It might not feel natural and at first, and we may be uncomfortable expressing our appreciation, but we will make a profound difference in their lives.

We will rarely regret generously expressing our gratitude and appreciation. When we learn to accept the people in our life, then we can experience a real relationship with a broken person who can be incredibly beautiful. Not only will we maintain influence, but we will often experience friendship, healing, joy, laughter, and delight.

I want to get practical for a few minutes. Parents, some of you have a son or daughter who is not living up to your expectations. His behavior is annoying. Her attitude is awful. When you have a conversation with him or her, do you focus on what he is doing wrong or on how much you value the relationship? We need to communicate to the people God has placed in our lives that we see their inherent dignity, value, and worth. If you are not careful, you will communicate rejection. You will leave the person you care about feeling like you will only accept them when they get their act together and when their performance matches your expectations. If you choose to focus on what the person you care about is doing wrong, then you will leave them with your disappointment.

Notice inherent dignity, value, and worth and speak it over them.

Every time you think something good about the people in your life, say it. This can be extremely difficult if you are not comfortable giving compliments. This can seem virtually impossible to half the population. I heard it said that there are two kinds of people in the world. Some people walk into a room and see everything that is wrong, broken, or not working. Other people can walk into the same room and see everything that is right, working properly, and functioning. The two people see the same room, but their eyes are drawn to completely different things. Neither person is completely right or completely wrong. Some people look at others and see all the things that are wrong, broken, and not working.

One way to communicate what you value is to keep a notepad, or use the notes app in your phone, and record the positive things your employees, parents, friends, and coworkers do. I had the amazing privilege of coaching my daughter's softball teams for eight years. I would keep a list of all the positive things the girls did throughout the season and during the end of the season celebration, I would speak to each girl personally in front of the other girls. Each speech lasted between two and three minutes. I would tell them about their remarkable accomplishments on the field and remind them of the times we laughed. I would highlight the important things about their character and how I believed in them. I would tell them how they encouraged their teammates or persevered through difficulties. Every year, the girls would ask why this part of the program had to be so short.

The encouraging words left a remarkable impact on the girls and communicated I was for them and believed they could accomplish great things. The girls would see me in public and acknowledge me even when they were surrounded by friends. Quite often, they would walk over to me and ask me how I was doing and update me on everything happening in their lives. They knew I cared.

One girl had never played softball before she joined our team. She could not even catch a ball from five feet away. The girls on the team encouraged her and helped her learn how to play the game. By the end of the season, she was making plays in the field and drove in a crucial run during playoffs. As I was giving her the two-minute speech, I could see both of her parents crying uncontrollably as they watched their daughter soak up the compliments from their coach. They both thanked me profusely and wanted to sign her up for another year of softball during the celebration. Solomon said it best in the book of Proverbs, "Gracious words are a honeycomb, sweet to the soul and healing to the bones" (Proverbs 16:24).

You can make a profound difference in the lives of other people when you see their inherent dignity, value, and worth and speak truth about it over them. When my children were young, I would often tell them, "I love you and I am committed to you no matter what." Your words can provide security. Life giving words can make an enormous difference. Learn to say things like: "I appreciate you," "I value our relationship," "I love the way you completed the project," "I am impressed with the way you answered that question," and "I noticed the extra effort you put in to include your sister."

Speak to their deepest longing.

Take the necessary time to get to know the hurts, fears, and vulnerabilities of the people you care about so you can speak to their deepest longing and answer their most important questions. The people you care about have been wounded and hurt by people. Some of them carry deep scars. As a result of their pain, they have unique fears. You are not responsible for their vulnerabilities, but if you are wise, you will pay attention to how their vulnerabilities impact your conversations and their well-being. The more you know about what they have been through, the more compassion you can offer and the better you can address their questions. Every person you know is human and flawed and most likely has real things they need to work on, but you do not want to be the critical voice that points out their flaws. Criticism will often activate a person's hurts, fears, and vulnerabilities.

> *Criticism will often activate a person's hurts, fears, and vulnerabilities.*

Generally speaking, whenever you criticize a man, you will activate his fear of being a failure and he will subconsciously want to avoid you in order to silence the emotional pain of telling him he is inadequate. Most men will do anything to avoid being told they are a failure. Whenever you criticize the women in your lives, you will activate all of her insecurities. She already sees all of her imperfections and criticism will often make her feel unlovable and activate her fear of being alone.

Ladies, the men in your lives want to know you believe in them. Your boyfriends, husbands, fathers, and sons are asking the question, "Do I have what it takes?" "Do you appreciate the contribution I am making?" and "Am I good enough?" They want you to believe in them because they are not sure they believe in themselves.

Men, the women in your lives want to know that you love them. Your daughters, mothers, and wives are asking "Am I worthy of your attention?" and "Do you love me and think I am worth fighting for?" Criticism is rarely conducive to real change because it often perpetuates a cycle of self-destructive thinking, sometimes followed by self-limiting or self-destructive activities. It is hard for them to function well when they know they are being criticized by someone they love. The people in our lives will feel a lot stronger and be more able to overcome the obstacles in their lives if they know you are on their side and believe that they have what it takes.

Receive them into your heart.

Intentionally focus on accepting the people you care about and receive them into your heart. We should do our best to love people. How do you accept unacceptable people? We live in a culture that teaches us that we should tolerate people and put up with their beliefs, values, and preferences. Tolerance does not value people, it simply puts up with their behavior or their beliefs. God calls His followers to more than tolerance. He calls us to accept people and receive them into our hearts. We need to move beyond putting up with people and begin loving the people we disagree with.

Acceptance is an act of the heart. When you accept someone, it means that you are for them, and you are glad they are in your life, and you long for the best for them. God wants us to receive them into our hearts. The word that is translated "accept" in Romans 15:7 actually means to receive them the way you would catch a football! God wants you to reach out and pull them into your heart. God wants you to treat the people in your life the same way he treated you.

How did God treat us? God demonstrated his love towards you and me by accepting us before we were acceptable. In fact, in Romans 5:6-8, we read, ⁶"You see, at just the right time, when we were still powerless, Christ died for the ungodly. ⁷Very rarely will anyone die for a righteous person, though for a good person someone might possibly dare to die. ⁸But God demonstrates his own love for us in this: While we were still sinners, Christ died for us."

> *God demonstrated his love towards you and me by accepting us before we were acceptable.*

In Ephesians 2:1-10, Paul said, ¹"As for you, you were dead in your transgressions and sins, ²in which you used to live when you followed the ways of this world and of the ruler of the kingdom of the air, the spirit who is now at work in those who are disobedient. ³All of us also lived among them at one time, gratifying the cravings of our flesh and following its desires and thoughts. Like the rest, we were by nature deserving of wrath. ⁴But because of his great love for us, God, who is rich in mercy, ⁵made us alive with Christ even when we were dead in transgressions—it is by grace you have been saved. ⁶And God raised us up with Christ and seated us with him in the heavenly realms in Christ Jesus, ⁷in order that in the coming ages he might show the incomparable riches of his grace, expressed in his kindness to us in Christ Jesus. ⁸For it is by grace you have been saved, through faith—and this is not from yourselves, it is the gift of God— ⁹not by works, so that no one can boast. ¹⁰For we are God's handiwork, created in Christ Jesus to do good works, which God prepared in advance for us to do."

We were objects of wrath because of our rebellious behavior, but because of God's great love, rich mercy, extreme grace, and incomparable kindness, he pulled us in and lifted us up. We must learn to accept people before they become acceptable. It is not easy, and it is not normal, but with some work, it is possible. God tells us how relationships work in the real world. How do you accept unacceptable people? We do this by intentionally

> *We must learn to accept people before they become acceptable.*

focusing on their inherent value instead of their present performance. We need to communicate to the people God has placed in our lives that we see their inherent dignity, value, and worth.

All of us are the products of the acceptance and the rejection we received as a child. We are attracted to acceptance like metal is to a magnet. God designed us to be acceptance magnets. Our hearts are attracted to the people who accept us. Most people choose their friends because they were the people who accepted them. Our hearts go where we find acceptance. Have you ever wondered why a husband will spend all his time at work? It's often because that's where he is accepted and affirmed for making a significant contribution, but at home, he does not measure up and he never quite gets it right. Have you ever wondered why teenagers get advice from their peers? It is not because their peers are smarter or have better advice! It's because we are far more open to the people who accept us than we are to the people who lecture us.

Trust God to bring about real change.

How do you accept unacceptable people? We must learn to stop trying to control the people we care about and trust God to bring about real change in them. We must learn to affirm and accept the people we care about for who they are, not for who we want them to be. If you want to communicate the most important thing, you will have to intentionally choose to focus on their inherent value. If you saw a priceless Rembrandt painting covered in mud, you most likely would not focus on the mud or treat it like mud. Your primary concern would not be the mud at all, though it would need to be removed. You would be delighted that you had something so valuable in your care. If you tried to clean it up yourself, you might damage it. If you were wise, you would carefully bring it to a restoration master and have him restore it to the condition it was originally intended. John Burke tells this story in an important book on this topic called, *No Perfect People Allowed*.[2]

When you look at the people in your life, do you see the mud, or do you see a masterpiece? God is in the business of changing lives. We are asked to love people and turn them over to God so He can change them. It is our responsibility to learn how to communicate our approval.

What if I don't know the most important message?

We are often so focused on what we need to say in the moment, that we have not thought through the most important message. We assume the meaningful people in our lives know how we feel because we've said it all before, but that doesn't mean they don't need to hear it again. Some people reach the end of their lives with regrets because they have either communicated destructive messages or failed to communicate meaningful ones when they had the chance. I suggest we protect ourselves from both outcomes by preparing the message in advance, so we know what to say when we get the opportunity.

It only takes a few careless words to cause permanent damage and destroy our relationships, so we must invest the necessary time figuring out what we want to say. Identify four people you really value. They could be a friend, coworker, employee, sibling, child, parent, or spouse. The words you say to them are extremely important. We can bring life into their soul if we communicate the most important message.

Ask yourself these four questions:

1. What do I want them to know?

2. What do I want them to feel?

3. What do I need to say and do for them to make sure they receive the most important message?

4. What do I need to avoid doing and saying to ensure they do not have to carry the weight of a destructive message?

Write their names below and take time to discover what is the most important message you want to communicate to them.

1.
2.
3.
4.

Here is an example so you can see how to do this with an actual person, my daughter, Grace.

1. **What do I want her to know?** I want Grace to know I take great delight in her, and I am extremely glad she is my daughter. She needs to know that I love her, and I am going to protect her from my words and actions. I want her to know she is deeply respected, highly valued, and genuinely appreciated. I also want

her to know she is a priority and has access to her dad's time and attention.

2. **What do I want her to feel?** I want Grace to feel my affection, attention, and approval. I want her to feel loved, close, and safe. I also want her to feel that her dad believes in her. He is fundamentally convinced she is amazing. He wants her to succeed, and he is willing to support her along the entire journey.

3. **What do I want to say and do to make sure she receives the most important message?** Grace needs to hear these words from me often. "You are enough." "You are worthy of love. "You are worth fighting for." "I am your biggest fan and strongest supporter." "I love you and enjoy spending time in your presence." Before I say anything to my daughter, I need to listen to her heart and get to know her. My most powerful tool in communicating with her is empathy. My daughter loves to talk and absolutely loves to be heard. There is something powerful about having her inner world seen and understood by her father. I won't try and fix her or her problems. I don't desire to lecture her by telling her what she needs to learn or do. My daughter needs my understanding and emotional support. She needs me to receive her sadness and care about her concerns.

4. **What do I need to avoid doing and saying to ensure she does not have to carry the weight of a destructive message?** I must manage my emotions and respond calmly without overreacting, especially when Grace makes mistakes. I will protect her from my anger and criticism, making sure I do not harshly point out her flaws which will trigger all her insecurities and make her miserable. I need to create a safe place for her heart by controlling the words I say to my daughter. I need to say words that are encouraging, hopeful, thoughtful, and kind.

What if I am carrying the weight of words that were spoken over me?

You may be your own harshest critic. Most people have an inner critic, but for some, it becomes the strongest voice. It is difficult to silence if you have experienced harsh criticisms, unrealistic expectations, or rejection. You may hold yourselves to an unrealistic standard of perfection, and when you inevitably fail to reach the standard, you say the same destructive words over and over again in your mind. What if the standard is an allusion because you are comparing everyone else's highlight reel to your own worst mistakes and biggest disappointments? If you were able to see the real lives behind the carefully crafted veneer, then you would not feel so inferior. It is time to silence your inner critic! You don't have to accept all the nasty, negative thoughts directed at yourself.

Pay attention to the words you say to yourself. If you are calling yourself names like loser or idiot or are putting yourself down by saying, "How could you be so dumb," "You will never get it right," and "You're not good enough," then it is time to stop. Calling yourself a screw-up or an idiot is demeaning. These words will increase your shame and keep you from making progress. Experience tells me that shaming yourself will not motivate you to do better or learn the tools to improve your relationships. In fact, it will often have the opposite effect because it will cause you to feel worse about yourself and less capable of making the right decisions. You will push people away.

Your internal dialogue can give you the encouragement you need to become a better person and the motivation to start solving the problems you are facing. Your words could help you properly frame the world around you. Think of how liberating it would be if you were free from the role of being your own harshest critic. What might be possible? What would you be free to attempt if you were not afraid of being criticized? What might happen if you invested the same amount of energy that goes into harshly judging yourself and instead invested it into learning better strategies, creating meaningful memories, and improving your relationships?

What if I need to correct my child's unruly behavior?

You may be saying that communicating the most important message is nice, but I need to correct my child's behavior before it becomes a problem. When a child is doing something wrong, the parent must let them know on the child's level that their behavior is wrong, and their actions will not be tolerated. Good parents discipline their children. If you allow your child to continue their disruptive behavior and refuse to discipline them, they will become unruly and out of control. But remember what makes all discipline more effective? Connection!

Connection is absolutely essential in effective parenting. If your children do not have a relationship with you, they will not care about what you think or what you want. If love or understanding are missing, then the entire experience will be painful. Your children need to know that you are on their team. They need to believe at the core of their being that you have their best interest at heart. Good parents never elevate the rules above the relationship. They guide their children with love and discipline, sometimes simultaneously. You can expect obedience when you explain to your children why certain behavior will be beneficial and why other behavior must be prohibited. Take the time to demonstrate how much you love them.

What if my employee needs to be held accountable for underperforming?

Employee underperformance must be addressed. What is the best way? It is not fun to reprimand someone, especially a full-grown adult, but it is possible to do it effectively and without ruining the relationship or weakening the company. Harsh criticism, public embarrassment, and humiliation will create an environment full of fear and job insecurity. Treat employees with respect, even when they have made a big mistake, is critical.

Before you go into a productive conversation, be honest with your motivation. Are you genuinely interested in helping your employees, or are you wanting to punish or terminate an underperformer at the first sign of weakness? People can tell if you are for them or want to get something out of them. According to *Crucial Accountability* by Kerry Patterson and others, holding someone accountable is in everyone's best interest because you can solve the problem and help them become a better employee.[3]

Taking the time to talk with the person instead of talking at them can make a profound difference and produce a significantly better outcome. During the difficult conversation, take enough time to understand the employee and care about their situation. Ask questions to get to the root of the problem. They may be underperforming because they don't clearly understand the expectations or have not been given the proper training. Take time to explain what you expect and how to move forward in the company. Most employees are open to receiving constructive criticism when they are told clearly what they did wrong and are given a legitimate opportunity to fix the problem. Even if you decide to terminate their employment, you can treat them with dignity and leave them with your appreciation and approval of them as a person.

If you focus your attention on the wrong things, you will communicate a dangerous message that will cause damage to your relationship. You will lose your influence and leave the people in your life feeling your disappointment and rejection. The apostle Paul wrote, "Do not let any unwholesome talk come out of your mouths, but only what is helpful for building others up according to their needs, that it may benefit those who listen" (Ephesians 4:29). Jesus taught His followers to slow down and think about what we wish they did to us. He gave us a new lens to see how to treat people. We can look at how we wish other people treated us to understand what to do.

What do you want from others when your behavior needs to be corrected? When I am acting badly, I want the person to gently correct me and help me see what I need to do differently. When I mess up, I want them to give me an opportunity to make it right. What do you want when you are underperforming at work? I want them to come alongside me and help me become a better employee. I want them to extend me grace and treat me better than my actions deserve. We have the opportunity to treat people the way we wish they treated us.

What if I am the one that has spoken harsh words?

The words you are speaking will have an impact on your relationships. In James 3:1-12, we are warned to be careful what we say because an entire forest can be set on fire by a single spark of the tongue. James also says the tongue is "a restless evil, full of deadly poison." Your words will either bring hope or cause damage. Your harsh words are destroying your relationships. Your critical words are impacting your children's confidence. Your thoughtless words are impacting the way your friends see themselves when they look in the mirror. What kind of words are coming out of your mouth?

In Proverbs 18:12 Solomon says, "The tongue has the power of life and death, and those who love it will eat its fruit." This proverb is a simple reminder of how much words matter. Your words either build up or tear down, motivate or discourage, inspire to greatness or to discourage people into mediocrity. There is the life and death in the power of your tongue. If you have not been careful with the words you have allowed to come out of your mouth, then it is time to take responsibility for the real-life consequences your words have produced. If you have spoken harsh words, then admit that your words have left people with a heavy burden to carry.

It is very difficult for our brains to go there because if we admit this is true, then we feel the weight of hurting the people who are important to us. It is our fault. We did not do it on purpose, but we did it. It is very difficult to indict ourselves. Some of our words have left people with deep scars and wounds that are difficult to forget. It is hard to accept the possibility that our words have caused hurt. Our first instinct is to reject the possibility that our words have caused pain. If we have used words carelessly, then we must admit it to ourselves, apologize to the people we have wounded, undo the deep scars we have caused, and start speaking life to the people we care about. What kind of impact are you having with your words?

How can we start speaking words that bring life? Paul tells us we can present our tongue to God as an instrument for good in Romans 6:13 and ask Him to fill us with His Spirit. We can start building others up and allowing God to infuse our tongue with life-giving power. Spirit-filled words please God and encourage people. We can submit our heart to God and hand Him control of our words.

Completing This Leg of the Journey

It is so easy to focus on what is wrong with people. We can see so clearly what is wrong with their behavior, their thinking, and their attitude. We can significantly increase the likelihood of being heard if we learn to ask ourselves a powerful question before we begin a conversation. The next time someone does something that disappoints us or says something that does not live up to our expectations, we can choose our response carefully.

We can place our emphasis on what they need to improve or on how much we value the relationship. This powerful question will bring clarity to what we need to say and how we need to say it. It will prevent us from doing significant damage to the relationship and increase our ability to influence the person we care about in the future. Remember the most important question to ask yourself when the stakes are high is, "What is the most important message I want to leave this person I care about with after our conversation?"

Questions for Discussion

- What negative messages have people left you with following conversations?
- What is the most important message you want to leave people with after your conversations?
- How have people treated you in the past when you disappointed them?
- What kind of emotions come over you when people refuse to express their appreciation?
- What would you need to improve in order to communicate your affection, attention, and approval to others?
- How would your relationships change if you stopped speaking in your critical voice?
- How can you silence your inner critic?
- Who needs you to speak in your hopeful voice right now?
- What is something you can do to repair the damage you have done with the hurtful words you have said?

Chapter Seven

Read the Road Signs

Discovering what is going on inside your heart so you can communicate from it.

Very few people have effective strategies to communicate when they have something important to say. Our passion to get the other person to see our point often overrides our compassion for them as a person. We often resort to one of seven strategies that destroy relationships. But there is a productive alternative that will significantly increase your ability to be heard even if the other person is resistant to what you have to say. If you want to communicate your heart, you will have to stop using your words as a weapon and shut down the habit of protecting yourself. Only a person in touch with their own heart can reach another person's heart.

> *Our passion to get the other person to see our point often overrides our compassion for them as a person.*

We live in a fast-paced world where everything happens quickly. We associate velocity with success and efficiency with productivity. We do life at a breakneck speed. We are on a mission to accomplish tasks and check things off our to-do lists. We get irritated when the thoughtless person in front of us in the grocery store forgets a nonessential item and wastes ninety seconds of our time to run to the back of the store to get an insignificant item that they could easily live without. We are incensed when we pull up to a stop light and the sensor that was designed to make things quicker does not recognize our car. We spend extra money on fast processors and lighting fast internet, so we do not have to wait.

We avoid anything that wastes our precious time. We would rather get a root canal than go to the DMV. How is it possible that someone can move so slowly? We wait in line to get a number and sit in an uncomfortable chair with a room full of cranky people, watching everyone move in slow motion. *Do they get advanced training in obnoxious behavior? How do they take such bad pictures?* We either end up grinning like an idiot or looking like some sort of criminal that was booked for aggravated assault. We take this same emphasis on productivity and speed and transfer it to relationships. Is it possible to have a great conversation in a hurry?

You cannot hurry an important conversation and check it off your to do list like you do the rest of life. The more you try and hurry a conversation, the more likely it will end up at the wrong destination with regrets. Conversations take time because relationships take time, and genuine connection requires trust and vulnerability to navigate the obstacles. Give important conversations the time they deserve.

If we want the other person to hear our heart when we talk, then we will need to get to our heart before we speak. To get to our heart, we must invest the time to discover what we would say if we could. We need clarity to know what to do and the courage to do it. There is an important question we can ask that will produce clarity if we are willing to sit with it long enough to get an answer. We will increase our likelihood of ending up at the right destination if we learn to ask this important question at every stage along the way. The question we must learn to ask is: *What is going on in my heart that needs my attention so I can have a productive conversation?*

Jesus made a profound observation that helps us form this question. He said, "out of the overflow of the heart the mouth speaks" (Matthew 12:34). If we are going to have a productive conversation, we need to discover what is going on in our hearts. And it is our words that will reveal what is going on in our hearts. When Jesus talks about the heart, He is including what takes place in our mind, will, and emotions. The words that flow from our mouths come directly from the reservoir that lies within our hearts. When I have a critical heart, I speak judgmental, disparaging, and derogatory words. When I have a kind heart, I speak gentle, compassionate, and encouraging words. When I have an insecure heart, I am self-centered, selfish, demeaning, and condescending, using words that promote my own self-interest. We speak out of the overflow of our hearts.

We often try and hide what is taking place inside of us. We want to manage the way people see us, so we use words in such a way that people will see us in a positive light. We can get away with it for a while, but eventually what is taking place inside of us will be evidenced by the things we say and how we say them. Whatever is inside our heart, whether good or bad, it will eventually come out in the words we use and in how we communicate.

It's on us to discover what is going on inside our heart before our words reveal it to others. If we do not deal with what is taking place behind the thinly veiled façade, our words will be spoken or shouted in moments of anger or disappointment, often causing irreparable damage. I have listened to people in my office tell me about the heartache that has come from saying words they did not mean to say. One man told his wife that she was so overweight that no one could find her attractive. He was then shocked to find out that she was uncomfortable with physical intimacy. Words can be so damaging. Is there a better way? Is it possible to prepare ourselves for a productive conversation? The husband wished he had asked the important question before speaking: *What is going on in my own heart that needs my attention so I can have a productive conversation?*

> We must discover what is going on inside our own heart.

How do you ask the question *before* the conversation?

It is a remarkable privilege to be able to work with people before they do damage to the relationship. After a person has been injured by hundreds of careless words and unproductive conversations, we need to spend hours unpacking the damage. We can start with practical strategies to have successful conversations. These strategies apply to every relationship. They can help you strengthen your relationship with a friend, business partner, grandparent, or acquaintance.

Not all conversations are important. In fact, most are not. Occasionally, a situation will have the potential for extreme danger. The best way to tell if you are in an important conversation is to pay attention to your own emotions and the reactions of the other person. If you can feel your own emotions getting heightened, then it is very likely you care about (or are nervous about) the outcome. The more important the person, the more the outcome matters. If the result of the conversation could impact your life in a meaningful way, then it is an important conversation. If you can see the other person reacting with more intensity than the moment warrants, then it is an important conversation.

Important conversations that end with productive outcomes require three essential elements: preparation, deliberation, and follow-through. We need to give each element proper consideration. I have divided this chapter into three sections. The first part will help you prepare for the conversation, the second part will give you principles to keep in mind during the conversation, and the last section will help you make necessary adjustments to improve your future conversations.

Prepare for the Conversation

It sounds elementary, but the first step in a productive conversation is to prepare for the conversation. Carefully choose the best time and best place. The right environment and emotional space will give you the best chance for success. If you or the person you are speaking with is overwhelmed emotionally, tired, hungry, or distracted, it may not be the best time. If there are too many people, noises, or distractions, then it may not be the right place. If you are trying to have a work conversation, pay attention to who could overhear (or be told about) the conversation.

We don't always get to choose the timing of a conversation. Sometimes another person will approach us at an inconvenient time, wanting to have an important conversation. If we don't see it coming, then how can we prepare for it? One option is to say this conversation is so important that you need a little time to prepare for it. To show how important it is to you, don't leave without setting a time and place to talk. It is much better to make someone wait then to have a conversation we are not ready to have. This wisdom rings true in the book, *The Way of a Shepherd*.[1]

You do not have to do it alone. If you have the courage to invite God into the process, He will help by revealing what you need to work on before the conversation. Pray for God's help and include Him in the entire process. God can and will help you communicate (James 1:8). You can prepare by asking God to help you discover your attitude, motivation, priorities, and words.

Attitude

Start with your attitude because that will determine how you come across to the other person. A good attitude will inspire, energize, and uplift the other person. A bad attitude will drain, produce stress, and discourage the people you care about. Your attitude has to do with your thoughts, your mode, the energy you project, and your attitude. Are your thoughts positive and hopeful or pessimistic and destructive? Are you calm and relaxed or anxious, frustrated, and irritated? Are you projecting peace and safety or danger and fear in the person you are going to talk to?

Motivation

Discover your motivation because that will help you determine the overriding message you want to leave them with after the conversation. If your motivation is to prove the person you care about is wrong, then your words will communicate your dissatisfaction, disapproval, and rejection. If your motivation is to leave them knowing they are valuable, then your words will leave them feeling accepted, important, valued, and respected. It is unlikely if you are in touch with your heart that you will want to leave them with an emotional injury. Ask the important question before you leave them feeling the weight of the blame you have assigned them. Make sure you end the conversation having created a safe environment to solve problems and a stronger connection for next time.

Understand yourself and what you really want. Do some self-reflection to determine what is going on inside you, and what you hope to accomplish. You also need to determine the best strategy to arrive at the appropriate destination. I have found it helpful to determine what I am feeling. I personally need to work hard to go beyond my secondary emotions of anger, frustration, and blame in order to focus on my primary emotions of hurt, fear, and sadness. I cannot move forward until I know what I want for me, for the other person, and for both of us. Sometimes other people have a stake in the outcome, and I need to determine what I want for them.

Take time to meditate on the real issue. Sometimes you will need to process out loud. Sometimes you will need time alone. It will take time, but everyone will benefit once you figure it out. Try and narrow it down as much as possible. Once you discover how you feel and what you want, then you can begin formulating what you should actually *say*. It will take moving beyond accusations and taking the risk to share your heart's longings.

Priorities

Figure out your priorities because this will determine what success looks like after the conversation. Sometimes we want the other person to apologize and sometimes we simply want them to know they are wrong. When bitterness and resentment are allowed to grow in your heart, wanting the other person to know they are a useless waste of space is not an uncommon desire. When we ask ourselves the remarkable question, we can discover what we really want for ourselves and the other person. *What is going on in my heart that needs my attention in order to have a productive conversation?*

When you sit with the question, you can prioritize each other's well-being while also finding resolution to the important topic of discussion. Treat the other person like you would your best friend. Conversation can be pleasant and productive if you are willing to value the other person more than making your point or winning the argument. You must choose between being right and being close, but you can't have both. The greatest gift you can give another person is to learn how to share your negative emotions in constructive and honoring ways.

> *You must choose between being right and being close, but you can't have both.*

Words

Your words, one conversation at a time, will either bring life or cause death. When we ask ourselves: *What is going on in my heart that needs my attention in order to have a productive conversation*, we can discover which words bring life to the people we care about. The right words can greatly improve your relationship. The Bible teaches that a kind word can encourage, nourish, and heal a broken heart. Proverbs 16:24 says "Pleasant words are a honeycomb, sweet to the soul and healing to the bones."

Affirming words can build confidence, renew hope, and restore purpose to a person who feels discouraged, overwhelmed, or unimportant. Choose your words carefully. Words are dynamite; they can destroy people (Proverbs 15:4), or they can bring incredible life

(Proverbs 16:24). It is far too easy to let emotions take over and we often speak before we think.

One man, named Jeffery, said to me in front of his wife, "There is nothing about Bethany that is loveable. I can't even think of one thing about her that is appealing." He was about to continue when I stopped him. His wife was hunched over, looking like a vacuum had sucked the life out of her soul. His words cut like a knife and did significant damage to her ability to function. A person who is so crushed they can't function is not going to carry much "appeal." This couple was in deep on a very destructive cycle!

It may take you twenty minutes, a couple hours, or even a month to prepare. If you don't get to your heart, then what is in your heart will spew out on the people you care about. Preparing your heart for the conversation may mean writing things down, practicing, or asking a friend for help. This is very difficult for people who are highly reactive or who feel they are good at thinking on their feet. The truth is that it often takes time to discover the hurt and bitterness you carry. You may even need to consider forgiving the person (or people) that hurt you. It is possible to let go of resentment and thoughts of revenge and experience freedom from the control of the person who harmed you. Holding on to the hurt will rob you of the joy and peace God has for you. You don't have to be defined by your wounds. You can live in your true identity as a dearly loved child of God.

Principles to Keep in Mind During the Conversation
Avoid These Seven Destructive Strategies

Let's look at seven destructive strategies that people employ to get people to do what we want. All seven get people's attention and often produce immediate results. Anger, intensity, threats, guilt, manipulation, nagging, and character assassinations rarely ever make things better and almost always leave residual damage. All seven will significantly decrease your ability to influence the people that matter to you, both now and in the future

1. Anger

Pay attention to your anger. Anger is unproductive and frightening no matter who does it. Anger gets immediate results because the other person must pay attention to you, but they are now afraid, and the relationship is unsafe. Most men have no idea the devastating impact their anger has on a woman. If a man gets angry in the presence of a woman, she will remember his angry outburst at least 500 times. She will be terrified and feel like she is in danger of it happening again. When a man raises his voice, a female may not be able to hear anything they say.

The impact of anger is often difficult to see during the moment. Adriana and Calvin were colleagues working together on a project. They were both experiencing pressure to finish before the deadline. Calvin was frustrated by multiple external factors including the CEO's insistence that the project needed to be turned over to her by the following morning so she could present it to the board. Calvin and Adriana were making progress when Adriana suggested a new idea that was revolutionary to her. Without warning, Calvin dismissed her idea and stormed out of the room. Adriana followed him into the next room and asked him why he was so angry. Calvin moved within three inches of her face, gritted his teeth, waved his arms around, and with great emotion, accused her of making everything into a big ordeal. Adriana was terrified and backed away sheepishly. Calvin stormed out of the room, mumbling that he needed to leave.

The next day, Adriana brought up the outburst to Calvin and said, "I don't like the way you treated me last night. Your behavior was inappropriate in the workplace, yelling and threatening me like that. Storming out when we had a deadline to meet was immature too."

Calvin, feeling dumbfounded, said, "I have never yelled at you or anyone else in this company." Before you characterize Calvin as a chronic liar, you should know that in his mind, he never had. In fact, when he went home, he recounted the whole encounter to his wife and asked her if he was inappropriate. He repeated the words he said to his colleague, Adriana. His wife reassured him that his behavior was appropriate and that Adriana overreacted because she was under stress.

Calvin later approached Adriana and said, "I have thought about what happened last night and not only did I not do anything inappropriate, but I did not threaten you nor did I yell at you. You are projecting things upon me that I am not responsible for doing, and I am offended that you falsely accused me this morning." Adriana was afraid of Calvin because she already experienced his anger, and his unwillingness to see his behavior as destructive increased her fear and caused her to feel extremely uncomfortable whenever around him. From that moment on, she walked on eggshells and did everything she could to avoid spending time in close proximity to Calvin.

How can two people be in the same conversation and have two completely different experiences? The simple answer is that there is a gap between how we see ourselves and how other people experience us. When you dig under the surface, you can see that the more complicated answer is connected to how people experience uncomfortable emotions. We evaluate our interactions with other people by looking at our intentions and what we hoped to accomplish, and we see our emotional responses as normal because they are directly connected to the circumstances.

We minimize our emotional responses and factor them out of the equation. When Calvin told his wife what happened, he did not even mention his anger, facial expressions, or arm waving because to him, they had no bearing on the situation. When he got angry, he felt he was provoked by Adriana changing the subject and preventing them from finishing the project on time. He thought he was justified in his frustration, and for the sake of meeting the deadline, needed to put a stop to her idea, plus make it clear other ideas were not welcome either. And to be fair, Calvin did the right thing by leaving before he said something he would regret.

The impact of anger is often invisible to the person who is angry, but the anger itself is the most important factor in the entire experience for the person witnessing the anger. In other words, when a person is upset, they are focused on the *reason* they are angry, while the person experiencing anger is keenly aware of the threat that is posed by the *anger itself*. We evaluate our interactions with other people by looking at their uncomfortable emotions and the destructive impact we are left carrying. We elevate their emotional responses because they are the most significant factor in the equation. The person on the receiving end of the anger is focused on the danger and fear produced by the unsafe situation. Any time you shout, glare, scowl, or grit your teeth, it can be a traumatic experience for the person opposite you. Many women have a visceral fear of harm whenever they experience anger. For them, anger can be terrifying.[2]

2. Emotional Intensity

Pay attention to emotional intensity. Most women have no idea the devastating impact their emotional intensity has on a man. He will be afraid, angry, uncomfortable, and confused all at the same time. The higher the intensity, the lower the understanding. David Clark compares the way men and women process emotions in conflict to a high-speed food processor compared to a kitchen worker. When a woman is hurt or feeling unheard, she can churn out a torrent of words with a terrifying intensity. She can slice and dice at warp speed, churning out mounds of emotional debris. The man in conflict is a ninety-year-old kitchen worker with arthritis in both hands and a dull knife.

> *The higher the intensity, the lower the understanding.*

As you read *Men Are Clams, Women Are Crowbars* by Clarke and Clarke, you become aware that when conflict breaks out, the man typically needs to slow down to think and process. He needs time and space to sort the vegetables and cut them into pieces. The woman is typically ready to slice and dice, whatever is needed to get the job done fast. When a woman gets intense, the man gets overwhelmed emotionally and becomes terrified and is completely unable to hear what she is saying.[3]

3. Guilt

People utilize guilt because it can have an immediate payoff and get someone to do something they would normally say no to doing. Guilt is a powerful emotion and can be a formidable tool used for manipulation. Trying to make someone feel guilty is an indirect form of communication that uses shaming or blaming someone with the purpose of convincing them to give in or to comply with a request. Guilt is a dangerous behavior designed to cause pain so that the other person will do what you want. People don't trust someone who is willing to intentionally wound them to get what they want.

We often resort to using guilt when we feel vulnerable, unloved, or unworthy. Something in our past makes us feel helpless, so we resort to guilt to gain control of a situation. Unfortunately, using guilt not only does not give us the closeness we want or the intimacy we crave, but it also destroys the trust we need to experience satisfying relationships. Whenever we use guilt-inducing statements, we will subject people to the painfully nauseating feeling of worthlessness for not being a good enough employee, friend, child, or spouse. This guilt tactic holds unconditional love hostage. The guilt that compels us to consider doing something we would not otherwise have done leaves us feeling resentful for being manipulated against our will.

4. Threats

Threatening to leave the relationship to make a point or get another person to understand how upset we are is rarely a good idea. It's also important to remember that thinking about cutting ties or dissolving a relationship and saying it are two very different things. Important relationships like business partnerships, marriages, and close friendships are based on the belief that both people are committed to each other. When we threaten to leave, we undermine the security of the entire relationship.

People often resort to threats when they are desperate and have a particularly important longing or desire they want to communicate and have no way of expressing it. What they really want is to have the other person hear their concerns and change their behavior, so they are reassured about how important the relationship is to them. Unless the other person is extremely mature emotionally, they will not be able to separate the threat of leaving with the longing for more love and reassurance. You see, the loud voice is pushing the person away and the soft voice is calling out for help. The louder one is the one people usually hear.

Threats often open doors that we do not want to remain open. They can be very difficult to close. They can be reciprocated. They will never be forgotten.

A threat to leave puts people on the defensive and sets them up to protect themselves from the threat, which decreases trust over time. Also, it is easy to hear threats as blame. The person you threatened will subconsciously begin thinking of life without you and pull away from you emotionally. The more important the relationship, the more dangerous threatening to leave will become. Hearing that a person you depend upon is threatening to leave can be very traumatic.

5. Nagging

We nag because we care. We find ourselves continually pestering people because they won't do what we want, or they won't stop doing something we know is bad for them. We are frustrated and don't know how to get through to them. So we nag. Nagging is often accompanied with anger because it feels justified and is borne out of serious concern for people that matter to us. Our employee doesn't turn in receipts or add them up correctly. Our spouse refuses to quit drinking. Our child won't pick up their room.

Nagging creates distance and leads to a downward spiral of negative thoughts and feelings about each other. We feel discounted, ignored, and unheard. The one being nagged feels controlled, criticized, and inadequate. Nagging may get people to react immediately, but in the long run, it is unproductive and makes things worse. The more we nag, the more people will tune us out and put up walls to avoid the constant pestering.

6. Manipulation

Manipulation is extremely dangerous because at its core, it uses deception to achieve our selfish desires. Being manipulated can really mess with a person. It affects their wellbeing, self-esteem, and confidence. It can be subtle, direct, relatively mild, or downright offensive. Regardless, it will not allow you to end up at the right destination. Here's why: It attempts to control people in a dishonest and harmful way. People who have been manipulated feel blamed because the problems are their fault, feel guilty as though they have done something wrong, feel crazy because there is something wrong with them, feel powerless because their choices are taken away, or feel inferior because their thoughts, opinions, and desires are dismissed and/or ignored.

7. Character Assassination

We should all be very careful not to attack someone else's character because of the irreparable harm that can come from public, critical attacks. As a matter of fact, *never* insult another person's looks, weight, intelligence, or character because this type of insult rarely goes away. When you're tempted to spew such venom, take a deep breath and hit the pause button. Words spoken in a fight that tear at the core of another person are extremely difficult to forget. Using profanity or cursing also pushes people away. This kind of attack will go beyond the other attacks because, instead of saying something is wrong with a person's behavior or feelings, we are saying there is something wrong with *them* as a person.

The person on the receiving end of an attack will most likely feel our disapproval and rejection and either question their value as a person or protect themselves from an unsafe person. When we receive disapproving messages from a person who is supposed to protect and support us, we feel terrible. Harshly attacking a person's character can destroy the connection and complicate all future communication. A character assassination is a recipe for a miserable, painful existence, not to mention the absence of happiness and satisfaction in relationships.

If we are not careful, we will sacrifice what we want in the future for what we want in the moment. All seven destructive strategies will produce immediate results but will leave residual damage and undermine the ability for people to trust us in the future. Most of us have experienced both sides of these but have definite tendencies that need to be addressed. It is difficult to develop or maintain emotional intimacy with someone we need to protect ourselves from. Without trust, a healthy relationship is impossible.

> Without trust, a healthy relationship is impossible.

Human beings are hard wired with the desire to feel safe. Our subconscious brains are constantly scanning our environment to determine if a person is safe or dangerous. Whenever we determine someone is dangerous, then we protect ourselves from them. When safety is not present, we are guarded, fearful, suspicious, and defensive. When power is misused, we walk on eggshells, have trouble being ourselves, and withhold our true feelings because we know the other person is willing to hurt us. We do not feel free to share our opinions, dreams, and desires. Without trust, it is very difficult for people to be vulnerable and express their honest feelings. When both parties are genuinely interested in the other person's wellbeing, then there will not be any reason to feel threatened or fear an attack. We must avoid this destructive behavior at all costs.

Eliminate extreme statements.

So, what CAN we do? We need to work to eliminate extreme statements. Words like *never* and *always* create an unnecessary barrier that can make it significantly more difficult to accept what you are saying. People often use exaggerated statements when arguing to emphasize or illustrate the merits of their position. Have you noticed this in others and in yourself? Be careful to not use words that people will have a difficult time accepting. Exaggerated words usually increase the defensiveness of the other person and lessen the validity of your feelings. They make it much more difficult for the other person to absorb what you are trying to say. Be careful whenever you use the words must, should, and shouldn't, because they generally serve no other purpose than to diminish the impact of your message. They can also put people off by making yourself sound like an authority who has some kind of hierarchical control over them.

Own your thoughts, feelings, desires, beliefs, and behavior.

A third thing you can do to contribute to better relationship health is to take ownership of your own thoughts, feelings, desires, beliefs, and behavior. Communicate what you think, not what they need to think. Tell the other person what you feel, not how they made you feel. Ask them for what you want them to do instead of telling them what they have failed to do. One of the most common communication killers is not owning what we really think, feel, or want. Sometimes the thing we want is selfish and we are unwilling to say it out loud because we don't want people to see us in a bad light. Sometimes we feel unappreciated, and we don't want other people to see us as needy. These feelings can cause us to not be honest about what we are feeling.

Other times, we are waiting for other people to go first, apologize, take initiative, assume blame, or take charge. If this is you, please know that other people can't read your mind. Our friends and loved ones need us to bring to the table what is going on inside of us so they can respond appropriately and with accurate information. We want to avoid conflict by refusing to own our thoughts, choices, desires, behavior, and feelings, but failing to bring essential information to the conversation doesn't avoid conflict; it often creates more conflict. Those who know us well can tell something is bothering us even if we are unwilling to admit it.

Clarify what you want.

The fourth healthy thing you can do is to clarify what you hope to accomplish during the conversation. If the other person understands what you want their role to be, it will make it possible for them to succeed. Try and help the other person understand what you want them to do. If you want the other person to listen, then consider saying something like "I am trying to figure out what I am feeling. Could you help me process what I am feeling for a few minutes?" If you need a solution, then you may want to say at the end of the conversation, "I have a deadline and I must come up with the best solution. I can't promise I will do what you say, but I would appreciate your advice and any helpful ideas." If you want support and encouragement then say, "I am not looking for advice or coaching on this. I just need a lot of reassurance and confirmation." If you need someone to step in and do something, don't give mysterious clues and expect them to pick up on your hints. Say, "I am desperate, and I need someone to sit with me and help me see a different picture of myself. Right now, I feel like such a failure that I am tempted to get a giant 'F' for Failure tattooed on my forehead!"

Express hurt instead of hostility.

The fifth tactic you can do to help stay away from the destructive strategies is to express hurt instead of hostility. It is okay to be frustrated, disappointed, and even angry as long as you are not lashing out in an unproductive way. Be careful because words said in anger are hard to take back and difficult to overcome. Give the other person an opportunity to respond by communicating your feelings and not just the anger (Proverbs 15: 1). When you are hostile, you stand up for yourself in a way that is inappropriate and causes other people to be afraid of you.

There is a reason the anger section above was the longest, and I feel we need to finish unpacking it here. Anger is such a potent emotion that we must be cautious with how it is expressed. Verbal characteristics of hostile and aggressive communication include sarcasm, yelling, intimidation, a harsh tone of voice and condescending statements that put others down. The nonverbal cues include intruding into someone's personal space, sneering, smirking, and aggressive gestures like pointing your finger or clenching your fist. Hostility can leave the other person exhausted, overwhelmed, drained, and convinced they need to protect themselves from another attack.

It is good to stand up and express hurt as long as you are cognizant of how you are treating the other person. It is healthy to express your hurt openly and honestly as long as you have compassion for the needs of others. It is okay to be firm as long as you are respectful of the other person's personal space and seek to have your needs understood so that they can be met.

Follow up after the conversation.

There are ways to follow up after a conversation to maximize the impact and connection. First, thank the other person for anything they did that you appreciate, no matter how little or insignificant. Whatever gets rewarded will likely be repeated. Second, evaluate your own attitude, priorities, motivation, and words. Evaluations produces wisdom and more connected relationships. When we ask ourselves the remarkable question, *What is going on in my heart that needs my attention in order to have a productive conversation?* then we can discover what we need to do in the future. Third, apologize for anything you said or did that damaged your connection or injured your relationship. Imperfect people (all of us) desperately need grace and forgiveness. Fourth, do whatever you said you would do. The best way to build trust is to keep your promises and be predictable, dependable, and reliable going forward.

Completing This Leg of the Journey

It's wise to have an effective communication strategy when we have something important to say. We cannot allow passion to get our point across because that can override the compassion we feel for the person we are talking to. We must stop using our words as a weapon and refuse the seven strategies that destroy relationships. Only a person in touch with their own heart can reach another person's heart.

To prepare for the conversation, keep in mind important principles during the conversation and make necessary adjustments to improve your future conversations. If damage has been done, this will take a concentrated effort! Let's increase our likelihood of ending up at the right destination by learning to ask the most important question at every stage along the way. *What is going on in my heart that needs my attention in order to have a productive conversation?*

Questions for Discussion

- Why are people in such a hurry when they are in important conversations?

- How does hurrying a conversation undermine the connection of two individuals and produce less than ideal outcomes for conversations?

- What is the negative impact of anger?

- What are some of the devastating results of emotional intensity?

- Do you agree that people speak out of the overflow of their heart?

- How do you prepare your heart for a conversation?

- How can two people be in the same conversation and have two completely different experiences?

- What is the difference between expressing hurt and acting with hostility?

- How can you effectively evaluate a conversation?

- What do you need to do before your next important conversation?

Part Three:
Decisions That Will Produce a Satisfying Adventure

Chapter Eight

Fill Up the Tank

Speaking from the heart to create thirst for future conversations.

How is it that when some people speak, everyone stops whatever they are doing to listen, and when other people speak, everyone tunes them out? Influence is a complicated thing. You do not have the power to make someone listen to you, but the way you talk and the things you say will influence whether they want to listen to what you have to say. If you are patient and gentle, the people you care about will want to hear what you have to say. The harder you push, the more your children will resist.

> *If you are patient and gentle, the people you care about will want to hear what you have to say.*

If you say things from your heart, then the important people in your life will want to hear from you, not because you pushed or cornered them and made them listen, but because they value your opinion and want to hear your ideas. Is it possible to increase your influence?

There is a decision you can make that will improve your relationship and make it possible to get to another person's heart. You will need humility to avoid or stop speaking destructive words and wisdom to see beyond what you want to say in the moment to get what you really want. If you make this decision, you will be able to bring up issues and end up connected. It will increase your influence at work, make you better equipped to redirect your friends, get your grown children to consider changing their behavior, and make you a more desirable spouse. You can create a thirst for future conversations if you make the decision to say things from your heart. This is how you improve relationships and increase your influence.

How do I talk in a way people will want to listen?

Stop speaking destructive words.

You must avoid destructive words and strategies to get what you want. Anger, intensity, threats, guilt, manipulation, nagging, and character assassinations may get immediate results, but will undermine all future conversations. Anger and intensity are effective strategies to get people to pay attention, but they will sabotage your ability to influence them in the future because they will tune you out before you even begin. If you genuinely communicate that you care about the person you are speaking to and value their ideas, opinions, and perspective, then they will trust you. The higher their trust for you, the more likely your perspective and ideas will be given consideration.

Not every comment is of equal importance. Some things are urgent, some are important, and some are insignificant. When you have something urgent to say, it is time sensitive, but rarely imperative. There will be times when you absolutely need your boss to pay attention to you and give your complaint consideration. If you are known to nitpick trivial things or say things in a harsh manner, your boss will likely protect themselves from your words and be resistant to your concerns.

If you are bothered by insignificant things, learn to let them go entirely without making them a big deal. I once heard a speaker say that the way to tell if a behavior needs to change is to run it through a one-year filter. If the person continues to do this irritating behavior in a year, would it be a game changer in the relationship? If the annoying activity is inconvenient but will not make a significant difference to the health of the relationship, then let it go and do not even bring it up. Wise people learn how to discern which concerns are important and need to be brought to the table for consideration. You will build influence by refraining from unnecessary comments, but that requires a decision to stop injuring people with your words.

Fill their emotional fuel tank with trust.

A potentially helpful way of thinking about trust is looking at it like putting fuel in your vehicle. If your truck has gas, then you can make it to your destination. If you allow the tank to completely run out, you will be stranded on the side of the road and unable to go anywhere. Every person has an emotional fuel tank. Positive words fill the tank and negative words empty the tank. Fill their emotional fuel tank with trust so you will have a voice when you have something important to say. If you use encouraging words, then they will look forward to hearing from you in the future. A person with a full tank will be significantly more likely to give you the benefit of the doubt and allow you to clarify when you say something insensitive or incorrect.

The more you fill up the tank, the more trust you have for future conversions. There will be times when you need to say something that they may not want to hear. As a parent, there will be times when you need to give your daughter feedback that may be critical to her future success. You want to have the important people in your life know that you have their best interest at heart and love them dearly. Pay attention to what you say. Every negative comment erodes trust and drains their emotional fuel tank. They say it takes six or seven positive comments to counteract every negative one.

Refuse to use manipulation.

Before we look at twelve strategies that will significantly increase your influence, we must slow down for a word of caution. These are not strategies to manipulate people. If we manipulate people to get them to do what we want, it may have an immediate payoff in one conversation but in the future, they will see through our fake or inauthentic behavior. Relationships are for the long haul. We need to do and say the right things today even if we don't have any pay off for months, years, or even decades. Influence must be earned. We pay attention to the people we trust who have our best interest and well-being at heart. According to fascinating book called, *Influencer*, manipulation is a very short-term strategy that ultimately destroys careers and relationships.[1] Instead, build trust and you will earn influence when you need it.

> Influence must be earned.

Learning to influence people is a fundamental skill that all of us need, but there is a fine line between influencing and manipulating. They can look similar, but they are not. The ability to recognize the difference between the two and make sure we stay on the right side of the line is a crucial long-term relational skill. Manipulation undermines trust, so it's important to understand the difference between influence and manipulation. It really comes down to our intent, their choice, whose best interest is the focus, and the future impact. Intent is about why we are doing it. What is the motive? We can manipulate to get what we want in the moment or build trust for future influence. Good persuaders and good manipulators understand what drives people to take action and know how to effectively utilize what they know to sway people. That is why there are few things more dangerous than a bad person with good persuasion skills. It's a good person who can influence people positively.

Do we want something for the other person and the relationship or do we want to get something from them that will satisfy our desires or only benefit us? Interest is about who the change will benefit. Being able to influence requires the knowledge of what motivates people and the understanding of what is driving their behavior. Convincing people to make changes can either be one of the most remarkable gifts or the most despicable acts of selfishness. There is nothing wrong with seeking to influence someone else as long we do it honestly and with their best interest in mind. Any time we lie or distort the truth, we will undermine future conversations because people don't trust someone who deceives them to get what they want. If you are providing true value to people on the opposite end of the exchange, then there's no reason to resort to deception or manipulation to convince them. If you want influence, you will have to give much more than you take.

That includes giving them choice. It's about who is in control. Influence is empowering people to make the best decisions that lead to internal peace and connected relationships. Manipulation is getting people to do what we want for our own selfish purposes. Are we willing to pressure, coerce, and demand, if necessary, in order to maintain control? Influence works best when we are transparent and not withholding essential information. If we are willing to wait for them to come to their own conclusions even when their choice is different than what we would have wanted, then we are not taking control. What impact can we have if we cause long-term damage? At the heart of influence is the future and how our present words affect it.

Twelve powerful strategies to increase your influence.

If we need to stop using destructive words and strategies (anger, intensity, threats, guilt, manipulation, nagging, character assassinations) to get what we want, then what can we do to increase our influence? There are twelve strategies that are significantly effective and will produce results. If we apply these strategies properly, we will earn influence and build trust. Each of these strategies will create a thirst in people for what we might want to say in the future. All of them can be used alone because they are effective by themselves, but if you want to make the conversation more persuasive, then you can combine two, three, or four in the same conversation. The more we can string together, the more influence we can have in people's lives.

1. Be uncertain. Talk in a way that communicates you need more information to be certain. This strategy is counter intuitive, but highly effective. It seems like we will be more influential by telling someone confidently what they need to do or how they should think. The opposite is actually true. The more willing we are to take a I-want-to-understand posture, the more willing they will be to consider what we have to say. When you are sharing controversial ideas with potentially resistant people, the more passionate and forceful you are, the less persuasive you will become. If we present what they want, think, or should do a little more tentatively, it will carry more weight. The more we remain curious and open to discover what the other person is saying, the more they will trust us. When we are willing to give consideration to their perspective, it reduces defensiveness and accurately reflects a willingness to consider the other person's opinion.

Why should we be uncertain? There are a couple powerful reasons to be uncertain. But let me first make sure you know that I'm not asking you to be disingenuous. I'm literally asking you to be less certain you know all the answers and to be sure that posture shows to others! First, it gives the other person the ability to change their mind and go in a different direction while maintaining their dignity, they will almost always choose to be a good person. You could say, "I may have completely missed what you were saying, and I am open to being redirected." Comments like these communicate a desire to understand.

Second, we don't actually know what another person is thinking or feeling because we are not them. We don't have the same temperament, motivational drivers, or life experience. Would you rather have someone tell you what you think, or would you rather discover your own thoughts after talking with a wise person? Do you want someone to tell you what you should feel, or do you want someone to care about how you feel? Would you want someone to tell you what to do or understand what you need? Whenever someone tells us they know what we are thinking or what we should do, we almost automatically resist. The best way to illustrate this principle is to give a real-life example.

Jeff came into my office because he had recently discovered his wife was having an affair. He was extremely angry and amped up. His six feet, four-inch frame, combined with 330 pounds of muscle, made him an imposing figure. Jeff wanted to crush the man that had the affair with his wife, and he was more than capable of carrying out his desire with his bare hands. He knew this man's schedule and where he lived. I immediately had two thoughts come to my mind: I am going to watch an awful story play out on the news this evening, and I am going to be arrested for accessory to murder.

What I wanted to say was, "That is a dumb idea that will end with your arrest, and will leave your children without a parent," but I have learned that people resist you if you tell them what they should or shouldn't do. I listened for over an hour and asked Jeff if he would be willing to hear my thoughts. I said very tentatively, "I might be wrong, and you have freedom to correct me. I think there are two things that you want right now."

He gruffly sighed and asked, "What do you think I want?

I continued, "It is obvious to me that you love both of your kids. I may be wrong, but I think you want to earn the respect of your grown children. I don't think that is what you want the most, though. You did not say this to me, and I may be on the wrong track so feel free to bring me back to the station. I think you want to win the heart of your wife, but you are terrified that it is too late. Did I miss it?"

Jeff put his head on the table and started crying like a little baby. After about five minutes, he lifted his head. I asked, "Can I help you accomplish those two things?" We spent the next ninety minutes having a meaningful conversation. The more uncertain you are, and the more tentative you speak to someone who is hurting, the more weight your words carry.

2. Affirm the relationship and the person. Tell the other person how important they are to you and how much you value being their friend, dad/mom, sister, or partner. Wise people say at least five positive things for every one criticism. If you see a friend or family member doing something good, then point it out. Affirming words can build confidence, renew hope, and restore purpose to a person who feels discouraged, overwhelmed, or unimportant. Consider making your home, work, and church a place where appreciation and approval are freely spoken. Words that are affirming motivate other people to draw close. You can say, "I appreciate you." To see how effective your strategy will be, you can ask yourself: *After I make this remark, will they be more or less likely to want to hear from me again?* Remember, you want to create a thirst for future conversations. If you want your boss to consider your brilliant idea for the company, start the conversation by saying "I appreciate you and am extremely grateful to have you as my boss. Thanks for creating a work environment where we can be successful in our jobs and feel like we can bring forward our ideas for improvement. It makes it so much easier to be passionate when I know that I am valued."

3. Share your longings rather than hurl your accusations. All of us have deep longings that are at the core of everything we say, think, and do. Behind every complaint is a deep, personal longing. Read more about this in *Disconnected* by Clark and Clark.[2] We all need to lean on God to help us move beyond saying things that are mean, cutting, and insensitive and communicate our deeper longings for help and connection. Jennifer wanted her boyfriend to invite her on more dates. She tried pointing out how her girlfriends who have boyfriends go on dates every weekend. She also said, "I don't understand why you don't do the simplest things to make me feel loved?" Telling a person they are not good enough and fail at even the simplest tasks is not the best motivator. We will get better results if we tell the people we care about our desires and expectations. Jennifer could say, "I want to feel closer to you. Could we go on a date next weekend? When you ask me to go on a date with you, I feel very connected to you."

4. Acknowledge the things that are frustrating for the other person. If something is difficult for the other person, let them know how you see it and why you care. Stephanie wanted her employee, Andrea, to fill out a form in the new database so everyone on the team could have access to the meaningful information. She could say, "I know this task might be extremely annoying. I realize I am adding something to your already-full plate." The idea is to create thirst for what else you might want to say. When you care about what the other person is experiencing and say it out loud, then they will want to have future conversations with you.

Joan wants her husband to attend their daughter's piano recital. She could say, "I care about how overwhelmed you feel right now because of the pressure you are under at work. I probably did not make it any easier by asking you to leave early last Monday." With this, she would acknowledge that she sees how difficult her husband's days have been. Joan could also say, "I know you hear her two-minute recital song at home all the time, and listening to other kids play the piano for two hours can be boring, but I also know how much you care." Remember, Joan is building influence by the words she says to her husband.

5. Appeal to what a person values. Try calling out their best and appealing to their values and desire to do the right thing. Kim values her relationship with her daughter and loves her family but has been very overwhelmed by her new job. Her husband, Frank, noticed that their two-year old has been missing time with her mom lately. Instead of shaming Kim for bringing her work home every evening, Frank could say, "You know, you are a great mom, and our daughter loves spending time with you. Can I help you schedule some special time with her in the next week or so?" Do you think this approach will make Kim more or less likely to want to hear what Frank says next?

The best way to illustrate this principal is from a true event from the Bible. In 1 Samuel 25, we find a desperate man on the verge of ruining his reputation and bringing guilt on himself that he can never escape. David's mentor, Samuel, dies, and David is exhausted and hungry from trying to remain hidden from King Saul's army and their relentless pursuit to kill him. He is hiding out on land belonging to a rich landowner named, Nabal. David's men are also trying to survive. They go above and beyond to protect Nabal's flocks from harm and keep marauders from stealing anything from them. (1 Samuel 25:15-16). David patiently waits for the perfect time when Nabal is likely to be in a good mood. David sends his men to respectfully ask Nabal if he will contribute whatever he can spare for the way David's men protected his flock.

It turns out Nabal is an arrogant fool who is impossible to influence because he does not listen. He does not care about his workers or his family. He not only refuses David's request, but he publicly insults David and his fighting men and questions their integrity. Nabal treats David's men so disrespectfully that they report every single word when they return to camp. David is so infuriated and immediately tells the men to strap on their swords. He is about to do something he will regret for the rest of his life.

One of the women notices how precarious the situation is and asks Abigail, Nabal's wife, to step into the chaos and do something about this dangerous situation. Abigail quickly repurposes a bounty of food that had already been prepared for Nabal's upcoming feast to give it to David and his men instead. She rides out to meet David. This situation was an inferno ready to be ignited. Angry men wanting to punish the person who treated them with contempt. It was like a valley of dry wood which had been doused with gasoline and 400 men were carrying matches. Abigail was the perfect person for this situation because she had a considerable repertoire of relational resources at her disposal.

Abigail was able to use at least four of the strategies to influence people in one conversation. She starts by bowing in a posture of respect, then she apologizes for not anticipating the need. She even acknowledges how difficult it would be to hear the contemptuous comments of her foolish husband. She starts speaking with gracious words filled with wisdom. She calls out the best in him and appeals to his values and his desire to do the right thing. She helps David remember who he is and what he is going to accomplish. She gently helps him see that God's hand is on him and one day will make him the leader over all of Israel. She reminds him of God's faithfulness in difficult circumstances and God's future plans for him despite insurmountable obstacles.

Look at her remarkable words in 1 Samuel 25:28-31: [28]"Please forgive your servant's presumption. The Lord your God will certainly make a lasting dynasty for my lord, because you fight the Lord's battles, and no wrongdoing will be found in you as long as you live. [29]Even though someone is pursuing you to take your life, the life of my lord will be bound securely in the bundle of the living by the Lord your God, but the lives of your enemies he will hurl away as from the pocket of a sling. [30]When the Lord has fulfilled for my lord every good thing he promised concerning him and has appointed him ruler over Israel, [31]my lord will not have on his conscience the staggering burden of needless bloodshed or of having avenged himself. And when the Lord your God has brought my lord success, remember your servant."

Abigail's appeal to David was so remarkable because it called out the best in him instead of pointing out his flaws and telling him what to do. David was clearly in the wrong in so many ways. Abigail guided him into better behavior. She did not get him to see a better path by emphasizing to David how wrong and angry and out of control he was acting, even though all of those were true. Instead, Abigail emphasized David's desire to honor God and fulfill His purposes. She pointed out his integrity and asked him to consider if his present course of action was consistent with who he wanted to be and what he hoped to accomplish. Abigail was able to put David back in touch with his values. She called forth the best in him and helped him see a better way. She appealed to his values and reminded him that he did not want to get revenge through bloodshed because that is not who David wanted to be.

David was so moved by Abigail's words that he abandoned his plan to get revenge. He even thanked Abigail for convincing him to walk away from his reckless plan. He complimented her judgement and told her he was going to grant her request. 1 Samuel 25: 32-35 says, [32]"David said to Abigail, 'Praise be to the Lord, the God of Israel, who has sent you today to meet me. [33]May you be blessed for your good judgment and for keeping me from bloodshed this day and from avenging myself with my own hands. [34]Otherwise, as surely as the Lord, the God of Israel, lives, who has kept me from harming you, if you had not come quickly to meet me, not one male belonging to Nabal would have been left alive by daybreak.' [35]Then David accepted from her hand what she had brought him and said, "Go home in peace. I have heard your words and granted your request."

6. Give them a choice by offering them a legitimate opportunity to experience it for themselves. If you want someone to try something, then invite the other person to try it for one week. Often, personal experience gives them an entirely different frame of reference. Sometimes you are describing activities and outcomes that the other person does not know anything about. Personal experience allows us to see and feel the benefits firsthand. If a person feels controlled or manipulated, they will resist you and get angry. Disagreements become power struggles instead of information exchanges.

Steve wants his friend Dan, who loves sports and has extra time on his hands, to play basketball on Thursday evenings. Steve could say, "Would you give it a try for just one week? If you don't like it, or it takes up too much of your time, I will understand."

If April wants Cheri to join her Life Group at church, she could say, "We are starting a new series on Sunday nights, and I think it may be exactly what you are looking for. If you do not feel like it is a good fit, or you are not comfortable, you can back out with no questions asked." The idea is to give them an opportunity to see how much they like it and what it would be like and if they decide to continue.

7. Apologize for your part. Sometimes you feel like the other person should apologize because they did much more offensive things than you. You can apologize for your part even when you are only partially to blame. It is extremely powerful when you acknowledge your part in hurting, disappointing, or frustrating someone you care about. Corey could start a conversation with his spouse, Jasmine, by saying, "I am sorry for hurting you with my inconsiderate words. I allowed my emotions to get the best of me. I want to treat you better than I did. Would you be willing to forgive me?"

Randy was talking with his son, Derek, whose behavior was pushing him over the edge. Derek left his half-eaten McDonald's cheeseburger in the car, ignored his sister, and did not turn in his completed homework into his teacher. Derek also got a ticket for driving twenty miles over the speed limit. Randy expressed frustration over his son's behavior by storming out of the room and initiating the silent treatment for the rest of the evening. Randy could get stuck on his son's offenses. Or Randy could say to his son, "I am sorry for walking away and giving you the silent treatment when I got frustrated, I value you and our relationship." An apology can be a powerful tool to create a thirst for what comes next. Remember you are not just focusing on the present circumstances because you want the people you care about to listen to you. You can string together more than one strategy if you want to make the conversation more powerful.

8. Tell a story. Few things can motivate people like a well-told story. In fact, a well-told story can engage the heart, the mind, the will, and even the behavior. This is a sophisticated strategy that takes practice and skill but is a remarkable tool. If a story is done well, a person can have a vicarious experience and understand an entirely different dimension to their situation. Nathan had the difficult task of confronting an immensely powerful king who was knowingly rebellious and unwilling to listen to correction. If the king did not like what Nathan said, the king could have him killed. In 2 Samuel 11:1-12, Nathan carefully confronted King David with the truth. I have no idea how long it took Nathan to prepare this message, but his approach was masterful and effective. He confronted David in a way that got him to admit he was wrong and want to change his behavior. Nathan also stayed alive in the process! He told him a story and connected it to his values.

David had an affair with Bathsheba and covered it up by having Uriah killed. Nathan said (and I'm paraphrasing), "I need your help because you are great at solving problems. Could you help me figure out what I need to do? There is a poor man that has one sheep, and it is the most valuable possession of his entire family. His children sleep with it at night and treat it like a sibling. Another man has thousands of sheep. When a legitimate problem came up because the wealthy man needed to show hospitality to a person that stopped by unexpectedly, he decided to bypass his thousands of sheep and take the one lamb from the family that cherished it. What should I do"? The story engaged David's sense of justice and he burned with anger. He said, "This man must die and pay back four times the cost of the lamb because he did such an awful thing with no pity. That man deserves to die." Once David's heart and mind were engaged, Nathan simply said, "You are the man." Be careful using this strategy because people can misunderstand your message.

9. Make a request for a specific change of behavior. Making requests can be terrifying because you must be vulnerable and risk rejection. What if they say, "no?" It is helpful if you give a straightforward description of the situation you want to address. Leave out analysis, interpretation, and blaming language. Try to make it as specific, kind, and objective as possible. Nobody wins when you only communicate your disgust, disapproval, and rejection. Give the other person a legitimate chance to connect and demonstrate care by fulfilling one of your desires.

Nancy wants to get Fred to do the dishes. She could say, "Would you put the dishes in the dishwasher before you go to bed?" The people we care about may say, "no," but the clearer we are in asking for a specific change, the easier it will be for them to say, "yes." Hearing, "no" is always disappointing, but we often don't get the results we want because the other person doesn't know what we are asking for.

10. Get to the bottom line before you share all the important details. Suspense and drama are important for telling good stories, but it can work against you in communicating something important. When Joann's car broke down, she needed to have it repaired. Her husband, Terry, was concerned about the repair cost. When Joann got home, Terry asked, "How did it go?" Although he didn't communicate this, his main motivation was to find out how much the repair cost.

Joann started by saying, "I invited my new friend Julie to go to breakfast. She needed to rearrange her entire schedule. We could not find the restaurant. Then it took forever to order because the menu was all changed. Actually, the waiter completely forgot us for twenty minutes, so it all worked out. We decided to share the most wonderful burrito. Oh, the chef uses this really special sauce that brings out the flavor. I wish I could buy a bottle of that sauce for our refrigerator. Anyway.... from there, I went to the car shop. I was a little late, but the mechanic was really nice about it. I waited in the lobby while they worked on the..."

The "extended version" continued as Terry looked like he was going to blow a gasket.

Ladies, guys need the bottom-line version first, then they will be able to hear the important details. In the first two sentences, Terry needed to hear how much the repair cost. Joann could say, "It is going to be ok. It cost $500.00, but the car is all fixed now." After he knows the cost, then he can hear about the rest of your day. If your grandson is in the hospital, it is important to include the outcome before you get to the details. If your daughter was in an accident, you can say, "Joy was in an accident, but it was minor. In fact, she's already back home." Tell them what they desperately want to hear before you share the details that will connect to your heart.

11. Accept them and communicate you are there for them. Other people sometimes make poor choices, act badly, and do things that hurt us. You can respond with contempt, look down on them, or judge them, but that will usually push them away and create another problem. When you accept someone, it means you are for them, you are glad they are in your life, and you long for the best for them. Words that show acceptance invite other people to share. People can tell if we are just putting up with them or if we are accepting them. We make our relationships stronger when we fundamentally accept who people are and choose to love and appreciate them despite their flaws. It will help us respond better if we invest the time to understand the other person's unique life experiences and how those experiences have guided their decisions along the way.

People make mistakes and don't always live up to our expectations. It's important to remember the happiness and joy their friendship has brought to your life. Their poor choices do not have to define everything. We can either judge them and look down on them or we can focus on who they are now and the person they are growing to be. Be patient because long-term growth and maturity always takes time. Acknowledge their personal struggles, recognize the hardships of their journey, and take note of the growth they have achieved. Compliment them on some of the things that make them unique, like compassion, patience, and thoughtfulness. Words that are warm and accepting encourage people to draw close.

If your son forgets to text you when he lands on his trip back to college, you could say, "That's okay. I am far from perfect, and I think you are amazing. I love you, and you are very important to me." The more a person feels accepted, the fewer barriers they will have to overcome in listening to what you are trying to say. When people feel criticized, disliked, and unappreciated, they are unable to hear what anyone is saying because they feel attacked.

Emily and Sam were in an argument that left Emily with unresolved hurt. She could point out all the things he did wrong which most likely caused more disconnection. She could say, "I was hurt by your comments, but I am committed to building a life with you. Can we talk about it?" Words that are forgiving release other people to admit failure.

What if an important person says no to us or makes a decision that is extremely disappointing? When we hear, "no" when we want to hear, "yes," we can either get annoyed, resentful, or angry and express our frustration and disappointment, or we can accept the person and graciously allow them to say, "no."

Joel was very disappointed with the decision his boss made when she asked his colleague to lead an important initiative that he wanted to take on. The opportunity would have given him exposure to other parts of the company and helped him build social and professional capital. He was so frustrated with her decision that he unleashed his frustration and let her have it. He said, "I just can't accept your choice. Who could follow the logic of your bizarre decision? To be honest, I question your ability to make sound judgements and lead this company. I am not even sure if I want to work for a company with such an incompetent leader." In a few short minutes, Joel lost the respect of his boss and all future ability to influence her or find favor in climbing the ladder.

Hearing, "no" is never easy, but it can be especially challenging when you really wanted something important. Take the time to carefully consider the cost before reacting poorly and saying something you will regret. We may have to change the way we see things. If we believe that allowing someone to reject us will make us appear weak and encourage them to walk over us in the future, then we are likely to respond to rejection with anger. We may feel like we are standing up for ourselves and refusing to put up with unacceptable behavior, but if we respond to our hurt by hurting someone else, it's not a recipe for personal happiness or strong relationships. Plus, consider the positive traits we display when we respond gracefully. We exemplify compassion, strength, and maturity, which are all qualities of a really good person.

When we feel rejected or overlooked, our disappointment can be too much to bear. This intense reaction makes sense because we lost something that we really cared about. Hurting people often hurt people. The way we respond today will often determine how close people will get to us tomorrow. It is okay to express our disappointment as long as it is not mixed with judgement and condemnation. If we say hurtful words, then our words will undermine our own wellbeing and damage the relationship.

What could Joel have said to produce a better outcome after his boss' disappointing decision? His best path was to be both tactful and truthful. He could have delivered his message by accepting the decision and expressing his disappointment without the harsh accusations and judgments. He could be direct, thoughtful, and honest. When he felt slighted, he could have said: "When I heard you went in a different direction, I was disappointed because I had been looking forward to the opportunity. I am hopeful the person you chose will do a great job, and I want to do what I can to support the initiative." Expressing acceptance and ending on a positive tone shows compassion and maturity. What we say to people when we are disappointed will determine how much influence we have with them in the future. Being told no and feeling rejection and disappointment isn't enjoyable or comfortable, but it can increase our influence and make us more successful if we can accept the person and graciously allow them to say, "no."

12. Use contrasting statements. This one requires some forethought. I would not attempt it if you use sarcasm often, as people will think you are messing with them or trying to criticize them. The idea behind this strategy is to contrast what you are not saying with the thing you want them to hear. Do your best to use words that keep them from hearing more than you intend. Trish wants to get her husband, Ian, to hear her heart and spend time with his seventeen-year-old daughter,

Sierra, who is hanging out with the wrong crowd. They have had several conversations, but all Ian heard is his wife telling him he is a bad father and his daughters' bad decisions are all his fault.

Trish could say, "I am not saying you are a bad father because I respect you very much. I am asking you to consider changing one thing. What would you think of taking Sierra out once a month for some father/daughter time. I'd love to support you in being able to do that!" Trish could also say, "I am not asking you to change your entire schedule, but I do have some ideas of how we could make it work. What do you think?"

I was able to watch my mother-in-law influence her entire family in a few sentences. The day before I married Darlene, both her brothers and her dad won the semifinal softball game to advance to the championship game. The only problem was the game was scheduled at the same time as our wedding rehearsal dinner. All three of them rightfully wanted to play for the championship. My future mother-in-law had been so careful with her words for decades, all she had to say was, "This is Darlene's one wedding, and we are not going to miss the rehearsal." She was known for keeping her cool, so when she showed her opinion with some intensity, everyone paid attention. My mother-in-law always acted selflessly, so when she asked for something, everyone knew the importance of her request.

Completing This Leg of the Journey

It is possible to increase our influence and get the people in our life to pay attention when we have something critical to say. The important people in our life will want to hear from us, not because we pushed or coerced them or developed more sophisticated arguments that compelled them to listen, but because we have earned their trust by consistently having their best interest at heart and caring about their well-being. They will want to hear what we have to say because we have stopped speaking destructive words and using manipulative strategies.

People will want to listen to us if we speak life and fill up their emotional tank. We all need to resist the urge to get what we want in the moment so we can get our friends and loved ones to pay attention to us when it matters. We will be able to bring up issues and even get them to consider changing their behavior when we take the time to get to know them, acknowledge their concerns, and speak to their values. We will improve our relationships when we make the decision to say things from the heart. It will create a thirst for future conversations.

Questions for Discussion

- Why are other people tempted to forfeit their future influence to get what they want in the moment?

- Why is it difficult to take the long view in your conversations?

- What hurtful things have other people said to you that have made it difficult to pay attention to them in the future?

- What are things you have said that have ended up costing you future influence?

- What role does trust play in your ability to hear what someone says to you?

- What are three things that the important people in your life can do or say to lose your trust?

- Why does passion and intensity lessen your influence in one-on-one conversations?

- How has someone else affirmed you in previous conversations?

- How much influence do you carry with the important people in your life?

- What could you do this week to increase your influence?

Chapter Nine

Follow the GPS

Listening so a person feels heard by receiving what they say before you respond to it.

+

Have you ever had a conversation that, despite your best intentions, did not go very well? Have you ever wondered why people you care about seem to resist you? Why is it that you can share the best possible solution to the problem someone you care about is facing, yet they refuse to listen to your advice?

Having a conversation is difficult because people often see things from entirely different perspectives, but when you add in personal preferences, temperaments, personalities, gender differences, and families of origin, it can seem almost impossible. To make matters worse, some people want to process conflict logically. They function best when things remain calm and reasonable. Their first reaction to most situations is to rationally work towards a logical solution. They operate in the arena of facts, empirical data, and rational thought. They see emotions as the silly ramblings of weak, unstable individuals.

Other people want to process conflict emotionally, by giving equal consideration to values, feelings, and the emotional impact on all the people involved. They function best when people are kind enough to give their feelings (and the processing of those feelings) time and consideration. They see logical solutions as the premature directives of cold, uncaring, and emotionally stunted individuals.

How do we have productive conversations with such vastly different people? Is it possible to navigate differences of opinions and end up connected instead of hurt? Does a logical person have to become illogical? Does an emotional person have to become unemotional? Of course not.

There is something we can all do that is both loving and wise. It is productive and amazing. This one thing will improve your relationship and make it possible to complete conversations on a positive note. You will need wisdom. You will need humility. You will need courage. If you make this decision, you will be able to navigate differences of opinions, hurt feelings, and end up connected.

The game changer is this. Make the decision to receive what the person you care about says before you respond to it. There is no way I could even begin to overstate the importance of this stye of listening.

> *Receive what the person you care about says before you respond to it.*

Six levels of listening.

There are six levels of listening. It may be helpful to think of listening as an action on a continuum. Each level promises a more meaningful experience for you but will require a deeper level of engagement and a higher level of commitment. Lower levels of listening are often selfish and designed to protect our hearts, whereas higher levels of listening tend to put the other person first and seek to fully understand them.

Why should you take the time to listen?
Listening helps the other person.

Hearing alone is not enough. The sense that we are not being heard is one of the most frustrating feelings imaginable. Toddlers throw fits, students move out, employees look for different jobs, and couples end relationships. Listening has the opposite impact and can be extremely helpful.

Six Levels of Listening

Understand

Highest level. We must do this with our eyes, ears, and heart. We hear people and empathize with their perspective and try to understand where they are coming from.

Explore

We are willing to hear something we don't want to hear from people and make a conscious decision to move past our discomfort and give their experience consideration. We move into their longings and begin processing their perspective.

Invite

We listen to people with our ears and also with our eyes. We encourage them to share more information even if it is uncomfortable or difficult to hear.

Defend

We take what people say personally and protect ourselves and our opinions. We hear their words as criticism or attacks and then we prove that we are not to blame.

Deny

Deny or **reject** people's emotional experience. We are not listening, but, instead, are formulating a response to change the way they think or feel.

Ignore

The lowest level is to **ignore** people as if they do not matter. We treat people with indifference when we do not engage them.

Sometimes people need to release their negative emotions by talking through them out loud. When a person is amped up or hurting, they do not have access to the part of their brain that can work toward solutions. Patiently listening can help to evaporate a lot of frustration and put people in a place where they are able to think creatively. *Couples Communication* by Sherod Miller and others talks about this concept in more detail. Listening helps them clarify what they want and make sense of their experience.[1] It can also help them feel valued and important. When a person feels emotionally supported, they feel appreciated and accepted.

Listening helps us gather enough information to solve the actual problem.

If we do not take time to listen, we will be answering the wrong question and solving the wrong problem. And we must wait. If we offer a solution before a person asks for one, they will resist us and get frustrated, angry, anxious, or stressed. Disagreements become power struggles instead of information exchanges. People are complex and their individual objections matter. Listening can help us respond appropriately. If we take time to listen, we can solve the actual problem or offer the comfort and emotional support they really want and need. Why are they resisting you? Why are they pushing you away?

We love to use GPS to get where we are going. If you use Apple Maps®, then you are familiar with Siri's voice. If you don't follow her directions because you want to take a side road instead of the major highway, then the app will recalculate and help you find your way. We have access to information but ultimately get to make the decision about which way we will drive.

One summer evening, I was headed to watch my favorite baseball team when I encountered an awful traffic jam. Siri chimed in and told me there was a hazard ahead and an alternate route had been identified that would save me eleven minutes. I had such a short distance left to reach the stadium, and I knew a better way since I'd traveled this route before. It was all I could do to ignore the constant interruption of Siri trying to get me on the "right path."

Convinced the information I was receiving was inaccurate, I yelled, "You don't have a clue what you're talking about." Frustrated with the pestering directions, I decided I had nothing to lose, so I gave in and surrendered to the recommended path from Siri. To my shock and surprise, I not only made it before the first inning started, but I also discovered a much better path for the future! From now on, I know a superior route to the ballpark. What can I say about listening and following the guidance I was given but did not ask for? It was pleasant, interesting, and surprisingly simple. I discovered a path that would save me valuable time.

I am so glad I got on the newly suggested route. I wonder what would happen if we learned to listen to others like we do our favorite GPS app. We see GPS as a tool we can't live without because it provides us access to essential information, such as updated traffic reports and road hazards, helping us get to our desired destination on time.

Listening is a valuable tool for gathering important information. It does not have to be complicated. What if we learned to think of listening as the tool that gives us access to the information we need in order to adjust course and arrive at the desired destination. We get to make the decision about which way we will go, but we are simply getting access to information that will help us make informed decisions. If we don't have the right information, we will not make the best decisions.

Who knows? You may discover a much better path to move forward in the future. I want to challenge you to change the way you interact with people. The only way you can know how to respond to a person that matters to you is to get to know that person and seek to understand their motives, fears, concerns, dreams, and joys.

In Proverbs 18:13, Solomon says, "To answer before listening is folly and shame." Not listening is a foolish activity that will leave you with a bucket load of regret. In Proverbs 18:2, he says, "Fools have no interest in understanding; they only want to air their own opinions." How many conversations are undermined by people who are more concerned with expressing their opinions than they are with receiving what the other person is saying? The half-brother of Jesus tells us why conversations are often unsuccessful. James 1:19-20 says, [19]"My dear brothers and sisters, take note of this: Everyone should be quick to listen, slow to speak and slow to become angry, [20]because human anger does not produce the righteousness that God desires." We should prioritize listening over talking and getting angry, two things that often undermine conversations.

Listening communicates we care.

Listening communicates a powerful message. I got to sit next to Brandon, a molecular biologist, on an airplane from Washington D.C. to Minneapolis, Minnesota. As the flight was getting underway, he struck up a conversation with me. One of the first things out of his mouth was, "Anyone who still believes in God is an intellectual moron."

I said, "Can you tell me more about that?" Brandon started telling me about several of the latest discoveries in science. He gave me several reasons why it doesn't make sense to believe in God. It was a *very interesting* conversation.

After about forty-five minutes of talking about his claim, Brandon turned to me and said, "What is it you do for a living?"

Aware it would make him uncomfortable, I replied, "I am a pastor."

He looked completely shocked and said, "No, you *are* not!"

I smiled and said, "Why, don't you believe that I am a pastor?"

He said, "I have talked with quite a few pastors over the years, and we always get into heated discussions."

He sighed and said, "If they're nice, they tell me they believe I am wrong. And if they're impatient, they get angry and tell me I have no idea what I'm talking about."

I surprised Brandon by saying, "I am sorry." I paused to listen to the white noise of the airplane and continued, "It seems like you have been hurt by more than one pastor."

Brandon sighed and said, "Yeah, I have been."

Knowing we had nowhere to go, I asked, "Will you tell me about what has happened to you?"

He lowered his head and told me he doesn't have time to tell me about all of them, but he could tell me about one encounter that happened the previous week. He said, "I started attending a church about two months ago. After my third visit, they sent me a letter telling me that people in my profession typically make a certain amount of money, and they actually had the audacity to tell me I owed them $250.00 for my tithe."

I could not contain the look of shock on my face and said, "Oh my, I would have been beside myself. I would have been livid. What did you feel? What did you do?"

Brandon said, "I was mad, like you said, but I was more disappointed than anything because I was considering the possibility that there may actually be a God. It turns out they did not care about me or my faith questions. All they wanted was my money. If they only knew. I don't even make that much money."

I sat there for what felt like forever, but it was only about thirty seconds. I finally said, "I don't even know what to say, except I am very sorry that happened to you. That is just awful."

We talked for another thirty minutes, and just before he got off the plane, he stopped and looked into my eyes and said, "If I lived in Minnesota, I would go to your church every week." I am so glad I got to listen to Brandon tell me about his hurtful experience. Listening, empathizing, and trying to understand where a person is coming from will communicate that you care enough about them to hear their heart and understand what they are saying.

Listening allows us to point other people to the God who listens.

God promised to receive everything we say to Him in prayer. Let's read three short passages of scripture to soak in God's wonderful promise that he will always listen to us and consider what we say.

1. Jeremiah 29:12-13: "Then you will call on me and come and pray to me, and I will listen to you. You will seek me and find me when you seek me with all your heart."

2. 1 Peter 3:12: "For the eyes of the Lord are on the righteous and his ears are attentive to their prayer, but the face of the Lord is against those who do evil."

3. 1 John 5:15: "And if we know that he hears us—whatever we ask—we know that we have what we asked of him."

Listening will help anyone improve their relationships, but did you know that if you are a follower of Christ, God gave you a mandate to treat others the way He treats us? The God of the Universe demonstrated how much He cares about us by listening to what we say. God takes human need to heart. We show our love for God by imitating

His love for us. Jesus called His followers to be the salt of the earth in Matthew 5:13.

Salt in the ancient world was an extremely valuable mineral that was used to preserve food, create thirst, bring out a food's flavor, and heal wounds. The salt-of-the-earth metaphor applies to the way we listen as well as how we live. Just the right amount of salt turns an ordinary meal into a delicious meal. How we listen can transform all our conversations. Our relationships will improve when we see our conversations as an opportunity to show people the love of God by the way we listen.

Paul encourages followers of Jesus in Colossians 4:5-6 to, [5]"Be wise in the way you act toward outsiders; make the most of every opportunity. [6]Let your conversation be always full of grace, seasoned with salt, so that you may know how to answer everyone." We will not know how to answer until we listen. The only way it could be possible to know how to answer each person is if we listen to understand their perspective. In 1 Peter 3:15, Peter tells us what we need when he says, "Always be prepared to give an answer to everyone who asks you to give the reason for the hope that you have. But do this with gentleness and respect." When we listen to understand and do it with gentleness and respect, people will feel heard and conversations will be more productive. When we get past ourselves and become fully present to hear the concerns of others, we point them to the God who listens.

How do you make the decision to receive what they say before you respond to it?

Learn a framework for communication.

I want to introduce you to a framework for communication that will improve all of your relationships. It will bring clarity so people can understand each other. Every time a person has an encounter with a human being, there are three important parts to the encounter. There are the facts, the experience, and the meaning. It is absolutely crucial that you understand the difference between the facts in the conversation, the experience of the conversation, and the meaning of the conversation before you move on.

1. The **facts** are what happened from our perspective. They include the words we heard and the behavior we observed.

2. The **experience** is what we noticed and felt during the encounter. This includes what was going on inside of us when we noticed the behavior. When a person experiences an emotion, they may not know exactly what emotion they have experienced, but they know they felt something genuine.

3. The **meaning** is our interpretation of what happened. Why did they do what they did and what was our interpretation of their motive? Is what they were doing good or bad, whether their judgement was appropriate or unreasonable (my judgment)? What do I need to do about what happened (my response)?

Logical people focus their attention on the facts, which happen to be the least important of the three parts of the encounter. I know it seems like I have completely lost my mind to the rational people reading this. Please hear me out because this will explain where the breakdown occurs in most conversations. I want to start by stating this principle I believe to be true and then giving you an explanation. An emotional question needs an emotional answer. A logical answer to an emotional question will never work.

> *An emotional question needs an emotional answer.*

I said earlier that you must decide to receive and process what someone says before you respond to it. I want to tell you why that decision is so important. If we lined up one hundred people and gave all of them the same exact encounter, there could still be one hundred different experiences and one hundred different meanings. A person's experience is their unique experience because everyone has a unique set of hurts, fears, and vulnerabilities. What happened to them in the past impacts what they experience in the present and colors the meaning.

Let's look at how this plays out in the real world. Jake and Kristen went on a date for their two-month anniversary. One week before the date, Kristin reminded Jake how much she enjoys going to see a good movie and her favorite part the popcorn. Jake invited her on a date. He was looking forward to getting her popcorn. On the way from their parked car to the theater, Jake got about nineteen feet in front of Kristen, purchased two tickets, and got a large popcorn with two drinks. He did it. Jake did everything he could to make this a special date.

Kristen was noticeably frustrated and tried not to say anything, but Jake asked her, "What is wrong?"

She said, "Nothing," but Jake insisted he could tell something was wrong. Kristen continued, "I am frustrated with you for being so insensitive."

Jake told her, "You have no reason to be upset. I took you where you wanted to go, and I even got the exact thing you wanted me to get you." They walked into the movie and remained silent throughout the evening. Both were feeling discouraged and frustrated with the inappropriate behavior of the other person. What went wrong and why did things get so tense?

Jake did so many things well, but he did not do the one thing that makes relationships meaningful and conversations complete. He listened to her the week before and paid attention to her interests. He invited her on a date and even got her popcorn. He paid attention to her enough to notice she was not happy. He encouraged her to share her feelings. He was genuinely trying to please his new girlfriend. He was trying to communicate and had good intentions.

But what was missing? Jake failed to receive and process what she said before he responded to it. I will show you a method that will help you find success with this. It is not complicated, and anyone can learn to do it. The difficult part is making the decision to do it in the heat of the moment. Jake asked Kristen what was wrong, but he did not receive what she said. When she reluctantly started revealing her feelings, he blocked them by saying, "You have no reason to be upset." He continued by telling her he had given her what she wanted. Jake is a good guy and he had great intentions, but he did not receive what she said before he responded to it. His response communicated she was either crazy or selfish or both. Most conversations do not end well when you block what the other person is saying. It doesn't stop them from feeling that way; it becomes an insult about their character. Before we know it, we have a much bigger conflict than the one we started with!

I want to slow down and help you understand what has happened in your past, unproductive conversations. Trust me, I am a fellow traveler, trying to avoid the road to misery. I had so many unsuccessful conversations until I learned what was taking place beneath the surface. I am going to start by showing you what will *not* work. I have had the wonderful privilege of sitting in on thousands of conversations, and I have yet to see anyone successfully navigate any of the following strategies. The three things that undermine conversations are to fixate on the facts, deny the other a person's experience, and undermine the meaning of their words. I want to help you see why all three are destructive. Do not try these strategies unless you want to hurt the other person and complicate all your relationships!

Stop listening reactively.

I want to introduce you to a three-step process that I do not recommend because it will virtually ensure that the people you care about do not feel heard.

1. You are not receiving what a person is saying any time you **fixate on the facts** by questioning details and pointing out inaccuracies. You are showing them that they missed what really happened. You are not really listening to them if you are preparing to make an effective rebuttal and undercut their arguments.

Here are examples of damaging things you can say: "No that is not true," "I don't agree," "I did not do that," "Yes, but," and "What about when...." The **main message** you communicate when you fixate on the facts is, *I don't really care about you*. *I am right, and you are wrong*. If you argue the facts, even if you are technically correct, you will push the other person away from you and weaken your connection.

Some people are argumentative. If this is you, you believe taking the opposing view is a good thing. You might even like it when other people do this to you. When you argue, you think you are doing people a favor by expressing your superior wisdom. When you prove them wrong, you are helping them learn something or find a better way. Have you thought about the way people experience YOU? The people you have enlightened are not necessarily grateful for the insight. You are annoying and obnoxious at best. When you are domineering, you injure people deeply and create lasting insecurities. Proving your point at the expense of another person clearly communicates to them that they are in the presence of an unsafe person that requires multiple layers of protection in order to continue on in the relationship.

2. You are not receiving what a person is saying any time you **deny, dismiss, devalue,** or **disregard** their **emotional experience**. You are also not helping the situation when you defend yourself or criticize their emotional experience. You let them know that they have no right to feel the way they do, and no one else would have those irrational feelings. You are not truly listening.

Here are some damaging things you can say: "You are worked up for no reason," "Calm down," "Wow, that's crazy," and "It is not that bad." The **main message** you are communicating is **what is important to you doesn't matter to me**. If you deny a person's experience, you will miss out on important information and leave them feeling like they don't matter to you.

I had a series of unproductive conversations with my wife after she lost both of her parents and our niece moved in with us. Darlene tried to express her fears and how she was alone without a partner. She was miserable and grieving the absence of the two most influential people in her world. I interpreted the words that she was alone as an attack on my character. I defended myself and I tried to prove that I would never do anything to hurt her. We had countless conversations without any resolution. I started withdrawing and pulling away from her emotionally. It felt like every time we talked, things got worse. We were at an impasse with no way to cross.

I loved God and was trying to love my wife, but her words were hurting my soul. I desperately wanted to be seen as a good-hearted, loving husband. I defended myself with passion. I repeatedly said, "That is not true." I would dismiss her feelings, deny responsibility, and complain about how painful it was to be accused of not being a good partner., I was focused on my own pain and unable to care about her perspective. I am not proud of this, but I actually took notes to prove that she was the one that was treating me badly. Keep reading and I will show you a better way.

3. You are not receiving what the person is saying whenever you **undermine their meaning** by questioning their logic and

dismantling their conclusions. If you attempt to convince them that they misunderstood you and your motives, then you are not hearing what they are saying. You are not listening when you focus your attention on what you want to say next.

Here are some damaging things you can say: "That's ridiculous," "You are crazy," "You always make a mountain out of a molehill," "It is not my fault," and "No one else would have come to that conclusion." The main message you communicate is **there is something wrong with you,** and I am not interested in understanding your perspective. If you undermine the meaning, you will leave them feeling misunderstood and unimportant.

Three helpful insights I have learned from observing people.

- If you offer a solution before a person feels heard or is asking for one, they will resist you and feel frustrated, angry, anxious, or stressed.

- Disagreements where a person is not heard become power struggles instead of information exchanges.

- A defensive response where you protect yourself by denying responsibility, dismissing concerns, repeating your views, or making excuses for your behavior leaves the other person feeling unheard, uncared for, and unimportant.

How do you listen so a person feels heard?
Follow the four-step process to attentive listening.

You can have productive conversations by using a four-step process to help the other person feel heard. This process will take time to learn, but you will experience so much success, you won't want to have conversations any other way. What allows a person to feel heard? A person will feel heard when you receive and process what they said before you respond to it. Attentive listening will work in almost every situation.

1. If a person is giving you facts, resist the urge to argue with them. Do nothing but **care about the person** until they feel heard. Listen by giving them your full attention, which includes facial expression, eye contact, and body position. Let them know that you are there for them and what they have experienced matters to you. Be compassionate, curious, and interested. You may

want to say, "Thank you for telling me about....," "That sounded important, would you go over that again?" "I want to understand more about what you are saying."

The **main message** you communicate when you resist the urge to argue is, **I care about you**.

2. If a person is revealing their experience, then **acknowledge their feelings**. Resist the urge to deny, dismiss, or disregard their feelings. Avoid defending yourself against their accusations or criticizing their emotional experience. You can always acknowledge their feelings even if you have some big, important things to work through.

Here are some examples of things you can say: "I didn't know," "Continue," "I want to hear more," "I can see how you feel that way," and "Wow, that makes sense." People feel heard when you validate their emotional experience. There is something powerful about having our inner world seen and understood. If you are willing to be influenced, you may even agree with part or all of what the person is saying. Then you have the opportunity to validate and affirm them by saying, "I can see why you think that," "I see your point," "I agree with what you are saying," or "That's a good idea." If you are able to identify what a person is feeling and name it, they will leave the encounter believing that this person gets me and has my best interest at heart. The most common feelings are anger, sadness, fear, surprise, happiness, and disappointment.

The **main message** you are communicating is **what is important to you matters to me**. If you acknowledge a person's experience, you will communicate the important message that they matter to you.

3. If a person is giving you the privilege of allowing you to see the meaning behind their words, then seek to **understand their perspective**. Try and see where they are coming from and how they came to the conclusions they did. Taking time to understand a person will communicate value and respect, but it also will lead to a faster resolution and a much happier life. This skill will help the person you care about feel accepted, respected, and valued. Commit to resisting a judgmental attitude. Don't undermine your friend or loved one's conclusions or tell them they are wrong. Try and see where they are coming from and explore what their experience has been like for them. Step

outside of yourself long enough to give their perspective thoughtful consideration.

Here are some things you can say: "I want to understand you," "Let me see if I've got this right," "I may have completely missed this, but here's what I heard you say...," and "Thank you for trusting me with your feelings."

The **main message** you communicate is **I am interested in understanding your perspective**. If you invest the time to understand the meaning, you will leave them feeling heard, understood, important, and valuable.

4. If you have cared about the person, acknowledged their experience, and understood the meaning, then it's time to **comfort their pain**. If you try to comfort their pain before they feel heard, they will resist you. Let them know that what they have experienced matters. Give them a soothing response that relaxes, reassures, and consoles.

Here are some things you can say: "That had to be really hard," "Is there anything I can do to help?" and "I'm sorry I did not help you sooner. I'm really glad we talked over all of this." The next time you see them, remember what they shared and honor their experience by asking, "How are you feeling?"

When we take the time to listen attentively, then we will be able to see the other person's perspective through their eyes. The more we use this framework, the more natural it will become. The more we value the relationship, the more important it is to use this model. Most people will feel heard and will be willing to move towards a solution in our crucial conversations (and the book by the same name) if they believe we genuinely care about them. Where there is trust, relationships will flourish. [2]

Listen with your heart to answer their internal questions. Listening is not just about what you do. It matters how you do it. We could follow the four-step process and leave the person feeling unheard. Attentively listening is more than mechanically going through the motions. That means we care about the person, acknowledge or validate their experience, understand the meaning, and then offer care and compassion. Doing it well requires curiosity, engagement, attention, and concern. The most important part of listening is making the person feel heard. A person will know they have been heard when we demonstrate curiosity and a desire to understand, give complete engagement with responsive body language, focus on the person with our full attention, and show concern with a caring attitude. When we are listening with our heart and not just our ears, we are in tune with the emotional questions under the surface.

Four essential behaviors to listen with your heart:

1. **Demonstrate curiosity** with a desire to understand: They are asking, *Do you want to understand me?* Show them you want to learn about them. Let them experience your willingness to discover what is going on in their inner world.

Ways to answer the internal question: A great way to demonstrate you want to hear is to ask follow-up questions. You can say, "I want to understand, would you help me?" Try to figure out what happened, what they are feeling, and what their experience means to them.

2. **Give complete engagement** with responsive body language: They are asking, *Does what happened to me matter to you?* The person is looking for a nonverbal response from your body language, facial expression, and tone of voice that demonstrates interest. They can tell when you are interested in finding out more information about them. They can see when you are engaged in what they are saying.

Ways to answer the internal question: Your level of engagement will communicate how important they are to you. Nod your head, lean toward them, uncross your arms, smile, and make affirming noises like, "yes" and "uh huh" to show that you are listening and encourage them to continue talking.

3. **Focus on the person with your full attention.** They are asking, *Is your focus on me or on yourself?* They want to have your undivided attention. They can tell when you are distracted, not paying attention, or would rather be doing something else.

Ways to answer the internal question: You can put your phone away, turn off the television, or stop reading your book, and turn your body towards them. If you are busy and can't give them your full attention, you can say, "I am not able to give you the attention you deserve, but I will be able to concentrate after 5:30 p.m."

4. **Show concern** with a caring attitude: They are asking, *Do you care about me?* They want to feel your compassion and empathy, so they know that what they are experiencing matters to you. They are looking for emotional support.

Ways to answer the internal question: Ask open-ended questions to show you are interested and emotionally involved in what they are saying. You could say, "Would you tell me a little more?" or "What did you feel when that happened?"

Let's go back to the failed conversations I had with my wife after she lost both of her parents. My wife needed me to receive what she said before I responded to it. When I finally learned how to listen, I stopped arguing the facts (and I stopped writing them down). I stopped denying the validity of her experience and undermining the meaning of her words. I quit protecting myself from her accusations. To my surprise, Darlene was not trying to tell me I was a failure. She was trying to communicate how lonely she felt and how much she missed her mom and dad. She wanted and needed more understanding and emotional support than I was giving her. She did not feel heard until I was listening with my heart, demonstrating concern, and acknowledging and validating her experience. I discovered she was feeling alone because the two most important people in her life were her parents, and all of a sudden, they were both gone. She was married but felt like an orphan.

Darlene desperately wanted to talk to her mom and dad and ask them for their advice. She wanted to pour out her heart to the two people who had always been there for her. But there was no bringing them back. The problem was not me, but rather, her loneliness. She wanted me to care about how difficult it was to be her at the moment and to give her emotional support and understanding. Darlene did not feel supported until she felt my genuine curiosity, engagement, attention, and concern. Once she felt heard, then she was open to receiving the comfort her heart was longing for.

Before we go any further, there are two big arguments people sometimes use against listening and trying to understand someone else's perspective. First, if we simply listen, then they will misinterpret our acceptance as agreement. Second, if we don't show them how they are wrong, then they will think we are condoning their behavior or encouraging their faulty line of thinking. If we take time to hear a person and communicate that we are for them, it will be much easier for them to hear the truth when we speak it, both now and in the future. We are not agreeing with them or condoning their behavior, we are simply demonstrating that we care enough about them to hear their heart and understand what they are saying. The conversation can continue after this important groundwork is complete.

Completing This Leg of the Journey

When Francis Schaeffer was asked how he would spend an hour with a non-Christian, he said: "I would listen for fifty-five minutes, and then, in the last five minutes I would have something to say." If we discipline ourselves to slow down our own instruction, wisdom, and agenda and truly listen to the other person, we will communicate volumes of care and attentiveness. Listening with curiosity, engagement, attention, and concern is such a gift.

Solutions often naturally arise when the person talking feels heard, connected, and understood. You will need to muster all of your humility, courage, and wisdom. Humility is needed to stop protecting yourself. Courage and wisdom are needed to navigate differences of opinions and hurt feelings. The one thing that will change everything is to make the decision to receive and process what the important people in your life say *before* you respond to it.

Questions for Discussion

- What message do you communicate when you argue the facts?
- Which one of the barriers for listening do you relate to the most?
- What kinds of emotions arise inside of you when someone denies, dismisses, or criticizes your emotional experience?
- Why does it feel so dangerous to explore the negative emotions of the people you really care about?
- How do you validate the people you care about when you don't agree with their conclusions?
- Should you listen to a person who is wrong? Why or why not?
- What happens when you solve the wrong problem?
- Why is it so hard to acknowledge and validate negative emotional experiences?
- The four-step process of attentive listening includes caring about the person, acknowledging their experience, understanding the meaning of their words, and comforting their pain. Which one do you appreciate the most from others, and which one is the most difficult for you to do?
- Can you think of a conversation that didn't go well and how it may have been different if you had each sought to first understand the other person?

Chapter Ten

Look Beyond the Biggest Obstacle

Turning accusations into longings to receive essential feedback to make the best decisions.

When you feel unjustly accused, everything inside you wants to prove your innocence and protect yourself from either looking bad or being wrong. Moments of defensive behavior can happen to anyone. They can occur with a business partner, coworker, friend, child, parent, or spouse. Everyone inevitably reacts to a perceived threat by first protecting themselves. We build fences, erect walls, and wear armor to protect ourselves when we feel threatened by other people's evaluation, judgement, and critiques.

Sometimes a person is attacking us and other times, they are simply stating a complaint. When we have been hurt, we wear armor as a protective suit to keep from being hurt again. It isn't a bad thing to be careful as long as we understand the stronger the fortress and the bigger the wall, the more difficult it will be for the people who care about us to communicate their desires. Keeping people out will increase disconnection and erode trust. Getting defensive is natural but being defensive is optional. The longer we remain defensive, the more damage we will cause. The sooner we realize we are being defensive and take steps to recover, the better the outcome will be for our relationships.

> *Getting defensive is natural but being defensive is optional.*

There is a better way. We can choose to look past accusations and see the longings of others. When other people criticize us, we can choose to see it for what it is, critical feedback that gives us access to essential information to make appropriate decisions and adjustments. This will improve our relationships and make it possible to continue conversations. We will need humility to stop protecting ourselves and courage to follow through on the decision once we have made it. If we look beyond the criticism, we will be able to navigate difficult conversations and end up more connected. We must make the decision to stop protecting ourselves from a dangerous enemy and instead, lean in to discover the important longings of a valuable person.

Why should you listen for longings?

Avoid pain.

The first reason to learn to listen to longings is to save ourselves pain. Accusations hurt us and cause us to respond in unproductive ways, often causing heartache and pain. When we first feel accused, we often respond defensively by minimizing the person's opinion or ignoring our feelings. When we return their judgment by judging them, we miss out on a wonderful opportunity to grow and can end up hurting ourselves and the people we care about, which makes us miserable.

Very few people are able to express their unmet longings because it requires emotional maturity and vulnerability to do so. Everyone we care about has deep longings that are at the core of everything they say, think, or do. Behind every accusation and complaint is a deep personal longing. Whenever people say their longings out loud, they run the risk of being rejected. Listening to someone bare their soul requires more vulnerability and maturity than very few people possess. We can either get stuck in the accusations or see their heart's desires that they might not be mature enough to express.

We all desire approval and fear rejection. Feedback from people we care about or have power to significantly impact feels dramatic because it threatens two of our deepest needs: security and acceptance. There are times when feedback does include financial threats such as, "I'm going to fire you," or relational threats such as, "I'm going to leave." In most cases, it is our defensive, argumentative, or angry response to feedback that puts us at risk more than it is the feedback itself. When we get defensive, it is

> *When we get defensive, it is our destructive behavior that causes the other person to increase their intensity to penetrate our defenses.*

our destructive behavior that causes the other person to increase their intensity to penetrate our defenses.

The harsh comments and deep wounds almost never come until we block the person and leave them no outlet for their overwhelming emotions. If we learn to see past the accusations to see their longings instead, we can receive feedback without having to push it back to the person who sent it. We can hear their heart without having to silence them or do and say things we will regret. The heartache and long-term trauma can be avoided if we can learn to respond in productive and healthy ways.

Enjoy successful conversations.

The second reason to learn how to listen to the longings of the people we care about is to create the best environment possible for successful conversations. You will no longer have to put your protective shield up. You can choose to stop seeing an adversary with the intent to harm you and start hearing how to have successful conversations. They can lead to understanding and also create opportunities for improvement and growth. If you are open to feedback, you can hear the idea you are looking for, the solution you desperately want, or the suggestion that improves a critical process for everyone involved. Successful conversations identify problems that need solutions which lead to changes that need to be made. Viewing colleagues, neighbors, or family as opponents and adversaries will make you miss incredible opportunities in the workplace.

Successful conversations can help produce satisfying relationships. When you listen defensively, you miss out on essential information that will make it possible to connect in a meaningful way. When we receive feedback from the people we care about, we are seeing through a window into the other person's heart. When we can identify their deepest longings and say them out loud, we connect in a way that will make it possible to heal the hurts of their heart and yours. When you give another person consideration and pay attention to their desires and longings, then your availability and responsiveness will create such a deep connection that they will want to hurry home to be near you.

Accomplish shared purpose.

When we stop seeing other people as an adversary or an opponent, then we can work together to accomplish a shared purpose. When we work together, we will improve our company's bottom-line results, positively influence our children, and experience more internal fulfillment. Employees perform at their best when they are engaged in their work and given the right resources and tools to get the job done. Everyone longs to spend time with people who give their perspective consideration, pay attention to their dreams, and take into account the ideas and feelings of others. When you respond in a considerate, kind, and respectful manner, the other person feels respected, accepted, valued, and appreciated.

When we lay down our protective armor, we can work together in a collaborative alliance with a teammate to accomplish a shared purpose. When we value the benefits of connection in our relationships, then we will have an easier time facing our fears and insecurities. With a sense of humility and purpose, we can experience the precious treasure that comes from hearing the longings of our spouse, child, or good friend. The good news is there are practical ways to overcome defensiveness and create a more supportive climate.

How do you listen to the language of longings?

Admit you are defensive.

You don't have to admit it to anyone else, but to overcome defensiveness, you must first acknowledge that you are defensive! This may be the most difficult step because you must admit you are doing something that hurts your relationship, holds your friends at arm's length, or damages your career. Genuine awareness includes understanding what you do and why you do it. Don't skip this step.

Start by asking two essential questions and sit with both of them long enough to get the answer.

- First, ask yourself, **what am I protecting myself from**? People often defend themselves when they feel attacked, threatened, misunderstood, or disrespected. You must understand why you defend yourself before you can move forward in a different direction. If you do not understand what you are protecting, you will keep blocking the people you care about.
- The second question is equally important. **Where does my defensiveness come from?** Invest the time to find out which of your buttons gets pushed and why? The deepest wounds often

come from childhood. Our wounds impact the way we see the world, ourselves, and our relationships. They can shape our expectations of ourselves and others and what we think we deserve. Our wounds may come from a recent relationship where a person you trusted broke your heart so deeply, they bruised your spirit and made you question all of your ideas about love.

Identify the language you use.

We need to gain awareness of the language we use. I like to break it down into two types: blocking language and receiving language. Let's start with blocking language because we often don't understand the long-term damage we cause when we defend ourselves. Sometimes we don't even mean to block people and other times our real motive is to block them until they change their mind. We can block subtly by placing doubts with words such as, "Yes, but, what about when." We can block by arguing the facts when we say, "No that is not true," "I don't agree," or "I won't accept that."

Other times, we can block by questioning the competence of the other person when we say, "That is ridiculous," "You are one to talk," or "Why do you have to see me in such a bad light?" All these statements prevent the other person from being heard or understood. It is hard to be close to someone who silences you or calls you crazy. With your defenses up, people don't have the energy to break through, and you lose out on vital information.

With receiving language, you will communicate volumes if you discipline yourself to slow down your instruction, wisdom, agenda, and truly listen to the people you care about. Few things will have a greater, more positive impact on your professional and personal relationships than learning when and how to acknowledge and validate the experience of others. Two-way conversation is an excellent gift. You may want to start by learning some key statements that you can use to demonstrate that you care about them and are open to additional information. Here are a few examples of receiving language: "That sounds important," "Take your time. I'm listening," or "Would you repeat that? I don't want to miss what you said."

Sometimes you may disagree with what they are saying. Before you stop the conversation or cause damage to future conversations, remember to hear them before you reach any conclusions. If you can remain curious, you may hear people say the exact words you have been longing to hear. Here are a few examples of constructive comments to feedback you might receive: "Thanks for sharing your thoughts with me," "You know, you might be right," "What would that look like?" "I hadn't thought about that," "Let me think about that," "That deserves a thoughtful response," "Yes, and...," "I am listening, tell me more," "I want to better understand," "I want to hear you," "I think we have common ground," "I never thought of it that way," and "How could we make that work?" The idea is to demonstrate that you want to know what they want and understand what they feel by showing that you will receive it and continue the dialogue.

Most people are reluctant to share important information until they are convinced the other person is listening. Compassion, acknowledgment, and validation, set us up for success in future conversations. Parents, your children may have some deep feelings or important information that they will only share if they feel heard. It is in your best interest to be the person they will tell what is really going on in their mind and heart. You must be perceived as a safe person who will listen without judgment. That is when they will feel safe to share their genuine feelings.

> *Most people are reluctant to share important information until they are convinced the other person is listening.*

Unless you know the real problem, you will not be able to work towards the most effective solutions. You can validate what people are saying by trying some of these supportive statements, "Wow that makes sense," "I can see how you would feel that way," or "I am so glad you shared that with me," If you are willing to be influenced, you may even agree with what the person is saying, then you can validate and affirm them by saying, "I can see why you think that," "I see your point," "I agree with what you are saying," "That's a good idea," or "Of all the important things you have said, which one needs immediate attention?"

Recognize the type of feedback.

Determine what kind of feedback you are receiving so you can respond productively. Feedback is essential information to make appropriate decisions and move forward with productive actions. Good feedback can be a remarkable gift because you can gain access to the information you need in order to solve your biggest problems. Bad feedback can destroy relationships and do damage to a person's wellbeing. When you hear the word feedback, who is the first person that comes to mind? Do you think of your workplace or the people living in your home? Feedback comes at all of us on a regular basis. The way we respond to feedback is up to us. Some people have good motives and want the best for us, but others may have bad intentions and want to cause us harm. It is important to distinguish which kind of information the other person is sending to us and how we are receiving it from them.

There are three primary kinds of feedback.

1. Appreciation (thanks)

2. Coaching (here's a better way to do it)

3. Evaluation (here's where you stand)

I learned a lot about the topic of feedback from Stone and Heen in their book, Thanks for the Feedback. Appreciation is the easiest kind of feedback to receive and often leaves us feeling good about ourselves and our relationship. Not only does it express gratitude, but it also conveys a deeper message that, "I see you." In essence, appreciation communicates two important messages: "I know how hard you've been working," and "You matter to me."[1] Appreciation motivates most people and gives them energy to work hard and improve their relationships. When people complain that they don't get enough feedback at work, they often mean that they wonder whether anyone notices or cares how hard they're working to contribute to the team's success. Most people don't want advice as much as they want appreciation.

Coaching is aimed at trying to help someone learn, grow, and improve their skills. It is often much more effective when people seek to be coached. This can be difficult to receive if you don't trust the person showing you a better way, or if you don't believe they know what they are talking about. However, when we get the coaching we need, we will see substantial gains in our performance and significant improvement in relationships because we are gaining the skills we need to succeed and grow. When you ask your boss for more direction, you're essentially asking for coaching.

Evaluation is, by far, the most difficult to receive because it tells you where you stand and comes with an assessment, ranking, or rating.

Evaluations often include comparisons to other people or a particular set of standards. Evaluation can be very helpful because it can align expectations, clarify consequences, and inform decision making. Evaluation can also elicit a strong emotional reaction and leave people with fear of being seen as a failure. It is natural to get defensive when you are being evaluated and judged. Some people associate all feedback with evaluation, and it causes their brain to panic and their stomach to tighten into knots.

The better you understand the feedback, the more likely you will find it useful. Before you reject feedback, decide what kind of feedback you are receiving. If it is appreciation, then receive it. If it is coaching, then give it some consideration and decide if you want to do it. If it is evaluation, then be cautious and evaluate the feedback. Evaluation may cause you the most pain, but it may also reap the biggest reward. If you are normal, you will want to reject feedback because it hurts, seems unfair, and can be given with the wrong motives.

Shift your mindset.

We can either look at criticism and accusations as a gift or a curse. If we see it as a curse, we will resist it and miss out on valuable information we desperately need to improve our relationships and accomplish meaningful tasks. If we look at feedback as an opportunity to grow and a window into another person's heart, then we will seek it out and reap the benefits from valuable information. We don't have to wait for official training or mentoring to receive feedback. It is the only way to see our blind spots. Our colleagues, friends, and family already have feedback for us. They're just not saying it aloud. If we let them know we want feedback and will receive it graciously when they give it and we show humility and teachability—two qualities that make us approachable and trustworthy.

Get feedback from the right people. This cannot be overstated. Not everyone is able to give you the kind of feedback or advice you need. Look for people who know what they are talking about—people who know you well and have already navigated what you are going through. People can see things that we do not have the perspective to see. Give feedback

> *The biggest waste of time is soliciting feedback or advice and then doing nothing with it.*

consideration and take appropriate action. Once we are aware of what other people want, we can take steps to make things better. The biggest waste of time is soliciting feedback or advice and then doing nothing with it. A word of caution: be aware of the natural tendency to seek out feedback from people you know will tell you what you want to hear, not necessarily what you need to hear.

How to give feedback people will want to hear.

1. **Take the time to prepare the feedback.** Craft your words carefully and assess your own motives. If you want to look smart, demonstrate your authority, condemn, or demoralize the person, then you are not ready to give feedback.

2. **Make it a two-way conversation.** Ask questions and listen to their answers. Give them an opportunity to express their perspective and concerns.

3. **Invest the necessary time to build trust.** People listen to people that have their best interests at heart, communicate that you are for them, and want them to succeed. People trust leaders who establish a personal connection with them. If people think you care more about yourself than about them, they won't trust you enough to listen to your advice.

4. **Remember that the purpose is to help them improve.** Be specific, helpful, and also realistic. That might mean withholding some of the details or harshness of your thoughts. Make your feedback clear so that they know what to change. Offer solutions instead of assigning blame. Focus on things that can be changed.

5. **Own your thoughts and opinions.** Don't speak for anyone but yourself. Say, "I have a concern," instead of, "Everyone has concerns."

Look in the rearview mirror.

Looking back at your family of origin can help you understand why you get defensive and react the way you do to feedback and criticism. Your family of origin refers to the environment you grew up in too. It profoundly shapes your worldview, causes some of your deepest wounds, and leaves you with some of the most difficult habits to break, but it can also set you up for success and leave a profoundly positive legacy worth repeating. Perhaps you were raised in a family you were proud of and want to emulate everything you witnessed. You may have experienced pain and heartache and want to avoid the same negative patterns at all costs. It is critical to see how your family and your childhood environment contributed to who you have become and how you behave within your relationships.

Everyone exhibits both healthy and unhealthy behaviors that can be traced back to their family roots. Two of the most common ways people react to what their family modeled is to repeat what they witnessed or do the opposite of what they observed. Both reactions can be done consciously or subconsciously. Your past does not define you, but it can explain why you are predisposed to act or feel the way you do. If you take a meaningful look at the way your family of origin influenced you, then your understanding can improve your present relationships and help you avoid common pitfalls and destructive patterns in the future.

Please understand, the purpose of looking at your family of origin is not to blame your parents, make excuses for your behavior, or fix your families, but to understand your own wounds, tendencies, and habits so you can make the necessary adjustments to enjoy a better future. There is hope because your past does not have to define you. Your past hurt can be the gateway to stronger relationships if you are willing to explore what happened and experiment with different ways of responding. How you deal with your wounds will determine the power your history has to keep hurting you.

> *How you deal with your wounds will determine the power your history has to keep hurting you.*

Look at why other people defend themselves.

Sometimes, it is helpful to look at why other people protect themselves. There are common reasons people go into defensive mode.

- Some feel inadequate or not good enough. They have a fragile image of themselves.

- Some believe it is unacceptable to be wrong. This often happens to children who grow up in emotionally abusive households where it is unsafe to be wrong. It also occurs when parents have unrealistic expectations or ridicule their children for making mistakes.

- Some take too much responsibility because they are burdened with the task of making sure other people do not get angry or feel sad or disappointed.

- Some react out of fear. When they are afraid, they do not know how to manage their fears, especially in relationships where there is a lot at stake.

- Some are protecting their ego. They want others to think that they are an intelligent, likable, good-hearted person, and want others to think the same.

- Some feel they have to justify the decisions they have made, the things they have done, or even the very person they have become.

Discover how your defensiveness has undermined your relationships.

What are some of the negative results from defending yourself? Before we can make things better and take action, we must figure out how our defensiveness has caused distance and/or chaos in our relationships. Defensiveness can cause conflict with our families, friends, co-workers, and even strangers. Acknowledging we played a part does not make us a bad person but allows us to start working on fixing the problem. If you do not find out why you defend yourself, you will leave the people you care about without a voice. Figure out what you are protecting.

Here are a few helpful questions to discover your part in the breakdown.

- Start by asking yourself how your defensiveness caused distance and/or chaos in your relationships? You must figure out what you did. It is difficult to see your part because what the other person did is often so clear to you. Ask God to help you see your part.

- Is it hard for me to admit that my defensiveness hurt someone else? It is worth my time to figure out why I get so defensive? For me, my mom spoke harsh words over me and told me I would never amount to anything. I was terrified of making my mother's prediction come true, so I learned how to passionately defend myself.

- What negative things happen when I become defensive? At the heart of our vulnerability lies the feeling that we've been hurt by someone we care about. We may want them to move towards us and reconnect, yet our behavior is the last thing that would invite them back. In the end, defensive response makes it much more difficult for us to get what we want.

Take responsibly for protecting yourself.

Each of us is responsible for our own thoughts, feelings, actions, words, choices, and beliefs. We often defend ourselves because we don't know how to take responsibility for the things we did or said that hurt people that matter to us. Sometimes, the path to satisfying relationships is admitting we wronged someone. Once we are aware of our defensive behavior, we can take steps to make things better. The way to accept personal responsibility when we have defended ourselves is to take the following simple but powerful steps.

1. **Own It** by taking ownership of your own behavior and admit what you did wrong or failed to do.
2. **Apologize** for your words or behavior by offering a sincere apology to the person you hurt. If you said harsh words, apologize for the words you spoke and the manner in which you said them.
3. **Make things right** by doing what is needed to make amends, if possible, to correct what you have done. The longer you take to own it and begin repairing, the more difficult it will be to repair the connection.

Identify longings so you will recognize them.

Get to know longings that are common to our human experience. It will be valuable for you to be able to identify them. I find it's helpful to think about them in two primary categories, Secure and Significant.

The four longings that help us feel SECURE:

1. **Acceptance:** Do I belong? I am longing for someone to include me and make sure that I belong. I am afraid of being alone.
2. **Attention:** Do you notice me? I am longing for someone to see me. I am afraid that I am not worthy of your time.

3. **Affection:** Do you enjoy spending time with me? I am longing for someone to light up when they see me. I am afraid that I'm not liked.

4. **Approval:** Do you see something good in me? I am longing for someone to see the good in me. I am afraid that I am not enough.

The four longings that help us feel SIGNIFICANT:

1. **Respect:** Do I matter? I am longing for someone to tell me that I have what it takes. I am afraid that I am a failure.

2. **Competence:** Do you value my contribution? I want to accomplish something significant, but I am afraid I will not measure up.

3. **Importance:** Am I important? I am longing to have a positive impact and make a difference. I am afraid that I am not enough.

4. **Adventure:** Will I experience something meaningful? I want to be courageous. I am afraid that I will have to live a routine existence.

Shaunti Feldhahn says that women are often drawn towards security and men are often more interested in significance. Those stereotypes don't always hold true, and everyone has all eight longings.[2] We find security in safety, familiarity, and predictability. We all find significance in what we do and what we accomplish. We all need to feel safe and secure in a relationship, but we also need a certain amount of adventure, exploration, mystery, and wonder. We want to feel as though our relationships have staying power and the ones we trust the most are not going to walk out the door. We want to feel appreciated, valued, respected, and worthy. We long to know that we can trust the people we rely on when we reach out to them. But as much as we long for predictability, we also want exploration, adventure, and risk.

Listen for longings.

Listen for the longings people have in your conversations. Behind every complaint or disappointment they express, there is a deep, personal longing. It is so easy to get caught up in verbal sparring when we let ourselves get wounded by the other person's intensity, generalized statements, or accusations. You do not have to react to what they say by taking things personally or defending yourself against their attacks. Be patient. It takes gentle care and patience to get at the deeper feelings, insecurities, and longings of your coworkers, friends, children, and even your spouse. You can learn to pay attention to their cries for connection and support and respond in a productive way that will improve the relationship.

How do you listen for longings?

Look for buried treasure.

Think of yourself as an explorer going on a grand adventure to look for buried treasure. Lay aside your preconceived ideas and ask open-ended questions and listen. Your single-minded purpose is to discover their deepest longings and desires. If you take it personally, then you will shut down the conversation before you find out what they really want or need. There are so many things you can say at that moment. You can say, "tell me more," "continue," or "then what." Invite them to continue as you show you care about whatever they say. Listen without judgment. Pay attention to your own body language. If you are squirming in pain or crossing your arms, then you are getting stuck on their accusations and are not listening for signs of their desires.

If you can remain present, receptive, and sensitive, you will be the salve that they need when they feel hurt. When all you hear is accusations, you misinterpret the intentions of the people who care about you. Nobody wants to fight through your defenses to be heard. The more defensive you have been in the past, the longer it will take for them to believe you are listening. Hear their concerns and care about the things that matter to them. There will be many opportunities to get sidetracked. Here is a helpful phrase you can say to yourself, "It is not about me until I make it about me and then it becomes all about me." If you make it about you then you miss out on the buried treasure.

Move into the torpedo before it is armed.

I want to introduce you to a very helpful principle. In the movie, *Hunt for Red October*, Sean Connery played a Russian submarine captain who was defecting to the United States.[3] Alec Baldwin played a Naval Intelligence Officer who figured out that Sean Connery's character was defecting. In the movie, you can feel the tension build when a team of four Americans take a huge risk by boarding the Russian submarine. Just when they start to relax, a different Russian submarine fires on their submarine with the characters played by Alec Baldwin and Sean Connery. The missile was coming to destroy the sub. Sean Connery's character told Alec Baldwin's character to turn into the torpedo. The American captain, played by Scott Glenn, tells the Naval Intelligence Officer, played by Alec Baldwin not to listen to bad advice but to turn away from the torpedo. Sean Connery's character, the defector said, "Trust me" and so the Naval Intelligence Officer did. He turned into the torpedo. The torpedo hit the submarine without causing any damage. Everyone was alright because the torpedo was not armed yet.

When you move into, or turn toward, a negative emotion, you can get to the longing before it is armed. If you block an intense emotion or try to prove the person has no right to feel their emotion, you are arming the torpedo and you will experience the shrapnel following impact. As you are thinking about this, you may say there is no way you could move into a torpedo. Try it for ten days and see what happens. It does not have to make sense to move into a negative emotion at first, but you will discover the best strategy to experience less pain is to move into the torpedo before it is armed.

Whenever we make it about ourselves, we miss out on what is really going on. When we get sidetracked with an accusation, we miss out on understanding the deep longing that is being communicated. If it feels like they are attacking our performance and our character, they might even be out of line in doing so, but the most important thing is we recognize that they are crying out with their perspective and their longings. We can put ourselves in their place and imagine what it would be like to experience things from their vantage point. We need to work to change the focus from the unfair way they see us to the unmet longing and deep desires they are sharing with us. It is surprising how often there are discrepancies between how we want other people to see us and how they actually see us. We long for the important people in our lives to see us in a positive light. What we truly long for is to be liked, to be loved, to be appreciated, and to have the people we care about think we are awesome.

We desire to be seen as a good-hearted person and hearing that someone is disappointed with us can cause us great distress. We are shocked when people describe us in a profoundly unfavorable light. We are completely taken a back when they accuse us of hurting them. At that moment, we can disparage their character with every word and tactic we can dream of, or we can give them a little latitude to discover and explain what they need. Our choices could directly affect the health of the relationship.

Even when the people we care about say mean, cutting, and insensitive comments, we do not have to take those things personally. Let the deeper cries for help and connection come through. Train yourself to watch and listen for them. When we find ourselves in the next situation, rather than getting defensive, we can try to remain curious by asking open-ended questions. Who knows, what they say may surprise us. They may tell us what we have been longing to hear. Our impulse to defend ourselves can be suppressed or eliminated with practice. Notice, I'm not saying that we should let people abuse us or deliver baseless insults over and over again. I'm saying that when people we love act out against us, we need to love them enough to get to the bottom of it.

The best way to illustrate this principle is with a real-life situation. Josh enjoyed working out at least five days a week. He also loved the outdoors and thoroughly enjoyed spending ten days with his closest friends every November. It was not just the hunting he enjoyed, but he relished the laughter, the competition, the playful banter, and the friendship. When he first married Jane, she would help him prepare for the trip and encourage him to go. When he returned, she would listen for hours as he would tell stories of their adventures. As time went by, she was becoming less than enthusiastic each fall when he would get ready to leave again. Right before Josh left for a trip one year, Jane began a conversation with three accusations.

Jane said, "You always prioritize your friends over me and the kids."

Josh responded to her accusation defensively by saying, "Your complaining takes all the joy out of the trip."

Jane responded, "You spend your time with everyone but me."

Jane was really frustrated and said, "All you do is work out and plan for your annual trip without me."

Josh responded sarcastically by saying, "You are getting worked up for no reason. No one else's wife makes such a big deal out of nothing."

Josh took a deep breath and said, "You are impossible to please. It doesn't matter what I do. You are never happy. You should be glad I take care of my body and have quality guy friendships."

Eventually, every time he worked out or went on his annual trip, they would argue. They would spend time attacking each other and defending their positions as if their lives depended on it. Their arguments were unproductive and hurtful. Eventually, they retreated into complete silence before each trip.

If Josh and Jane would have known how to go beyond the accusations into the longings, then Josh could have seen that underneath Jane's complaints about what he was doing "wrong" was actually a much deeper longing for his **attention**. She wanted to feel important to him, as if he wanted to spend some of his free time with her. If he cared about her concerns and validated her feelings, she could have felt loved and cared for.

On the other hand, if Jane knew how to see beyond Josh's accusations to his longings, she would have seen his criticism of her "unacceptable behavior" was actually a cry for her to see him in a different light. He was longing to be seen as a good-hearted person who had competence in many areas in life. He longed for her to express her appreciation for all the things he does for himself and for the family.

If either person would have received what they were saying, they could have experienced a much more satisfying relationship. Josh could have acknowledged Jane's desire for attention and put more effort into giving her time and the attention she was longing for. He would have felt competent, and Jane would have felt comfortable with him enjoying his time with other people. Jane could have cared about his desire to be respected and taken the time to point out how much she values his contribution to the family.

How do I get my longings met?

It is so easy to turn to the closest people in our lives to meet our needs, but what do we do if we've told them over and over what we need, and they remain insensitive and unwilling to address our concerns. We all need encouragement and support. We want a shoulder to lean on, companionship when we are feeling lonely, and approval when other people reject us. Is that too much to ask? Most of us who are married decided to tie the knot because we found the person who could give us the respect, attention, support, and affection our hearts long to receive. We have tried to tell them repeatedly how much we need help with the kids, a listening ear, an engaged partner, someone to help shoulder the brunt of the heavy loads and financial burdens of life, but they stubbornly refuse to meet our needs.

I have an important piece of reality I need to share with you. Regardless of what we do or say, our friends, boss, children, and parents will not meet our deepest needs. Even the most loving spouse is not capable of meeting our deepest longings. We could grumble and complain, manipulate people to satisfy our desires, or resign ourselves to living with unmet desires. All those options will be unfulfilling and make everyone around you miserable. The other option we have is to stop going to people who are not capable of meeting our needs. They were never intended to meet all our needs. God can meet not just one of our deepest longings, but all of them. Our greatest needs can only be met at the deepest level by the Creator of the Universe.

> *Our greatest needs can only be met at the deepest level by the Creator of the Universe.*

Allow God to meet some of your needs now.

God made us and created us with longings. He alone can satisfy them. We find ourselves so busy surviving daily tasks and dredging out a meager existence, that we forget He is available to us now. He made all of us for a purpose. That is why there is a yearning in your heart for your life to count for something. God wants you to participate with Him to accomplish something meaningful. You are invited to enjoy His friendship, to have a relationship with Him. God desires you to know Him intimately.

If you have decided to follow God, then you are a dearly loved son or daughter (Ephesians 5:1-2), with a heavenly Father who loves you perfectly, unconditionally, and infinitely more than any human parent could. God's love is wider, longer, higher, and deeper than you can imagine (Ephesians 3:18). He will lovingly protect you (1 John 5:18), and help you become who you were designed to be (Ephesians 2:10). He will redeem everything painful in your life (2 Thessalonians 2:13), and work everything together for your good (Romans 8:28-29). His love is relentless, selfless, and sacrificial. It will drive out your fears (1 John 4:18) and quiet your anxious heart (Philippians 4:6-7) because he cares for you (1 Peter 5:7). Nothing can separate you from His love (Romans 8:39). He will never leave you or forsake you (Hebrews 13:5).

At the core of every human heart, we long for security, significance, affection, and approval. Zephaniah sees a future so amazing it is hard to even imagine. He paints a picture of a world without war and people without fear and anxiety (Zephaniah 3:9-16). God is present and has removed everything that prevents people from genuine intimacy. We get to experience everything we have ever longed for. God will shower us with affection and recognize us for the meaningful contribution we're making in the lives of those around us.

Look forward to the day when God satisfies all our longings permanently.

One day, our amazing God will restore the world to the way He originally intended. Imagine an existence where you get to live in a secure world, in profoundly intimate relationship with the author of life itself! Everyone around you enjoys each other's presence and your heart is filled to satisfaction. The sovereign ruler of the universe will come as a warrior to judge the nations that rebel against His authority. God will provide a future beyond our wildest imagination. You and I were made to be loved and appreciated.

In Zephaniah 3:17, there are several promises explained in one verse. "The LORD your God is with you, he is mighty to save. He will take great delight in you, he will quiet you with his love, he will rejoice over you with singing." Every single human being has an unquenchable ache for someone to take delight in them. One day, those who know the Lord will get to experience everything their heart desires. The God that loves you and me will speak of His delight and shower us with his approval. We will be able to hear that we are loved and be told in a way that will resonate at the core of our being that we matter.

He will take great delight in us. God finds you a source of unending happiness and heart-bursting elation. You are known at the core of your being and are thoroughly enjoyed. He will quiet you with his love. Wordless adoration is the ultimate picture of contentment. You don't have to be afraid because He has removed all your guilt. You don't have to live with anxiety or shame because God has a deep, heartfelt, passionate, abiding love for you. He will rejoice over you with singing. God offers internal peace and satisfaction to anyone who is willing to crawl into his arms and encounter His presence.

I remember when my daughter was a little baby with beautiful blond curls. Whenever she was unhappy or needed something, I would pick her up and sing to her. I would hold her in my arms and sing off key, but it did not matter. I can remember that feeling I had when I saw her face fade into a feeling of contentment. She was experiencing the safest place on earth in a parent's arms. I remember, with great fondness, looking down at her face as she smiled up towards me. Even now as I close my eyes, I can almost feel those precious moments all over again. As I would sing, she would relax and experience peace.

God loves you more than I love my daughter. God loves you more than you love your daughter. The longings of your soul can only be satisfied in God's presence. All our deepest longings find fulfilment in the one who designed us. Take a moment to read Revelation 21:1-8. When people think of heaven, they can miss out on the most important part. They read about streets of gold and breathtaking structures and end up focusing their attention on the wrong things. God is not trying to compete with materialistic notions and all the amenities of this world. The reward of our salvation is not that we get to avoid work and live in luxury. All of history is working towards God's plans where His people are in God's place accomplishing His purpose. God does not and will not throw away the earth and start over. He will bring to fruition everything He has been working on all along.

There will be no more sin, no more sorrow, no more cancer. Relationships will be perfect. The broken relationships between God and human beings will be healed, and people will get along the way God intended. John sees heaven as the fulfilment of every dream of the entire Bible. We will have no more painful disconnection and separation. Curses will be replaced by blessings, and we will get to see His face. The entire Bible is moving towards a day when God satisfies the deepest hunger in the heart of every human being!

Completing This Leg of the Journey

We do not have to see the people who criticize us as a dangerous enemy that we need to protect ourselves from. We are not at war, and no one needs to win or lose any battles. We can stop being our own biggest obstacle by taking down our defenses, getting rid of our walls, and removing our protective armor. We can put down our weapons and work together in a collaborative alliance with a teammate to accomplish a shared purpose. When other people make accusations, we can choose to see it for what it is, critical feedback that gives us access to essential information to make appropriate decisions and move forward with productive actions. Listen to the language of longing. They are giving us a rare opportunity to learn and grow, along with a rare privilege to connect with an important person's heart and understand what is going on in their world.

Because of God's great gift to us, we get to avoid the pain that comes from our own destructive behavior and the pain that we feel when other people have to increase their intensity in order to penetrate our defenses. We can experience successful conversations with people we care about who carry inside themselves deep and driving longings that are, at the core, of everything they say and do. We can respond in a productive way by hearing their heart and understanding what they want. And we can choose to meet some of their needs and address their concerns. God loves us and wants us to treat other people the way He treats us. By the grace of God, we don't have to take things personally. We can ask open-ended questions to discover what is going on in their world. Our relationships will improve when we make the decision to stop protecting ourselves from a dangerous enemy with threatening accusations and lean in to discover the important longings of our most valuable people.

Questions for Discussion

- What are some reasons why so many people speak the language of accusations?

- In what ways do you take things personally?

- Is it possible to be able to identify the longings behind every complaint?

- If you are constantly falling short in the eyes of the people you care about, why should you keep trying to uncover their deepest longings?

- Why is it so difficult to overcome patterns set in childhood? In what ways did your family shape the way you see the world?

- In what ways did your family set you up for success?

- Describe one or two of the wounds your family inflicted upon you that impact how often you defend yourself?

- What are the three primary types of feedback and how can understanding each type help you respond better to the important people in your life?

- How is it helpful to see past the accusations to the longings when you are receiving feedback?

- Do I recognize when a loved one is setting aside my accusations in order to listen to me and show care for my unmet needs?

- What makes it difficult for you to speak the language of longings?

- What can you do to bring into focus what God has done to meet your greatest needs, both now and into the future?

- Which one of the eight longings do you have the strongest

Chapter Eleven

Avoid Overheating

Maintaining access to as much of your brain as possible.

Why is it that people are so fascinated by watching people lose control of their emotions? Reality television has become extremely popular because the creators of the shows place people in high-stress situations and gradually increase the pressure until somebody snaps and completely loses their mind. When Hollywood celebrities or sports figures have a meltdown, the media will show it over and over on television. For some weird reason, we are drawn to it and enjoy seeing people lose control. Can we relate? Are we glad it's not us? Does someone else's outburst make us look less emotional? There is nothing that complicates relationships more than losing control of our emotions.

What happens to you when you get overwhelmed emotionally?

There's a part of the brain called the amygdala. It's a primary place in the brain that experiences very strong raw emotion, like rage and fear. Normally, when input comes into your brain, it goes to a place called the neocortex where it gets processed. It's where the sensible mature stuff happens like long-term planning, executive function, impulse control, and emotional regulation. *The Emotional Life of Your Brain* by Davidson and Begly, can help you learn how to take the best course of action when there are so many paths to choose from.[1]

About 5 percent of the time, when we are afraid or overwhelmed, we experience our emotions in the amygdala. When this happens, the thinking part of our brain gets short-circuited. Every one of us has experienced this. When this happens, our muscles clench and everything in our body becomes tense. Our blood pressure rises. Our heart rate accelerates. We have neurotransmitters that give us a surge of energy. Our amygdala has the ability to overtake the entire brain!

We can do and say things that cause ourselves and the people we care about significant damage. When our brain is flooded, we literally can't see beyond our own limited perspective. To make matters worse, you don't even have access to the parts of your brain that can take steps to improve the situation. You are lightyears from listening to the other person with empathy and understanding.

Keep the conversation train on the track.

When the hurts, fears, and vulnerabilities of either person get activated, then the conversation can easily get derailed. When we get off track, for any reason, we can lose our focus or get overwhelmed emotionally. So how do we keep the train on the track? We do so by only addressing one topic at a time and paying attention to what is happening with our emotions.

The best way to illustrate this is to share a conversation between work colleagues, Jackson and Sheila. They often get put on the same projects and are both respected and valued employees. The conversation started with Sheila expressing her annoyance with Jackson for not listening to her requests to tell their boss they will not be able to present their findings at the weekly team meeting.

Sheila: "Why do you ignore my clear instructions? Yesterday I emailed you and communicated explicitly that you needed to tell Eric (their boss) we will not be ready."

Jackson reacted: "This is out of line. You are being unreasonable. The team meeting is still two days away. I will let him know this afternoon or tomorrow morning if it looks like we can't make the deadline. I volunteered to manage your accounts for five days while you were in San Diego for the conference, but now you are acting ungrateful and entitled."

Sheila unleashed her pent-up frustration and said: "You are patronizing me, and I'm done. Your comments are just rude."

Jackson interrupted her and sarcastically said: "I can't even begin to tell you how wrong you are in this conversation. You should have thanked me for everything I did for you, but instead, you got overly emotional and attacked me without provocation. Why do you have to always be so controlling?"

Sheila responded with sarcasm: "Oh really! You think I am emotional?! Exactly what should I be grateful for? You don't even listen before you decide to completely ignore everything I say. I am the least controlling person I know. I hardly ever ask you to do anything, and when I do, you dismiss me and do it your own way. Talking to you is like talking to a brick wall."

Jackson rolled his eyes and said: "What is *wrong* with you? Would it kill you to say thanks or to ask nicely? I don't get it. I go out of my way to help you, and this is the thanks I get. The only thing you do is attack me and tell me everything I do that is wrong."

Sheila said: "You missed everything I said, Jackson. You don't listen to me or give my ideas any consideration."

Conversations stay on track by addressing one topic at a time.

What happened here? And how did the conversation get derailed? If we slow down, then we can see what is happening to Jackson and Sheila. They both got overwhelmed by their hurts, fears, and vulnerabilities, and their emotions were elevated, causing them to temporarily lose access to their entire brain. Let's start with Jackson. He became emotionally overwhelmed when he felt like Sheila was trying to control him. He also felt unappreciated. Jackson switched topics and started talking about feeling controlled and unappreciated.

Sheila was also flooded with emotion when she was talking about being unheard and inadequate. The original message she was trying to communicate was you did not listen to me, and we need to correct the situation.

Once Jackson felt controlled, it became an entirely different conversation. When Sheila said, "Why did you ignore my clear instructions? Yesterday, I communicated very clearly that you needed to tell Eric we will not be ready." Once he felt like she was telling him what to do by stepping out of her lane and barking out orders, he got triggered. The conversation changed tracks and became about control.

If Jackson understood what derails conversations, he could have kept the conversation on track by listening to Sheila's complaint and caring about what she was saying. He could have responded in several different ways. For example, he could have acknowledged her concern by saying, "It matters to me that you felt ignored and we do need to contact Eric immediately." He could have validated her concern by saying, "I may have missed it. If I would have listened then I would have known what to do." He could have apologized, "I'm sorry, Sheila. I should have talked to you about this and contacted Eric. I will do that today and explain that the delay was my fault." He could have cared about her and said, "Tell me more. I want to hear about what you were feeling." Once we learn how to listen well, then we will know what to do. We have so many different options at our disposal, even when we disagree with everything they are saying. We can always care about the person, acknowledge or validate their experience, and try to understand the meaning of their words.

Addressing one topic at a time.

It is the best way to communicate. Jackson could have received and addressed Sheila's concern and then circled back later about how her comments landed on him. Switching topics usually derails conversations. Both people are putting their topic up for consideration and talking past the other person. Neither person is listening or understanding. If you continue to speak about your topic without receiving the other person's message, you will derail the conversation. If you continue talking over each other, you will damage the relationship.

When you notice that there are two topics running simultaneously, then consider addressing one topic at a time. There are two separate but related topics that need to be addressed. Each one is important and needs to be discussed. You will end up at the right destination if you address each topic fully but separately, giving each topic the consideration it requires. Only after you have finished discussing the first topic is it wise to circle back and address the second topic.

Conversations stay on track when people notice what is happening internally and take the appropriate action.

Switching topics is only part of how the conversation got derailed with these two colleagues. What else happened? And what can we do about it when we find ourselves in a similar situation? Both Jackson and Sheila got triggered emotionally and contributed to the derailment of the conversation. Once Sheila's triggers were activated then she was under the grip of her overwhelming emotions. She was ready to fight, wanting to prove that her perspective was valid and needed to be considered. Jackson's refusal to pay attention to her request fueled the fire that was already lit inside her. When he rolled his eyes and said,

"What is wrong with you?" that seemingly small comment activated her deepest insecurities. She heard Jackson saying that something is wrong with her because she felt disappointed. Sheila's father had been overly critical of her and consistently communicated through words and actions that she was not good enough. When she felt unheard and inadequate, her emotional brain had completely taken over. Her stress hormones were released, and she was ready to fight and willing to do whatever was necessary in order to be heard.

When Sheila increased the emotional intensity and said, "You are patronizing me, and I'm done. Your comments are just rude," Jackson was feeling unjustly accused, hurt, and angry. The combination of her words and her intensity hit to the core of Jackson's vulnerability. His activated amygdala brought him to the edge, ready to fight. His heart rate was high and everything inside him felt like the threat needed to be neutralized. When Jackson was in middle school, he was bullied, and that helpless feeling made him promise he'd never allow it to happen again.

Destructive emotions undermine entire conversations. Conversations where two people are talking over each other are great indicators that something is going on under the surface that is bigger than the conversation at hand. What should we do to make things better? Start by paying attention to what is happening internally. The first step is to learn to recognize when the emotional part of your brain is activated. As long as your amygdala is driving your actions, your relationship threat indicator will be sounding the alarm. Your hijacked brain will be so busy protecting yourself and/or fighting a dangerous enemy, that you will be unable to connect with the part of your brain that can see things accurately and make things better. When your blood stops pumping and your hormones stop raging, your neocortex will be able to comprehend what the other person is communicating. You can learn to manage your own emotions and keep access to your brain, but it will take a greater awareness of what is happening and the things you need to do in order to make things better.

Take steps to regain access to your entire brain.

How do we take appropriate actions? We need to recognize when the emotional part of our brain is activated. How do we do that? Let's look at a story of an ordinary father in a grocery store. He was in a hurry, and he needed to grab three things quickly. He needed tampons for his wife, orange juice, and batteries. They were all on opposite ends of the store. He was feeling the pressure of time because he knew that the sooner he could get back to the house, the more time he would be able to devote to the last-minute touches to the presentation.

As an added handicap, the busy dad had a three-year-old next to an eighteen-month-old riding in the shopping cart. The three-year-old kept grabbing stuff, but he was hoping to keep moving quickly so she had no time to do any damage. Instinctively, the dad grabbed the orange juice and said to his eighteen-month-old to not drop the glass bottle or it would break. He hurried to the far corner of the store to the tampon aisle. Who knew there would be eleven different brands and five different sizes? He was feeling his window of time closing in on him, so he rushed to the front of the store where he planned to grab the batteries. Meanwhile, his three-year-old kept grabbing stuff. Just then, a cashier went on break, so the dad took his place at the back of the line. When he finally got to the front of the line, his three-year-old reached out and grabbed a candy bar. He turned to deal with putting it back and realized the batteries were not where they should be! He turned around to get out of the line so he could retrieve the batteries. That's when his eighteen-month-old dropped the glass jar of orange juice on the ground. It shattered (and splattered) in front of (and on) everyone who was nearby!

What happened to the dad at that moment is called an amygdala hijack. We all go there from time to time. Rational thought is no longer in control, it's just anger, frustration, and blame. The way to recognize it is to pay attention to what is happening in your body. When your hurts, fears, and vulnerabilities get activated, you can significantly increase the likelihood of remaining connected if you **learn to maintain as much access to our brain as possible.** It's a choice you have to make ahead of time. The more you get to know yourself, the better you will be able to respond to the people you care about during stressful moments.

The purpose of emotions.

Why did God give us emotions? Emotions add meaning to our experiences and inform us of how to respond to what is happening around us. Emotions give texture, color, and purpose to life. Emotions transform life from an objective series of events into a living, breathing experience. The main reason God gave us emotions is to show us what to do. If we are paying attention, emotions can motivate us to take the appropriate action. Our emotions were not designed to punish but to motivate behavior that will help our situation. Emotions do not tell us we are a bad person; emotions make us aware that we need to do something small to make things better. We will often continue to feel an emotion until we respond to it with the appropriate activity.

How do we learn to manage our emotions?

I have good news we can learn a strategy that will work. From my experience, the journey will take several months to be able to learn how to do it. Learning to manage your emotions may be the single most productive thing you can do. If you do it consistently, then you can master it sooner than you thought possible. Let's look at three verses from the book of Proverbs and one verse from the book of Colossians that will lay the groundwork for us to learn how to manage our own emotions. The first is found in Proverbs 25:28. To paraphrase, it says that a person who can't control their emotions is like a city without walls. In the ancient world, a city without walls was a disaster waiting to happen. Walls provided protection and security. When there were no walls, the people were helpless and completely vulnerable to attacks from the enemy. If we are unable to manage our emotions, we will be vulnerable to the words and actions of everyone around us. So, ask yourself, how vulnerable are you to the words and actions of other people?

> *Learning to manage your emotions may be the single most productive thing you can do.*

The second verse is equally powerful and communicates the same principle from the opposite vantage point. In Proverbs 16:32, Solomon says, "Better a patient person than a warrior, one with self-control than one who takes a city." A person that can manage their emotions is more powerful than a warrior that conquers an entire city. The third verse is in Proverbs 13:3. It says, "Those who guard their lips preserve their lives, but those who speak rashly will come to ruin." Those words are intense, but the reality is that unregulated emotions cause untold damage.

Our biggest wounds come when other people fail to control their emotions and unleash hurtful words or actions on us. Their uncontrolled emotions cause us a great deal of pain. Likewise, our biggest regrets are from times when we failed to control our emotions. We say harsh things to people we care about. We hurt the people we love the most. Words can cut like a knife. If you want to complicate your relationships, then unleash your negative emotions. You will lose trust and leave the people in your life feeling anxious and hurt.

Colossians 3:15 says, "Let the peace of Christ rule in your hearts, since as members of one body you were called to peace. And be thankful." There is a connection between how we treat others and the internal peace we feel. Peace is more than the absence of conflict, passive indifference, or detachment from reality; it is an internal feeling of serenity and calmness that everything is going to be alright. Managing your emotions *will* bring peace.

Use the P E A C E process to manage your emotions.
PAUSE to prepare yourself to act in a productive manner.

Pause. Pay attention to what is happening around you. Instead of reacting and doing or saying something destructive. Take a few seconds to pause and calm yourself so you are better able to respond in a healthy manner that will produce a much better outcome. It is easy to get overwhelmed emotionally. It may be helpful to think of your emotions like you do the warning lights that appear on the dashboard of your car.

When you are driving down the road and a warning light appears on the dash, every driver knows it's important to understand what it means. The yellow light that looks like windshield wipers is not terribly urgent, but it is helpful to know that your windshield washer fluid is low. It is something to address soon, but you are not in imminent danger. As we all know, there are some dash lights you should never ignore. If a red engine temperature light comes on, pull over immediately and shut off your engine before it overheats. On your car, there are three kinds of warning lights that appear on your dashboard: green, yellow, and red. The same three categories could apply to your emotions. Some are green and need to be noticed, some are yellow and need eventual attention, and some are red and need immediate action before driving anywhere. When you notice your emotions are running red hot, stop what you're doing before you cause irreparable damage to the relationship. If you pause, take a breath to slow down, and make a

> *When you notice your emotions are running red hot, stop what you're doing before you cause irreparable damage to the relationship.*

choice to manage your emotions instead of cutting off access to your brain and doing something you will regret.

EXPERIENCE your emotions.

Allow yourself to experience what you are feeling. This may be difficult because you have spent your entire life avoiding your emotions. Ask yourself an extremely important question. *What am I really feeling?* Allow yourself to sit still for five to twenty seconds while you feel what is going on inside your inner world. Go beyond the harsh secondary emotions to the tender primary emotions.

Examples of:

- **Secondary emotions**: anger, frustration, defensiveness, criticism, irritation, and blame

- **Primary emotions**: sadness, fear, disappointment, shame, loneliness, and hurt

Primary emotions are tender and private. We long to be close, and we want to be connected. It takes vulnerability to discover what we are really feeling. Secondary emotions are harsh and critical. We are afraid and work to protect our hearts from harm. So, how do we manage all this? We have to look past what other people are doing to us and how we need them to change and discover what we are feeling instead. We can figure out how we need to respond, but first we need to identify our own feelings.

In order to focus on what we want in the future, we need to be able to look past the intense emotions we might be feeling in the moment. Sometimes, we can be so upset that we forget there is even a future! One man got so enraged when his boss said something offensive that he stuffed an ice cream cone in his boss's face. Heat-of-the-moment actions have prolonged consequences. It is amazing how the desire to hurt someone you care about can be so strong in one moment, and in the next moment, you experience pain and regret. The greatest gift you can give the people you care about is to learn how to share your emotions in constructive and honoring ways.

> *The greatest gift you can give the people you care about is to learn how to share your emotions in constructive and honoring ways.*

Practice identifying specific feelings when you have them. Allow yourself to rest in those feelings long enough to understand them and to keep your focus on the end goal.

Examples of emotions:

- **Afraid**: When you feel like something bad is going to happen or you are going to be hurt.

- **Inadequate**: When you feel like you have failed and let people down. You feel like you are not good enough. No one could love the real you. No one ever will.

- **Alone**: When you feel like you are by yourself. You feel like you are invisible and unworthy of being noticed. When you feel like your opinions, desires, and emotions are not worthy of consideration.

- **Unloved/Insignificant**: When you feel totally unimportant, not mattering at all. To be so unimportant that your thoughts are not worthy of consideration.

- **Sad**: When you feel pain as a result of having experienced loss, grief, or sorrow. Prolonged sadness can lead to depression.

- **Accused/Guilty**: When you feel you have done something wrong. To hurt someone and cause harm. To have betrayed someone or to have acted against your values.

- **Rejected/Devalued**: When you feel completely unacceptable, put down, thrown out, or abandoned. When you feel disregarded and treated without value or told your contribution is insignificant.

- **Controlled/Powerless**: When you feel completely without power over your internal experience. To be out of control in your thoughts, your emotions, and your behavior.

ACKNOLWLEDGE your desire.

Admit to yourself what it is you really want. The entire next chapter will help you discover what you really want, but for now, ask yourself three sets of important questions. The answer to each set will give you clarity to know how to proceed. You often can't do both so you will need to choose.

1. Do I want to be close, or do I want to be right?
2. Do I want the other person to be heard, or do I want to make a point?
3. Do I want to be seen differently, or do I want to get my way?

If you take a few moments to figure out what you want, then you will be able to know which direction to head. If you want to be right, make a point, or get your way, then you are either a selfish person or chances are good that you are still overwhelmed emotionally and do not have access to your entire brain. Saying out loud what you want will help calm your emotions.

CARE about other people.

It comes down to compassion. Having compassion for yourself and the other person is critical. When we have compassion, we have a different lens to see what is happening around us.[2] We see the people in our lives as they really are, human beings with dignity and worth. We put ourselves in their place and imagine what it would be like to experience things from their shoes. We must change the focus from ourselves to the other person. We are not managing our emotions when we only see our own viewpoint. We care about the person when we demonstrate that they are important and their perspective matters to us. Listen in a way that leaves them feeling heard. Care about what they are saying, then acknowledge their feelings. Try and understand their perspective and comfort their pain. Receive their emotions and care about their situation. Listen to what they are saying so that you can respond to their experience with understanding and support.

Here is a practical example. If your friend or loved one is feeling sad because they are alone and don't have anyone to talk with, show you care about their situation by telling them, "I am so glad that you shared your feelings of loneliness with me." Acknowledge their feelings by validating their experience. "I can see how awful it must be to spend so much time alone." Share your emotions in a way that is constructive. Tell them what you feel and what you want. Don't attack their character or hurl accusations. One of the greatest gifts you can give the people you love is to learn how to share your emotions in a constructive and honoring way.

A person with the ability to manage their emotions can:

- Hear criticism without taking it personally
- Learn from their mistakes without feeling like a failure
- Admit they are wrong without blaming someone else
- Demonstrate compassion without invalidating other people's feelings
- Hear things about themselves that they desperately wish no one would ever say to them
- Receive the emotions of the people that matter to them

I had the privilege of talking to a man named, Sebastian, who was emotionally overwhelmed by a text message his wife, Phoebe, sent him. She said, "I am sick of living with constant disappointment. You will never keep your promises. You don't listen. In fact, I don't see how you make any positive contribution at all. I don't even know how you can call yourself a man. If I were you, I would be embarrassed to even call myself a man."

Sebastian said to me, "I want to work on my relationship with my wife, but I am tired of being a doormat. She unleashes her emotions on me with no regard for how badly they hurt me. To keep this marriage going, I'm going to have to suck it up, I guess I'm going to have to endure painful words and let her emasculate me."

I said to Sebastian, "I am so sorry your wife said such harsh words to you. I am having a hard time imagining how distraught I would be if my wife said those words to me. I don't want you to suck it up and endure her painful words. I want you to learn to regulate *your* emotions, so you can care about your wife and become the man that you desperately want to be. I want you to love your wife in a mature way and act in your own best interest. I want to empower you to respond in a way that doesn't sabotage your relationship, leaving you disconnected and alone. I want you to focus your attention on the only person you have the power to change, which just happens to be *you*. I want you to do the kind of things and say the kind of words that would encourage your wife to connect with and feel safe to pursue and desire genuine intimacy with you. I want you to act in a manner that will please your heavenly father and make you a man of honor, leaving you feeling good to the core of your being."

We can better care about the important people in our lives when we manage our own emotions. The most caring thing we can do is to respond to their experience with understanding and support. One of the most powerful ways to care about a person is to receive their disappointment without having to minimize or dismiss it. We can manage our emotions when a person we care about is hurting, frustrated, or sad because of something we did to cause it. When we experience their disappointment, it feels awful. It is frustrating and disappointing to be seen in a way that makes us uncomfortable. We feel like we have been unfairly placed in the basement. We desperately want to be seen in a positive light and come upstairs, but there is a lock on the door preventing us from leaving the basement. We want to break the door down and force the other person to hear all the reasons why they have come to the wrong conclusion.

We can waste all our energy determining why they see us in a negative light or assigning blame to the person who sees us unfairly. Emotional suffering is greatly increased and unnecessarily prolonged when we become preoccupied with why something happened or protesting that it should never have happened in the first place. The most caring thing we can do is to allow the other person to see us in a negative light without forcing them to change the way they see us. We make things better when we accept their disappointment and take steps to improve the relationship. How can we do something so unnatural and difficult? How do we accept and improve when we feel such deep and uncomfortable emotions?

EXCHANGE our emotions for what we really value.

We must pay attention to what we feel so we can exchange it for what we value. Remember, our emotions were designed to point us to actions. Our emotions were not designed to punish us or make us miserable, but to motivate behavior that will improve our situation. Emotions do not make judgements on our character and tell us we are terrible; they make us aware of what we need to do in order to make things better. At the end of the day, our life will have meaning and purpose when we acknowledge our emotions and allow them to motivate us to treat people well. That's what I mean by exchanging our emotions for what we value. Steven Stosny wrote about this in *Love Without Hurt*.[3] We feel good about

> *We feel good about ourselves when we live out our deepest values.*

ourselves when we live out our deepest values. Our ability to experience lasting happiness will depend on how we treat others.

If we value compassion and are acting in alignment with our values, we will care about people and consider their perspective. If we dismiss it and yell at them, we will feel awful because our actions are violating our values. Whenever we treat someone in a way that is consistent with our most important values, we will feel internal peace and our continued kind behavior will improve our relationships. Every time we treat someone in a manner that is out of alignment with our values, it will destroy relationships and undermine our own happiness. When we act in a manner that is consistent with our values, we may be disappointed with the outcome, but we will be far less likely to regret our behavior.

Take some time to identify and record your top seven values below, on paper, or on your favorite notes app. It's important to identify your top values so you can live by them. Put them somewhere you can see often. If we don't internalize our values, we will not act according to them in the heat of the moment. We will not live out what we believe in until we can rely on their strength in real time.

Top Values:

1.
2.
3.
4.
5.
6.
7.

Not all choices lead to freedom. If we are not careful, the things we do and say when we are emotionally overwhelmed will close doors that will be difficult to reopen. We can unleash our emotions and react to what we are feeling, or we can exchange the feelings for what we value. You absolutely need to go past your hurt to what really matters to you. Learning to manage your emotions is not learning to ignore all unwanted or unhelpful feelings, but to say *yes* to something better. Allow your emotions to put you in touch with something higher, better, and more meaningful. To determine what is most important to you, I have three very important questions to consider:

1. What is the most important thing about me?

2. What are the most important qualities I want to be known for?

3. What are the most important qualities of my most important roles as a boss or employee, teammate, parent, son or daughter, and/or husband or wife?

We are the best version of ourselves when we are living out our core values. When we are out of alignment with our values, we hurt the people we care about. Knowing who we are and what we stand for can lead us to who we are meant to be. Our core values can provide us with a sense of stability, direction, and peace of mind. However, acting upon our core values when we are overwhelmed emotionally is an entirely different challenge. It requires more than awareness that a specific behavior needs to change. The most difficult part about it is that we need to implement the behavior when we are overwhelmed and before we receive any of the benefits. The only way to implement lasting change is to develop habits that produce productive behavior when we are overwhelmed emotionally. This is next-level behavior. It is very difficult! We will need to practice responding with purpose and dedication until we can change our automatic response.

We can choose to take the high road or the low road. Traveling down the low road is like walking downhill. It is the easier of the two options, especially when we are overwhelmed emotionally. For some of us, it's a well-worn path! If we want to withdraw, we walk away and hide from the tough conversation. If we feel like blaming, we point out how the other person is responsible. People tend to follow the familiar path formed by the habits they have developed.

Taking the high road is much more difficult. It is like walking up a hill without a path. We have to make a path, clear out the rocks and brush, and step over obstacles as we go. We must choose to go in a direction that is contrary to what we are feeling. Changing habits is a slow process that always feels awkward in the beginning. With practice, we will be able to gradually build the skills to be able to do it consistently in real time. Anything we do repeatedly will become automatic if we give it enough time. New behaviors will feel more natural the more you enact them, and eventually, you will be able to do this on auto pilot.

We must make a conscious choice to treat people better than their actions deserve and act in a manner that is productive. One of the most crucial aspects to relationship success must be implemented at moments when it feels like the other person is making our life difficult.

> *The ability to respond effectively when we are feeling rejected, criticized, ignored, and disregarded will determine the quality of our relationship.*

The ability to respond effectively when we are feeling rejected, criticized, ignored, and disregarded will determine the quality of our relationship. It is precisely at these moments when we feel strong emotions that we will need to take the high road. Over time, we can train our brain to choose what we value. But it's critical that we develop the habit of taking the high road by exchanging our emotions for our values.

The more we choose the high road, the easier it will be to go down it again. At first, we will be forming neuropathways in our brain. It will feel awkward, but every time we go down the path, it will become easier and more familiar. The more we experience the benefits of the high road, the more motivation we will have to repeat high-road behavior.

When we are under stress, when our fears are activated, and when our emotions are heightened, we need to exchange what we are feeling and replace it with the high-road behavior we value. What are the behaviors? I've identified seven behaviors we can choose that will make things better in our relationships. Repeating these behaviors will bring us freedom and improve all our relationships, even the ones that are the most difficult. The habit of exchanging what you feel and want to do in the moment for doing something that makes things better, and to do it consistently, will produce results.

Let's start by looking at the high-road behaviors and a few real-life examples.

1. If you feel like assigning blame and proving the other person is responsible, then own your part of the breakdown and take responsibility for your behavior.

2. If you want to cause pain, harm them, or say something mean, then protect them from harm by controlling your words and actions.

3. If you feel like you need to withdraw or pull away, then intentionally move towards them to be close.

4. If you want to give up, feel helpless, want to quit, or stop trying, then do something small to improve or make things better.

5. If you feel the need to criticize, point out their shortcomings, or tell them what is wrong with them, then notice the good in them and tell them how much you appreciate them.

6. If you feel like getting revenge or making sure they receive punishment, then forgive them by letting them off the hook and canceling the debt they owe you.

7. If you want to silence them and stop them from communicating their feelings, then understand their perspective and try and see things from their point of view.

What does this look like with a real person? When we are overwhelmed emotionally, we want things in the moment that could cost us everything. If we stay in the amygdala, the almond-shape place in the brain that experiences very strong raw emotion, we will blame, hurt, withdraw, give up, criticize, get revenge, or force silence. If we can get to the place in our brain called the neocortex, then we can process our options and act maturely through the high-road behaviors that are consistent with our values.

We may feel like we want to say something mean or cause pain, but in order to protect the person we care about from harm, we need to control our words and actions. We've all felt the injustice of hurt that is caused by the actions and harsh words of others. It's natural to want to reciprocate the pain or say something mean to get back at them for hurting us. Hurt upon hurt causes damage to the relationship and everyone feels awful about themselves. Jack was dating Justine for a few months when she said he was acting just like his dad. Her comments cut him deeply, because his dad was a selfish jerk without any regard for other people. Jack reacted to what he perceived to be harsh criticism by calling Justine judgmental and insensitive. If he was managing his emotions and taking the high road, then he could have resisted his momentary desire to respond in kind and hurt her with harsh words of his own. He could have protected her from his cruel words by refusing to point out her unjust comments. When we protect the people we care about, even if we leave words unsaid, we are doing something noble that will leave us feeling good about ourselves. If Jack would have taken the time to develop a habit of identifying the impulsive urge to give it right back and instead chose high-road behavior, then hurt feelings and relationship damage could have been avoided.

Seven high-road behaviors to make things better

Cause pain
If you feel like you want to hurt them or say something mean.

Protect them
Control your words and actions to keep them from harm.

Assign Blame
If you feel like accusing them by proving they are responsible.

Take responsibility
Own your actions. Take responsibility for your part of the breakdown.

Pull away
If you feel like you need to run away or hide.

Move towards
Intentionally move towards them to be close.

Criticize them
If you feel like you need to point out their shortcomings or tell them what is wrong with them.

Appreciate them
Notice the good in them and tell them how much you appreciate

Quit trying
If you feel helpless and want to give up or stop trying.

Improve things
Do something small to make things better.

Silence them
If you feel like stopping them from communicating their feelings.

Understand them
Give their perspective credence and see things from their point of view.

Get revenge
If you feel like making sure they get punished for their crime.

Forgive them
Let them off the hook and cancel the debt they owe you.

If reading this chapter has given you a new awareness that managing your emotions will require you to make changes in habits and behavior, I celebrate that with you! It will be overwhelming at times, and those who bear the brunt of your low-road behaviors will be surprised and so pleased with your new choices. To start out, you will need to practice responding with resolute dedication until it all becomes more automatic. Motivation will get you started, but it will take discipline and commitment to follow through. You will need to practice going through common scenarios in your mind and intentionally plan out another way. Be determined to practice your responses over and over so when you encounter a real-life situation you will be able to overcome your automatic reactions. If you devoted ten minutes a day for at least two months, it would become a habit. The more deeply rooted the habit becomes, the easier it will be to respond productively in the heat of the moment.

To live out our values, we may have to give ourselves permission to challenge our own conclusions and question our own assumptions. When we feel an intense emotion, we know what we experienced is real, so we rarely ever challenge our own feelings. We justify them all day long. But where do these emotions come from? Do they come from the other person's behavior or the assumptions we make about their behavior? At first glance, the answer seems obvious because the obnoxious behavior came right before we experienced the intense emotion, but it might not be that simple.

To bring this all together, let's circle back to the work colleagues from the beginning of the chapter, Jackson and Sheila, and honestly evaluate if they were experiencing the only possible emotions? Jackson was convinced that Sheila was ungrateful and did not even care about how much he did to help her. Was his conclusion an assumption or completely based on undeniable evidence? What if Sheila really did appreciate him and was thankful when he covered all of her accounts for five days while she was in San Diego for the conference? Could he have made the wrong assumption? Sheila was convinced that Jackson wasn't willing to give her request any consideration. What if he really did respect her and value her opinion? Could Jackson have made the wrong assumptions?

When we experience a strong emotion, we do three things in less than a second.

1. We assign motives to the other person. Why did they do what they did?
2. We make judgments about the other person's intentions. Were they good or bad?
3. We also determine our response to the situation. What do I need to do now?

Question your conclusions.

As soon as we feel our emotional temperature rising, we should give ourselves instant permission to question our conclusions. We should ask ourselves if it is possible that we may have assigned motives and made judgments about the other person's intentions. When we are emotionally overwhelmed, we can become a prisoner to our assumptions without even knowing it. If Jackson or Sheila were able to have compassion and understanding, it would bring down their temperature and help them to regain access to their brain so they could treat each other more in line with their values. When we see the other person as the enemy, we treat them like a dangerous threat. Mature people give themselves permission to question their assumptions and reconsider their own judgements. We will live out our values when we take steps to manage this process.

Imagine you are in a meeting where your boss fails to celebrate your project success but takes the time to celebrate the endeavors of three other people. Before you become completely overwhelmed and say something awful, ask two helpful questions. What am I missing and could there be another reason my boss did this? As we begin to look for answers, our negative emotions will often dissipate. When our empathy and understanding replaces judgment and condemnation, we are reunited with our values. Our boss may have forgotten about us, he/she may be feeling inadequately prepared for the next part of the meeting, or he/she may have a better or different recognition planned for your hard work. Considering other options will bring down your temperature and help you act in the best interest of the relationship.

Upgrade your wardrobe.

Managing your emotions can be helpful for anyone, but if you are a follower of Jesus, then it may be the one thing you need to change to become the person you really want to be. My kids tease me all the time that I need a complete wardrobe makeover. According to them, the clothes I wear are outdated, out of style, and downright embarrassing. My clothes don't fit properly, look awful, and convey the wrong message, they say. I must admit, I have some low standards when it comes to the clothes I wear, getting most of them from the thrift store. I like clothes that are affordable, comfortable, and casual. Five dollars is an expensive shirt to me. I wear a different sweatshirt most days, usually promoting the teams or destinations that bring me joy.

My family tells me the clothes I wear reflect who I am and what I represent. When I had an important presentation, Darlene purchased five brand new dress shirts. She was excited when she brought the shirts home and wanted me to try them on. When I asked how much they cost, she assured me she got a great deal because they were 40 percent off the regular price. Imagine my shock when she reluctantly told me the sale price was still over eighty dollars per shirt! I wanted to take them back, but I love my wife, and the effort she spent to go shopping for me, so I reluctantly tried them on. To my surprise, the shirts were comfortable and fit perfectly. They looked good and did not distract from my upcoming presentation. They helped me convey the most-important message. I still enjoy these shirts and wear them often. The bonus is my family is not embarrassed whenever I wear them.

The Apostle Paul told followers of Jesus that they needed to put on entirely different clothing in Colossians 3:12-14. Paul said, [12]"Therefore, as God's chosen people, holy and dearly loved, clothe yourselves with compassion, kindness, humility, gentleness and patience. [13]Bear with each other and forgive one another if any of you has a grievance against someone. Forgive as the Lord forgave you. [14]And over all these virtues put on love, which binds them all together in perfect unity."

Christians have been given an entirely different closet to dress from! Paul lists five characteristics of Christ that we can wear wherever we go. He slows down to remind us who we are before he calls us to change our clothing. If we are a follower of Jesus, then we are chosen by God, set apart as unique and dearly loved. In Christ, we are loved. We were created with a purpose. We are not a convenient carbon copy of someone else. We were lovingly designed with intention and intricate design. God was not obligated to include us in His family and allow us carry out His plans. We are chosen, wanted, and forgiven. We do not have to define ourselves by our past mistakes, our present performance, or our future accomplishments. We are not a mistake. We are dearly loved.

Paul tells us we have access to a better closet with a wardrobe that always looks good on us, because other people experience the best versions of ourselves. The clothes are comfortable and fit perfectly because when we wear them, we are living out who we are meant to be. The clothes are stylish and elegant because they convey the most important message. We experience peace by becoming the person God made us to be. Internal peace is only possible when who we are on the inside matches what we do on the outside. We are at peace when the person we want to be is the person other people see.

> *We are at peace when the person we want to be is the person other people see.*

The first item of clothing we can put on is **compassion**. When we wear this, other people experience a person with sympathetic ears who hears them and has empathy for what they are going through, combined with a willingness to consider their perspective. The second item of clothing we can wear is **kindness**. When we wear this, people feel cared for because we are thoughtful, caring, helpful, and considerate. The third item of clothing we can wear is **humility**. When we wear this, they feel respected because we put them in a position of honor by placing their needs above our own. The fourth item of clothing we can wear is **gentleness**. When we wear gentleness, they can relax because we are not going to force them to do anything that will harm them. They can feel safe because we are careful with them and respond tenderly to their vulnerabilities. They get to witness inner strength from someone who is strong enough to allow them to get what they need. The fifth item of clothing we can wear is **patience**. When we wear this, people can take their time because we have prioritized them over our need to get what we want in the moment.

The people in our world do not see what we feel on the inside, they only see what we display on the outside. The same is true for everyone else. That's why it's so important that we take the high road and clothe ourselves with the wardrobe identified in Colossians, chapter 3. Our internal feelings have a big impact on what we do, but people are not aware of what is driving our actions. They can't see the hurt we carry from the people who have treated us very badly. They were not there when we were betrayed and deeply wounded. All they can see is how we treat them. It is unfair, but true. If we want people to see us differently, then we will have to change what is taking place on the inside.

Are you willing to allow God's Spirit to develop compassion, kindness, humility, gentleness, and patience in a way that shapes your character, influences what you say, and changes the way you treat people? When we are not controlling our emotions, people only see our behavior and see people who are mean, inconsiderate, critical, selfish, and dangerous. Those traits don't exactly make people want to spend time in our presence. We have been given a wardrobe upgrade. Let's put it on and wear it well. It's time we reflect our true identity in Christ.

When we are managing our emotions and maintain access to our brain, we can live out our deepest values. We are able to bear with others when they annoy us. Bearing with one another implies willingness to overlook the irritating things other people do and the frustrations they cause. It is one thing to put up with someone; it is altogether different to forgive them when they hurt us the way God forgave us. He concludes by asking us to put on love which binds them all together. Love is like the perfect accessory that completes the entire outfit. When we get dressed in these characteristics, they will be evident (and attractive) to others.

Release the hurt other people have inflicted upon you.

If you have ever been wounded, betrayed, abandoned, or violated, then you probably carry some deep injuries that reverberate all the way into the depths of your soul. Before you can manage your emotions, you will have to release the pain of your past to move into a better future. Forgiveness is a wonderful gift. Before we talk about forgiveness directly, or give you reasons why you should consider doing it (or show you how), let's start by looking at what life would look like without forgiveness.

Imagine the hurt you caused could never be erased; the relationships you have damaged could never be repaired. No matter what you did or how hard you tried, you would never be let off the hook or released from the guilt. Everywhere you went, you had to carry the shame of all your failures. That's a heavy thought! Forgiveness is a wonderful thing because it allows us to repair broken relationships and to be released from the guilt we carry. Forgiveness is one of God's greatest gifts, because it allows us to gain freedom from the hurt that has been done to us. It is a gift from God.

Author and theologian, Lewis Smedes, said there are four stages to forgiveness (Hurt, Hate, Healing, and Coming Together). When we are hurt by someone else, our initial instinct is to focus on the hurt we have received or do something hurtful back. Thoughts of retaliation dance around in our minds. Injustice and revenge are usually the things that preoccupy our minds.[4]

The only way to break the chain between your past and your future is to decide to release the hurt that you have experienced. You may be thinking: *They don't deserve it. You don't know what they did to me.* And you are 100 percent correct I don't know what they did, and they probably don't "deserve" forgiveness. But here's the flipside—you and I don't deserve forgiveness either. But the good news is God grants us forgiveness even though we don't deserve it. God wants to forgive you and the people who love you want you to experience it. The best thing you can do to move into a better future is to decide that they don't owe you, even though they were wrong, and that you are not going to force them to "pay you back." Forgiveness is about uncoupling yourself from the person who hurt you, deciding to let them go, and refusing to allow the pain to follow you into the future.

Forgiveness allows us to put the event into its proper historical perspective. We don't repress the memory, but neither do we dwell on it. It is a chapter of our story, but it is not the whole biography. When we forgive, we are saying we are not going to allow someone else's actions to have power over our life anymore. Why should we consider forgiving the people who have hurt us? Don't we have enough friends and loved ones to not need this complicated relationship? Refusing to forgive will destroy our soul and ruin this relationship and likely others as well. It becomes a barrier to moving forward and discovering all that God has planned for us.

Forgiveness is about uncoupling yourself from the person who hurt you and letting them go. It is about refusing to allow them to follow you into the future. Some of you are allowing the person who hurt you to live rent free in your mind. They preoccupy so much space in your head that you have lost track of the cost. Today is the day to evict them from your thoughts. Forgiving them will force them to move out of your mind. Do not allow what they did to you to define you. They may have stolen your childhood, but don't let them have the rest of your life. They may never apologize, but you don't need it to move on. They might not even be sorry for what they did, but that isn't a requirement either. Forgive them anyway.

> *Forgive them anyway.*

You have truly forgiven when:

- You refuse to allow your past hurt to justify your present bad behavior.

- You stop telling other people about the awful person that hurt you. (You no longer have a desire to tarnish their reputation).

- You no longer give them free rent in your head or heart.

Forgiveness may result in tender actions that fit the relationship. Forgiveness almost always brings a kind of peace that helps you go on with life. The offense is no longer front and center in your thoughts or feelings. Your hostility and misery have made way for compassion, kindness, and peace. Instead of dwelling on the injustice and revenge which will only make you miserable, you can move toward a life of empathy, mercy, compassion, and joy. "To forgive is to set the prisoner free and discover that the prisoner was you". – Lewis Smedes.[5]

We can release the pain of our past and move into a better future if we identify the person who hurt us and determine what debt they owe us. Before we can forgive, we need to determine what is owed. Maybe it is your boss or your son, your neighbor or your dad. Many times, when we feel hurt or disappointment, it is because someone has taken something away from us. Forgiveness in the Bible means that, with God's help, we make the decision to cancel the debt.

When a relationship falls apart, we may feel like our stability and self-worth has been stolen. When we are let go from a job, our dreams and financial security can be stolen. When your spouse divorces you, they rob you of precious time and influence with your children. You can't forgive hurt until you identify what has been taken away from you. I could not forgive my mom until I admitted her alcohol abuse stole my ability to be a child. I had to grow up way too fast.

How do we release hurts others have inflicted upon us? One answer is to focus on how much we have been forgiven. The more we understand how much we have been forgiven, the more motivation we will find to forgive others. The more grace and mercy we realize God has poured into our lives, the more grace and mercy we will extend to others. Forgiven people forgive. Before we can really forgive other people, we need to stop and reflect on all the ways that God has forgiven us. Think of all the destructive words we have spoken over other people. Think of the judgmental attitudes that have dishonored others and destroyed the work of God.

It's time.

Think of forgiveness as a process and reconciliation as a final (but optional) step. Reconciliation does not always happen. If there has been abuse, it may not be wise or safe to reconcile. Forgiveness is for us, not for the person who hurt us. It is a gift from God that will bring *us* freedom. People often confuse forgiveness with reconciliation, as if they were the same thing. They are not. The difference between forgiveness and reconciliation is that forgiveness requires nothing from the person we choose to forgive. The person who hurt us doesn't even need to know we are forgiving them.

Reconciliation is about restoring the relationship and requires an understanding from the person who hurt you that they did something wrong, combined with a willingness to change direction. Reconciliation requires some level of regret, remorse, humility, and a genuine concern for the damage caused. In your attempt to restore the relationship, do not engage with anyone who continues to make excuses and is not willing to make lasting changes in their behavior.

When we forgive, we decide to cancel the debt and give up the right to be repaid. We may not feel like it, and they do not deserve it, but we forgive them anyway. Forgiveness is an act of trust that God will bring about the justice so we don't have to. Freedom will come in time. We can release the pain of our past and move into a better future if we focus on how much we have been forgiven, identify the person that hurt us, determine what they owe us, and decide to cancel the debt, never to be repaid.

Clean out your closet and take it to the curb.

Paul tells us we have to clean out our closet and get rid of the articles in our wardrobe that do not look good on us anymore. When we wear these clothes, people experience the worst versions of ourselves, and we are not living out who we are meant to be. Paul says to take off anger, rage, malice, lying, and hurtful words. All five of those behaviors happen when we are overwhelmed and not managing our emotions. Take them out to the trash and throw them away. We must get rid of the hate growing inside us.

If we are not careful, we will close off our own soul. One of the most important steps in learning to manage our emotions is to get rid of bitterness and resentment. Evil done to you can grow into evil inside of you. Don't get stuck in the hate. If someone at work takes credit for your idea, you could make it your priority to undermine them in front of the entire organization, but be careful.

> Evil done to you can grow into evil inside of you.

Bitterness and resentment can distance your soul. Thoughts of retaliation dance around in your mind. Injustice and revenge preoccupy your mind. Hatred hurts the one doing the hating the most. It gets in the way of the peace God has for us. We justify our bad behavior, but bitterness is nothing but self-induced misery that produces chain sinning. Jim Wilson gives an excellent definition in his forty-page book of essays on Christian relationships. He says, "Bitterness can be defined as "an intense, deep-seated feeling of indignation. It is a cancerous condition which can consume us."[6]

The Bible compares bitterness to a "root" and declares that it causes a lot of trouble. Many have been "defiled" by it because its potential effect upon our life can be widespread and deeply embedded. As the action of spreading roots takes hold and entangles us, it becomes an increasingly deadly and destructive problem that chokes out every area of our existence. If left unchecked, it will completely contaminate and eventually undermine all of our relationships. Bitterness will poison our soul from the inside out and make it impossible to be kind or experience closeness with anyone. Resentment will eat away at our ability to love, which will lead us to blame other people and justify our own bad behavior.

When we are hurt by someone else, our initial instinct is to focus on the hurt and use our energy to assign blame. If the pain, we are experiencing is someone else's fault, then we can justify our bad behavior.

Completing This Leg of the Journey

If we want to enjoy satisfying relationships, then we must pay attention to the way we react when we are overwhelmed emotionally and make the necessary changes to our own behavior. We can keep the conversation train on the track by only addressing one topic at a time and paying attention to what is happening internally. We are responsible to keep our own engine from getting overheated. If we feel our temperature rising, then we must pull over immediately and do what is necessary to cool down the engine before we cause extensive damage to the relationship.

We are called to take appropriate steps to manage our emotions by developing habits to automatically exchange intense feelings for high-road behaviors that align with our values. Emotions do not make judgements on our character and tell us we are terrible; they make us aware we need to do something to make things better. Compassion and understanding will bring down our temperature and help us act in our own best interest. We must exchange our emotions for what we value and then act in a manner that is productive. When our hurts, fears, and vulnerabilities get activated, we can significantly increase the likelihood of remaining connected if we learn to make the decision to maintain as much access to our brain as possible.

Questions for Discussion

- What happened to you the last time you lost control of your emotions?
- Why is it essential to talk about one topic at a time?
- What happens inside you when people switch topics with you?
- Do you feel past hurts are making it hard to manage a current relationship? Why do you think that is?
- What are the signs to look for so you can recognize when another person is overwhelmed emotionally?
- How do you know when your amygdala has become hijacked?
- How well can you access your own emotional temperature?
- What are some of the things you have done to elevate someone else's emotional temperature to an unsafe level?
- What steps can you take to regain full access to your brain?
- Of the five articles of clothing Paul instructs us to put on in Colossians 3, which do you feel most called to work on "wearing" right now? Compassion, kindness, gentleness, humility, and patience. What action steps will you take to accomplish this?
- Which of these five do you need to clear out of your closet: anger, rage, malice, lying, and hurtful words? What action steps will you take to accomplish this?
- Is there someone you need to forgive? What steps will you take to do so?

Chapter Twelve

The Productive Path That Brings Resolution

Working together to solve the problem.

One minute you are having a harmless conversation with someone you value and want to be close to, when without warning, you are ducking incoming grenades in the form of angry comments and harsh criticism. You hurl a few yourself in the form of insults and nasty looks.

Carter was fifteen years old and having a pleasant conversation with his dad, Tom, about a get-together he was planning on attending. Trying to make conversation, Tom innocently asked who was going to attend. Carter felt controlled and unintentionally used a particular tone of voice as he responded, "Who cares?" to his dad. The tone combined with the words were interpreted as disrespect by his dad.

Tom's reaction moved from initial shock and disbelief to frustration and anger because his son was so disrespectful. Tom's mood changed from relaxed to anxious and the conversation was transformed from a casual connecting conversation to an outright power struggle.

Carter sensed the change and got defensive. He was no longer talking with a friend, but with an overbearing, authoritative, and unreasonable parent. Carter was incensed and quickly retorted with accusations to his dad about the intent of the conversation, noting that his dad was a control freak and pulled rank whenever he didn't get the information he wanted. Tom reacted with full-fledged disgust and unleashed some of his pent-up rage as he stormed out of the room. What they do next will determine the long-term satisfaction in their relationship. They can continue to escalate and say increasingly harsh comments, or they can go down a different path with the potential to end up at a different destination.

Wise people do not ignore the problem and pretend it will get better. They refuse to blame their opponent, silence the enemy, or demonstrate the guilt of their adversary. They recognize they are on a dead-end path and get off the merry-go-round of misery and get on the **productive path towards resolution.** This means that wise people take steps towards resolving conflict and deal with unfinished business. They take steps to get closure so the relationship is not left with the tension of the damaging conversation. As we bring together several different pieces of the puzzle, lets incorporate questions and decisions that come into play during real conversations. If you learn to do them well, you will be able to complete a productive conversation in minutes instead of in hours.

Like anything complicated, coming to a resolution will take some practice. It can be awkward or even seem silly that you must repeat things or clearly acknowledge you received a message. That awkwardness will fade away and you will find yourself being able to get more done with less headaches. The more you communicate your care, show your concern, and demonstrate your interest, the more the people will trust you. It takes work to edit yourself in real time, but the effort is worth it as you communicate in a way that brings you closer to others.

Completing Conversations.

Making the decision to complete conversations becomes a powerful way to connect with your loved one or friend. Every time you have a conversation about an issue that does not get resolved, you are left with an open loop. I introduced them to you in chapter two and will unfold them in more detail now. The more you travel around on that open loop, the more it becomes second nature to travel around that loop again and again. The unresolved conflict destroys hope and leaves you with an unsettled feeling that you will not be able to solve problems with this person in the future.

Deana and Lucas had been dating for four years. Lucas really wanted to get married, but he and Deana never seemed to be able to complete the conversation. They both enjoyed spending time together, but when they talked about the future, intense emotions derailed the conversation. They never got very far because Deana got overwhelmed and found a way to stop the conversation. The loop remained open because they were not working together to identify or solve the problem.

Here's another example. Fred and Jose were working as mechanics in their shop and both were frustrated because their boss had been grumpy for twenty days straight. The city denied issuing them a permit because they needed a picture of the inside of the electrical box. Both Fred and Jose were convinced the other person was supposed to take care of this, but the boss had the contacts with the city and was ultimately responsible. They started a conversation and agreed that someone needed to take a picture of the electrical box, but the loop remained open because they had not clearly decided how the task was going to be carried out. Two key factors in having clear communication are understanding when a decision has been made and what role each person will play in carrying out the decision. When the conversation is not completed, the task is not completed.

One of the most powerful things you can do is close loops and complete conversations. A loop is closed when both people are working together to solve the actual problem. There are sequential steps that will make it possible to know that you've completed a conversation. Unresolved conflicts can take place in our relationships with one another at every level.

Ask yourself what it would take to have closure between lifelong friends, competing companies, or new roommates? Other times, unresolved conflict exists between a boss and employee, a parent and child, or a husband and wife. When you follow the four-step process, you get on a productive path that brings a listening ear to your ideas and a resolution to the conflict.

The productive path that brings resolution.

Step #1: Identify the Issue

The first step on the productive path that brings resolution is to identify the issue and agree on what topic you will be discussing. The more you can clarify the particular topic, the higher your chances of resolving the conflict. Be specific and make sure you are addressing the real issue you are facing. The more clarity you have, the more likely you are to have a productive conversation. Taking the time on the front end will keep you from getting side-tracked from what you need to talk about.

Don't talk about a general topic like parenting teenagers. It will be more effective if you talk about the specific problem of your daughter breaking curfew. Don't talk about having a good relationship with your coworker. It will be more effective if you talk about the specific problem of what happened last Tuesday during the team meeting. You need to address the actual topic and speak about what you perceived happened. If you believe your coworker lied to the team and told everyone that you sabotaged the project, then you have to share that from your perspective. Remember, problems are solved when people talk respectfully and have compassion. The more you can narrow down the topic, the better chance you will have to come to a resolution.

On this first step, work together to identify the issue. It is equally important to have full participation from both people because if you can't agree on the issue, you won't have a chance of solving it. Don't start the conversation until both people are fully engaged in the process. If you are unable to agree on a topic, you may need to have two separate conversations. In order to have a productive conversation, both people must be willing to follow the guidelines and fully participate in the process. Often, one person wants to talk and the other person prefers to avoid the conversation altogether. Take some time to create a safe environment where both can participate. You can only close the loop in a conversation when both people are listening and talking from their hearts. You cannot rush important conversations. Make sure you both agree on the issue and are willing to actively participate in the process.

Step #2: Determine the Designated Talker

After you identify the issue, determine who gets to talk first, then work together to proceed to the second step. When the designated talker unfolds what happened from their perspective, they get to share their thoughts, feelings, and conclusions without judgment or interruption. The process is simple but far from easy because most people have the habit of jumping in to defend themselves and argue the facts. Once you start to experience success, you will never go back to the destructive patterns that leave you feeling alone, frustrated, and unheard. The reason it's important to start with listening is because it is key to releasing angst and deeply held assumptions.

If you have a history of unproductive conversations with this person, you may need help from a third party who can make sure that you are following the process. It is critical that you are both listening to understand, talking from the heart, and caring about the other person as best you can. If you attempt to follow the process and have three unsuccessful conversations about the same topic, then get someone to help you.

The person listening must work towards opening their heart, so they can receive what is being said before responding. There is something powerful about being heard and understood without any resistance. We can give that gift to each other. We must care about the person, acknowledge what they are saying, validate their experience, and seek to understand the meaning of their words. We cannot allow ourselves to argue the facts or deny their experience. The idea is to make sure the person talking has experienced compassion, empathy, and understanding so they will be able to get to their own heart in order to begin the next step in the process.

The person talking must see that the listener understands their perspective. This step is about communicating the desire to understand and making the person speaking feel heard. It is not possible to communicate that we understand without demonstrating that we have listened. One way to show we are listening is to reiterate what has been said, even going as far as to repeat their words so they understand they have been genuinely heard. They need to know that we get them and want to understand where they are coming from.

Repeating back the speaker's words might seem awkward or even silly, but this simple habit will summarize the main concepts and prevent misunderstanding. **We must demonstrate that we have received the message before they will believe it**. That awkwardness will fade away and you will find yourself being able to resolve disagreements simply because the other person will feel your care and concern. Listen with your heart. You will not be able to pretend or bide your time to make your point. Only genuine interest will allow their relational threat indicator to relax and keep their past hurts, fears, and vulnerabilities from becoming part of the conversation. Quite often when the person sharing feels heard and understood, the problem will be solved, trust will be rebuilt, and the connection will be restored.

It may be easier to see this in a real-life conversation. Tyler and Hannah were on the way to the hospital to have their first child when Hannah asked Tyler to make a quick stop at the grocery store to get some snacks to eat in the hospital. Tyler went into the store to get snacks and was in there for less than three minutes. As he was paying for the snacks, he talked to the attendant who he happened to have dated in high school. The entire conversation happened in under a minute. The reason they know the exact timeframe is because Tyler and Hannah had argued about it over a hundred times. When Tyler came out to the car, Hannah was noticeably upset, but Tyler had absolutely no idea why. He got the snacks that had been requested as quickly as possible.

Hannah asked if Tyler enjoyed the conversation with the attendant.

Tyler was taken back and confused. He asked what Hannah meant.

Hannah retorted that in her time of need, his main concern was talking to his ex-girlfriend.

Tyler thought this was ridiculous as he was just trying to get food for the hospital upon her request.

Every time they tried to discuss this topic, Hannah became withdrawn; Tyler became frustrated. By the time Tyler and Hannah came into my office, their son was nineteen years old, and the argument was very familiar! Usually, it would come up when Hannah was feeling disconnected or unloved. Sometimes, Tyler would try to listen until he felt falsely accused and disrespected, which was sometimes seconds into it. He would try and prove to his wife she was being ridiculous and that he did not do anything wrong. The more he defended himself, the more intense she became until the conversation would escalate out of control and stop abruptly.

Whenever Hannah reopened this conversation and Tyler was not receptive to hearing her pain, she would increase the intensity. She would bring up the original incident on the night of the birth of their first child. Tyler would respond by saying one or any combination of the following statements: "Not again. You are crazy! Here we go again. It was your idea to get the food. I can't believe we are still talking about this. So, what if I happened to know the store clerk that night. I don't know how much longer I can put up with this nonsense. I am done. See you later!"

This had tortured Tyler and Hannah for almost two decades. They loved each other and were miserable at the same time. When they finally were in enough pain to bring someone else into the conversation, they came to see me. We were able to work our way through all four steps to get to a resolution. We will look at the first two now. They both agreed the subject of the conversation was the trip to the hospital on the day they were having their first child. Hannah was the person that became the first designated talker.

Hannah started by saying, "A day that was supposed to be special turned out to be the worst day of my life."

Tyler added, "And that day has produced hundreds more miserable days."

I stopped Tyler and reminded him that he was the listener, and his role was to care about her and allow her to tell what happened from her perspective. I asked if he could stay on the productive path that could possibly bring resolution.

Tyler agreed to give it another try. He had been listening, so he repeated back what he heard her say, "That day was the worst day of your life."

Hannah took a deep breath and agreed that is exactly what she had said. They both sat silently for one entire minute.

Tyler finally looked at me and said, "What do I do now?" I reminded him that he should engage Hannah to tell him more. So, he turned to Hannah and said, "Tell me more." It wasn't totally natural for him, but he said it.

Hannah continued to share her heart, admitting she was hurt, angry, and frustrated that her husband doesn't understand this. She said she felt abandoned at a time when she really needed him.

Tyler interrupted her and said, "But I have never abandoned you."

I interrupted him and said, "What is it I want you to do right now, Tyler?"

Tyler said, "Hannah just falsely accused me of abandoning her. I can't stand by and let her lie like that."

I reminded him that interrupting and defending himself is a dead-end path and not the path we are on. Adversarial conversation filled with hostility has made them miserable for almost twenty years. The path they have been taking is not producing the desired outcome, but it sure was familiar. Tyler agreed this was true.

I then asked Tyler to continue to follow the process and receive what she says without any resistance. His part is to care about her and acknowledge her experience. That's it. To take it a step further, he should validate her experience and try to understand the meaning of her words. After this, a step further, is to offer her comfort.

Tyler said, "This is crazy. I don't see how listening to her will make any difference." We sat in silence for about a minute more before Tyler agreed to give it another try. He looked at Hannah and reluctantly said, "Tell me more."

Hannah continued to describe the hurt, confusion, disappointment, and anger she felt that night. Then Hannah stopped mid-sentence and said, "I don't think this is going to work."

Tyler stepped in and demonstrated he was listening by repeating again what he heard her saying, including the part about how she didn't think this was going to work. He then proceeded to ask her to tell him more about how she felt abandoned that night.

Hannah leaned forward and noted she was uncomfortable and terrified to share more. She hesitantly explained that she was not only literally in the process of having her first baby, but she also felt emotionally exhausted, physically drained and, well, "Huge," she said. For several nights, she had not been sleeping and felt cranky, mean, vulnerable, and helpless. As she recounted watching Tyler talk to his ex-girlfriend at the checkout through the convenience store window, she stopped talking, and started crying.

Tyler moved in and said, "You were feeling vulnerable and scared and ugly. I heard you loud and clear, but what else were you about to say?"

Hannah continued on through her sobs and told Tyler that she felt alone, like she couldn't trust him, and that she felt awful all over again every time she brought it up and he told her she was crazy."

What Tyler did next changed the entire conversation.

Tyler said, "Wow, Hannah, I had no idea you were feeling alone, vulnerable, and afraid in the car. When I was talking to my former girlfriend, you felt like you couldn't trust me. That had to be an awful feeling while you were just starting labor pains. Can you tell me more?"

Tyler was not listening to make his point or prove her wrong or even to follow promptings from me; he was listening to her heart and caring about her experience. He continued repeating what she was saying but was also validating her experience.

Hannah said, "It was awful. It was terrifying, but that is not even the most painful part."

I took a deep breath knowing that the way he responded to the next sentence may be a defining moment for the rest of their relationship. I was not sure Tyler was ready for the moment. I wanted to stop him and prepare him for the moment, but I felt a nudge from the Holy Spirit to let it ride.

I underestimated his compassion.

Tyler leaned in and said tenderly, "Sweetheart, what was the worst part?"

Hannah said, "I was feeling vulnerable and wondering if you would abandon me with a newborn. I wanted to share my fears and have you reassure me. I wanted you to tell me I was the woman you loved, and I was enough, and you were not interested in any other woman."

Hannah paused and continued, "In my most terrifying moment, you silenced me and called me crazy. You told me I was ridiculous and that my feelings were my fault."

Tyler was operating in his heart now and he said to his wife, "I think I get it. You were feeling unlovable, I was talking to another woman, and you were questioning my love and trustworthiness. You wanted to trust me, but you needed me to demonstrate in that moment that I would always love you, and you could always trust me. I did not hear you. I've never heard you. I am sorry, Hannah! I did not hear you. You were afraid, and I was unavailable to meet your needs."

Hannah sighed and took another deep breath. She was feeling heard and said, "Exactly! Thank you, Tyler. But that is not all."

This time, I was not nervous for Tyler. He was doing great.

Tyler grabbed her hand and said, "I am listening. I want to hear what you experienced. What else?"

Hannah was feeling cared for and valued. She said, "Through the years, I wasn't feeling connected to you, and I wanted to make things better. That's why I kept reaching out. I know I was far from perfect. I was angry and hurt and feeling cast aside. I lashed out so many times to try to get your attention. I wanted to be close to you, but every time I brought it up, you called me crazy. Sometimes you even threatened to leave. Those times really hurt me, Tyler. One time after my parents left, you screamed at me that you did not know how much longer you could put up with this nonsense. I have re-lived that moment over and over. When it got too painful, I tried to bring it up, and you harshly rejected me and told me again I was crazy."

Hannah was crying uncontrollably now.

Tyler was fully engaged and full of compassion. He said, "I am so sorry, Hannah. You were reaching out to me because you wanted to be close. You wanted me to comfort you and I called you crazy. Now I get it. You desperately wanted me to tell you that I loved you, and instead, I screamed at you and threatened to leave. I had no idea. I thought you were telling me I was a failure. I thought you were trying to convince me I was a miserable husband."

I interrupted him and said, "You will get to share your experience with Hannah later. Tyler, you are doing so well. I am impressed. Trust the process and let Hannah finish first."

Hannah said, "That's okay. I want to hear what Tyler experienced. Thank you, Tyler, for listening. I can tell that you get it. I do not have words to express what it means to me that you cared enough to listen and to understand me today."

Why did this conversation help when so many others had failed? What happened in that moment was exactly what Tyler and Hannah needed to begin healing the relationship. Tyler's compassion and understanding changed everything. Hannah had previously concluded that she could not trust Tyler. Every time she brought it up, he confirmed that she was not worth it, and she could not count on him. Hannah was asking an emotional question from the heart, and Tyler was giving her a logical answer by arguing the facts and rejecting her feelings.

Hannah was hurt so badly that it damaged her ability to connect with Tyler at a heart level. Experts call it an attachment injury of the heart. An attachment injury is different from other relationship hurts because it requires more care and often more guidance. Dr. Sue Johnson defines an attachment injury as "a feeling of betrayal or abandonment during a critical time of need."[1] When an attachment injury has occurred, a person sees the relationship and the person who hurt them through a different lens. The impact of the injury leaves them feeling completely unsafe in a previously safe relationship.

Tyler loved Hannah, and he was indeed trustworthy, but despite his best intentions, his defensiveness from an unresolvable accusation prevented him from receiving her message. His defensiveness made it impossible for Hannah to reach his heart. Tyler's attitude and actions communicated to her heart that he did not love her, and she stayed alone in her fears.

In Tyler's moments of frustration, when he said things like, "I don't know how much longer I can take this," he communicated he would consider leaving her, which only heightened her fear of abandonment. His silence and withdrawal spoke loudly to her soul that he might literally leave her. The problem could not be argued or word-smithed away, it needed to be cared about, acknowledged, validated, and comforted.

Hannah's injury of the heart left her with the inability to trust Tyler. The broken trust made vulnerability almost impossible and damaged their connection. The relationship that was once solid felt unreliable, and it happened at such a critical time during the birth of their first-born child. Their constant attempts to talk at or past each other made it impossible to get to the real problem. Every time Tyler defended himself and minimized Hannah's concerns, the wound was reopened, and her conclusions confirmed.

Even with this breakthrough moment in my office, Hannah's trust would need to be rebuilt over time through repeated compassion and understanding from Tyler. His willingness to receive her concern demonstrated he was available and receptive, and it was a powerful first step to restore the connection. His willingness to hear Hannah's heart and communicate his emotional availability strongly demonstrated he would be there for her in the future.

Every situation is different, and layers of painful interactions can cause people to arrive at vastly different conclusions. If you want to bring unresolved things to closure, you must first receive what someone says and demonstrate that you have received it. It takes time to show a person how much you care. You are not on the productive path that leads to resolution until they believe you are willing to get to know them and genuinely want to understand where they are coming from.

Taking the extra step of repeating the words that were just spoken back to the speaker is remarkably effective, especially when your heart is open to genuinely receiving the message. Simply saying the same words back to them can feel awkward and disingenuous. Tim Kimmel writes about how it will be more effective and feel more natural if you can accurately summarize the main concepts.[2] People feel heard when you let them know that you are there for them and willing to receive what they are saying without any resistance. It can be helpful to ask the speaker questions to make sure you received the message but be careful to not ask "loaded questions"—questions that have the intent of disputing a fact or disagreeing with a statement. Here are a few examples. "Did I hear you?" "Was I close?" "What did I miss?" and "I really want to hear you."

Any time you summarize, you face the possibility of misunderstanding the message. If you attempt to summarize, but miss the message, it will be tempting to try and prove to them that you did not miss it. That is a dangerous dead-end path. It may even seem like a good idea to prove to the speaker that they either misspoke or actually intended to say the message you thought you heard. Both of those paths will undermine the entire process. Resist those destructive paths. Neither of them will bring resolution.

Simply say one of the three potential options: "I am sorry I missed it," "Would you please give me a chance to try again?" or "I really do want to hear it. Would you say that again?" Don't sabotage the progress you have made by trying the strategies that have caused disconnection in the past. Take the high road and give them a gracious path to maintain their dignity and change their mind. Thank them for sharing their heart with you. If you receive their pain, demonstrate you care, validate their experience, understand the meaning, and comfort them, then you are ready to begin the next step in resolving the problem.

Step #3: Say Things From the Heart

The third step for the speaker is to say things from the heart, that will create a thirst for future conversations. This requires identifying your longings and putting them into words. This can be difficult because you must move beyond your fears and accusations to ask for what you actually want and need. During the third step, the person talking expresses their desires in the form of reasonable requests. This makes it possible for the person listening to respond to their requests. How does this work in a real conversation?

Thomas and Francis worked together to sell hotel rooms to families and groups. Francis did not always pay attention to important details, which caused Thomas to have to speak with angry customers who did not get the rooms they were promised. Instead of attacking Francis and telling him he was incompetent and lazy, Thomas moved beyond accusations and shared his longings.

He said, "I want us to be able to satisfy our customers, but it is more than that. I really enjoy saving people money and providing an opportunity for families to enjoy vacations. When I was growing up, our vacation was the highlight of our year. I have so many fond memories. Our yearly vacation was the lifeline that held our family together. When I hear the disappointment in their voices because they miss out on the hotel they had their hearts set on, something happens inside of me. I know it does not even make sense when I say it out loud, but I feel like in our work, we are saving families. I am sorry, Francis, for getting angry and unleashing my anger at you. You don't deserve it. I know you work hard and care about people too. I respect you, and I want two things for you. I want you to be highly successful, and I want you to enjoy working with me. As for me, I would really like to be able to trust that the requests will be finished on time, or at least know when you are unable to meet the deadline."

Conversations are completed when people get to the feelings in their hearts. It is not the formula that magically makes everything better. It is important for Thomas to share from his heart what he wants for himself and for Francis as well as for the company. Thomas could also create a better working relationship by acknowledging the stressful environment they both have to operate within. He could say, "I know you have a lot on your plate. Would you be willing to let me know which projects you completed and which ones you are unable to finish by 4:00 p.m. each day? I am open to how you want to get the information to me."

After Thomas asks from the heart, it's time for Francis to receive the request and give it some consideration. He can start by acknowledging his request. Francis could say, "I hear you asking me to let you know the progress of the projects by 4:00 p.m. each day because you want me to succeed. You also want us to work well together and satisfy our customers. Thank you for sharing your past experiences because it helps me see why you are so passionate about helping families." After Francis acknowledges the request, he can either accept it or take a moment to think about it.

Francis could say, "I can let you know by 3:30 p.m. each day." He may say, "How about if at the end of the day I only let you know which requests I could not complete." Or he could say, "I will give you administrative rights to our tracking software and you can see the information for yourself. Does that work?" If Francis agrees to the request, then they can work together to solve the problem. Sometimes the listener may need to talk for a while and give some additional information or circle back and unpack some raw emotions. Often when people talk in a respectful manner and get to their hearts they can work as problem-solving teammates instead of adversaries.

Step #4: Solve the Problem

The last step is working together to solve the real problem. Every time we resolve conflict and bring about closure, we build a deeper connection. Taking care of unfinished business will give us hope, knowing that we can navigate disagreements and become collaborative allies and problem-solving teammates. When we can work together to defeat a common enemy or accomplish a shared purpose, we thoroughly enjoy spending time in each other's presence and develop a connection that goes beyond words. Coming to a resolution requires a collaborative environment to consider solutions It is virtually impossible to solve the problem until you understand the other person's perspective. If the listener has taken the time understand the problem, then it is time to work together to start seeking solutions.

> *It is virtually impossible to solve the problem until you understand the other person's perspective.*

Ending a difficult conversation without an action plan is like hooking up the boat and driving two hundred miles to a pristine lake without ever putting the boat in the water! This is the step that makes sure you get closure and end up with a sustainable solution.

The speaker and listener must work together to bring about resolution. Work together to **gather possible solutions**. You can brainstorm ideas or take turns offering suggestions. Once you get some good ideas, then **chose the best option** or **set a time to find a solution**. You must cooperate to solve the real problem. You will be tempted to rush this part of the process but completing the conversation will help prevent the frustration that leaves you disconnected.

Both people must take responsibility for **creating an action plan** to make things better, **agreeing on the next steps**, and following through on everything you say you will do. Always confirm the actions that are to be taken, **setting realistic deadlines** and **creating a time to evaluate progress**. Making firm, clear commitments with due dates helps you make progress and gets things done. For example, "I agree to plan three tasks with due dates by next Tuesday." It can be helpful to set a time to reconnect and follow up before ending the conversation.

If we want to get closure and complete the conversation, we need to decide exactly what needs to get done by identifying specifically who does what and by what time. We can't leave any of these important details up for interpretation or we will be disappointed with the results.

As you are reading this section, it might sound like a great solution for a business but too rigid for a family. We have all had conversations where we were certain everyone knew what to do, only to find weeks later that nothing was done. At the end of any important conversation, it can be very helpful to summarize what was discussed by asking, "Is there anything you are unclear about? Do you have questions?" Before the conversation is completed, we need to work together and establish what we are trying to accomplish with clear goals, detailed parameters, and accurate deadlines. No matter how competent, committed, and responsible people are, they will not effectively meet expectations without clarity and a willingness to follow through on their promises.

Routinely checking in ensures decisions get implemented and helps to make everyone accountable for their responsibilities. For long-term solutions, consider setting a weekly thirty-minute check-in at a set time. Following through on your promises builds trust. Having a clear plan also ensures accountability and acts as a reference to return to if an issue arises.

Even the best relationships have periodic episodes of poor communication or a complete absence of any compassion, leading to misery and pain. The breakdowns can have an impact, not just on understanding each other, but on the wellbeing of a person. The more you are able to successfully navigate conversations by closing the loop and bringing about resolution, the easier it will be to trust each other and move forward again when there is another problem.

Completing This Leg of the Journey

You don't have to remain disconnected and living in misery. You can have the difficult conversation and take steps towards resolving the conflict. Deal with the unfinished business and get closure, so your relationship will be free from the unresolved tension. Stay on the productive path that brings resolution by completing conversations and working together to solve the problem. Your relationships are worth the investment!

Reviewing Our Entire Journey

Over the course of our trip, we've discovered a lot about how to have more connected relationships and productive conversations. If you want your relationship(s) to get better, then you must choose to stop the chaos, get off the merry-go-round of misery, and get on the productive path that will bring resolution. Invest the time necessary to understand what is happening under the surface and what causes your conversations to get off course. Your relationships will improve in direct proportion to your willingness to change your interactions. With the important people in your life, develop habits to change your own behavior. It is time to stop your deeply entrenched patterns and see things

> *Your relationships will improve in direct proportion to your willingness to change your interactions.*

from a completely different lens. You can stop seeing people through the lens of your unmet desire. You can treat people the way you want to be treated—the way God treated you.

My hope is that your journey is already producing better results. Remember to choose the best route to arrive at the desired destination. Your connection is the one thing you will need to enjoy the journey. Blaming others and making excuses will lead you to the destruction of any and all of your relationships. Don't become your biggest relationship problem. Take ownership for your own thoughts, emotions, beliefs, behavior, and decisions. If you find yourself going down a dead-end path, get off as soon as you recognize you are on it!

Ask clarifying questions to help you stay on course. Take the time to discover if you are you headed in the right direction by asking what is the most important message in every conversation? You do not want to leave the people you care about with your rejection and condemnation. Stay on course. All four of the destructive modes will create an additional problem. Be careful before you attack, defend, withdraw, or freeze. Ask: *What mode am I in right now?* Pay attention to the road signs before, during, and after every important conversation. Asking what is going on inside your heart will bring clarity to your actions.

The seemingly insignificant choices will improve your relationships and produce a satisfying adventure. Follow the GPS and receive what the important people in your life are saying before you respond to it. Keep the engine from overheating by maintaining as much access to your brain as possible. You will not regret learning how to manage your emotions. Fill up the emotional fuel tank by speaking from the heart in order to create thirst for future conversations. You can learn to talk in such a way that will significantly increase your influence. Don't be your own biggest obstacle by taking down your defenses, getting rid of your walls, and removing your protective armor. You can listen to the language of longing and get the essential feedback to make the best decisions. Stay on the productive path that brings resolution by completing conversations and working together to solve the problem at hand. With God's help, you can experience a satisfying adventure.

Questions for Discussion

- What What are the four steps to the productive path that brings resolution?

- What is the cost of not closing the loop in your conversations?

- In what ways does addressing general topics make it difficult to come to a resolution?

- Why does making it specific give you a better chance to come to a resolution?

- How do respectful interactions improve the likelihood of getting to a shared purpose?

- What conversion loops do you need to close in one of your closest relationships?

- What is keeping you from having a difficult conversation?

- What are the two most important next steps you need to take after you have invested time reading this book?

About the Author

Bob Leinberger has guided thousands of people through significant challenges in their relationships over the last twenty-five years. Each conversation has helped him gain a deeper understanding of what fuels negative communication patterns and how to better guide people in the future. Bob has a rare ability to bring clarity to why the people we care about act the way they do and how to repair the damage that's already done. He is an ordinary guy who has experienced God's grace, is learning to extend it to others, and is passionate about encouraging others to do so too.

Bob has been married to Darlene for thirty-eight years. They have two incredible grown children, Zach and Grace. Bob received his M.Div. degree from Denver Seminary, and during the past nearly four decades, has served as a pastor in three churches. He is passionate about teaching God's Word, developing leaders, and guiding people into satisfying relationships. Bob is a gifted communicator with a strong desire to see people become all that God intended them to be.

Bob regularly teaches at retreats, camps, and conferences, and he also contributes to podcasts and radio programs. He serves as a consultant to train employees in healthy relational skills. He coaches executive teams in creating a healthy culture for entire organizations. Bob writes curriculum and serves as a mediator for executives, companies, couples, in-laws, and families who are facing relational roadblocks or other significant conflict. His greatest passion is connecting people to God and helping them improve their relationships. Bob enjoys traveling, sports of all kinds, and eating dessert.

Socials:
Website: www.Relationalmap.com
Instagram: @therelationalmap
Facebook: Relational Map
Linkedin: "The Relational Map"
Email: Bob.leinberger1@gmail.com

Acknowledgements

I am deeply grateful for the remarkable people who have made this book possible. I am humbled by the people who shared their struggles with me and trusted me to guide them through their challenges. All the examples in this book are based on real people, but some of the specific details and all names have been changed to protect their identities. In some cases, I have created a composite picture from several interactions, but I have tried to maintain the truth of what happened.

I adore my wife, Darlene. Her encouragement has given me much needed energy, her sacrifice has allowed me to focus my attention, her wisdom has provided me with incredible insights, her respect has supplied me with courage to risk rejection, and her admiration has motivated me to become a better man. There is absolutely no way I could have written this book without Darlene!

I want to thank my son, Zach Leinberger, and my daughter and son-in-law, Grace and Nathan La Blanc, who are the inspiration for this book. I appreciate how they have tolerated my obsession with this project and allowed me to read countless paragraphs to them throughout each of the numerous ideations of the material. They have encouraged me through every obstacle, supported me through each setback, and made time in their busy schedules to help me through each step in this incredible journey. I am grateful for their belief in this project and for their helpful suggestions. Zach and Grace, I love you, and I am glad that you are my children. You have grown into wonderful adults, and I am very proud of you. Nathan, I am so glad you are part of our family. I can't wait to see the amazing things you are each going to accomplish!

Dan Johnson has referred at least a thousand people to meet with me and has mercilessly nagged me for the past several years to write this book. At first, he employed numerous unsuccessful strategies to motivate me. He finally got my attention when he said, "You need to write a book to expand the scope of people that can be helped by your incredible material. Not everyone can sit across a table from you, you know." Thank you, my friend and colleague, Dan Johnson.

Corey Koskie has encouraged me on a weekly basis to spend time on the book in order to expand my reach to a larger audience, specifically to reach more people in the business world. He firmly believes that people become better leaders when they learn how to better interact with the important people in their lives. He got me started when he set up a pilot of my material with his business leaders. Thank you, Corey, for your friendship and encouragement.

Aaron Felty has kept me busy meeting with the hundreds of people he has encouraged to speak with me. He has a unique way of commanding them by saying, "You have got to meet with Bob." His unwavering belief in the material has encouraged me, but his encouraging words have made the biggest difference. Aaron constantly tells me, "This content is important and can change lives. You need to get this out there." Aaron, working alongside you in ministry has been a great privilege.

April Kunze read the first draft and helped me with the content, layout, structure, flow and transitions. She also encouraged me by saying. "This is so important, and the world needs to hear your voice! Keep going!" April I am very thankful for your friendship and help.

Randy, April, and Paige Stensgard have given me tireless support and much-needed encouragement. They have even gone on vacation with us three times in order to give Darlene something to do while I stay in the room to write. Many thanks, Stensgards!

Doug Leskee, Brian Dobson, Sarah Schultz, Tom Prichard, Dan Thompson, Steve Michel, Di Schafer, Amy Dyvig, Emily Leskee, Will Shultz, Tracy Lohr, Cathy Hilary, and Grace La Blanc all read an early draft of the manuscript and gave me extremely helpful feedback. Their words gave me the encouragement and motivation to write two additional chapters and make important changes throughout. Thank you!

Clay Schafer, Wayne Severud, and Don Brisco have listened to me share the stories going into my book during our weekly workouts. They not only listened to me, but they also gave helpful feedback. These three men have helped me become a much stronger person and have given me the courage to move into the gifts and passions God has designed me to share. Thank you.

Steve and Cheryl Michel, Doug and Emily Leskee, Monte Niemi, and Molly Wenck have provided their wonderful homes or cabins to give Darlene and me a wonderful place to write and edit without the interruption of normal life. Thank you for your overwhelming generosity.

Kristen Taraszewski, Sam Lamphere, Ron Lyric, Brian Dobson, and Will Schultz have given me great ideas, wonderful suggestions, and solid advice on how these principles relate to business relationships.

Benjamin and Crystal Woods deserve appreciation for the many wonderful conversations and our growing friendship. I am in awe at how well they have faced adversity and the gracious ways you model how to LOOK OUT FOR THE LEFT OUT®. Thank you, both.

Bobby Tarnoski has encouraged me through our quarterly breakfast meeting. Thank you very much, Bobby.

Charles and Cheri Daws have given me so much encouragement despite both having separate battles with cancer. You are both inspiring to me and to countless others. Thank you.

Sue and Nate Pelto, Vinay Wankhede, Kia Bihl, and Sonja Hettinga, thank you for consistently praying for me through each step of this project. Your prayers have made an enormous difference. Thank you.

The Plymouth Covenant Re-engage leaders, Brian and Jennie Dobson, Adam and Rena Gess, Charles and Cheri Daws, Jim and Ruth Buezis, Joe and Monica Lomando, Steve and Anne Hatton, and Steve and Bethany Kennedy have graciously listened to content of the book on Sunday nights during the large-group talks for the last five years. Their graciousness has allowed me to make numerous revisions to improve the material. The friendships and partnerships in ministry within this group are priceless. Thank you, all.

To the 150 couples that have trusted me with their pre-marriage counseling by allowing me to customize the material to their unique situation, thank you! Each conversation has helped me gain clarity and develop language that will bring greater understanding to the reader.

Chris Taylor has done a great work on the content edit of the rough draft. She was willing to roll up her sleeves and help me make some much-needed changes. Thanks for forcing me to do the hard work to make the book better.

As stated earlier, I really appreciate my wife, Darlene. (She can't be thanked enough!) I also very much appreciate my friend, Molly Sanborn, speaker and author, whose publication timeline of her own book, *Cheeseballs for Jesus*, was about nine months ahead of mine. (I highly recommend her book, by the way!) Molly meticulously read every word of the final draft, and both she and Darlene caught tiny errors and overall, gave me tremendous feedback. Thank you, both!

I could write many paragraphs on how helpful my editor, Heidi Sheard, has been, but she would edit them out. I am willing to limit my appreciation to four things. Without Heidi's help, I would still be talking to my friends about "a book I am writing." She has gone above and beyond to help me carry this project over the finish line. I appreciate Heidi's belief in the project as well as her tireless, detailed work and helpful suggestions. This book is a significantly better book because of her contribution. Thank you, Heidi.

Most importantly, I want to thank the God who I love. He is the source of everything good in my life. Every meaningful principle and every helpful insight came directly from Him. He has modeled how to have a satisfying relationship with an imperfect person. He makes me feel loved and secure. He meets my deepest longings. I am grateful for His life-giving words and faithfulness to an ordinary guy like me. I will spend eternity praising Him for everything He has done in my life!

Endnotes

Part One

Chapter One

1. Grant, Adam, *Give and Take: Why Helping Others Drives Our Success*, (Penguin Books: Westminster, 2013). Personal success is driven by how you interact with others. Selfishness and mean tactics may get immediate results but will not produce the kind of success worthy of your time, energy, or devotion.

2. Louw, Johannes P. and Nida, Eugene A., Editors, "Agape," *Greek-English Lexicon of the New Testament: Based on Semantic Domains*, (Fortress Press: Minneapolis, 1999). This is a great tool for advanced or intermediate Greek studies. Focusing on the contextual aspect of words, the authors use categories called "semantic domains" to navigate the dictionary and help discover the meaning of the Greek terms in the context of the passage.

3. Ramsey, Dave, *The Total Money Makeover: A Proven Plan for Financial Fitness,* (Thomas Nelson: Nashville, 2009). Dave Ramsey provides a step-by-step process for saving money, getting out debt, creating a personal budget, and investing for long-term wealth. The keys to winning with money are time, diligence, determination, and unleashing your greatest wealth-building tool: your income.

Chapter Two

1. May, Sharon Morris, *How to Argue So Your Spouse Will Listen: 6 Principles for Turning Arguments into Conversations,* (Thomas Nelson: Nashville, 2007). Drawing on the latest research in neurobiology. Sharon Morris May helps the reader understand why people argue so you can understand how to unravel disagreements. Understanding the anatomy of an argument can make it possible to develop effective strategies to approach conflict.

2. Burns, Jim, *Creating an Intimate Marriage*: *Rekindle Romance Through Affection, Warmth, and Encouragement*, (Bethany House: Bloomington, 2007). Jim Burns does a wonderful job of providing a blueprint for physical, relational, and emotional intimacy.

3. Allen, Jennie, *Get Out of Your Head: Stopping the Spiral of Toxic Thoughts*, (WaterBrook & Multnomah: Colorado Springs, 2020). Jennie Allen clearly communicates how our thinking shapes how we live. We can learn to stop thoughts that leave us prey to toxic patterns like victimhood,

anxiety, and distraction. Drawing on biblical teaching and neuroscience, she shows how to fight the enemies of the mind with the truth of God.

4. Reina, Dennis and Michelle, *Rebuilding Trust in the Workplace: Seven Steps to Renew Confidence, Commitment, and Energy*, (Berrett-Koehler Publishers: Oakland, 2010). This practical book helps to rebuild broken trust by reframing the experience, taking responsibility, letting go, and moving on. Trust is essential to a productive work environment.

5. Lewis, C.S., *The Four Loves*, (Deckle Edge: Jersey City, 2017). This is a repackaged edition of the revered author's classic work from 1971 that examines the four types of human love: affection, friendship, erotic love, and the love of God. It is part of the C. S. Lewis Signature Classics series. Lewis explores the topic of love by looking at the four ancient Greek words for love. He separates love into two categories: need-love, where something is received and gift-love, where it is altruistic.

6. Lencioni, Patrick, *Getting Naked: A Business Fable About Shedding the Three Fears That Sabotage Client Loyalty,* (Jossey-Bass: San Francisco, 2010). According to Lencioni, our reluctance to be vulnerable is driven by three fears: 1) the fear of losing the business, 2) the fear of being embarrassed, and 3) the fear of feeling inferior.

Chapter Three

1. Stanley, Andy, "Own It," *Starting Over: A four-part sermon series*, Northpoint Community Church, July, 2018. YouTube: https://www.youtube.com/watch?v=u7oYW-zdzyk. Pastor Stanley says one reason history repeats itself is that we don't own our part of our history. We can't own it if we don't think it's our fault! But if something important has come to an end and you are starting over, we must look back and own our part in order to move ahead.

2. Tavris, Carol and Aronson, Elliot, *Mistakes Were Made (but Not By Me): Why We Justify Foolish Beliefs, Bad Decisions, and Hurtful Acts,* (Mariner Books: Boston, 2020). This fascinating book draws from hundreds of research studies of how people deal with their mistakes. It shows that most of us, to maintain our confidence and self-esteem, routinely fail to admit our mistakes and reject information that questions our beliefs, decisions, or preferences. We thrive on self-justification at the expense of the truth.

3. Wagner, Todd and MeGee, John, *Re-engage Workbook* (version 2.1), (Watermark Resources: Dallas, 2019). Re-engage is a nationwide ministry out of Watermark Community Church in Dallas, Texas, and helps reconnect, reignite, and resurrect marriages.

4. Keller, Timothy, *Forgive: Why Should I and How Can I?* (Viking Press: New York City, 2022).

Chapter Four

1. Weiner Davis, Michele, *The Divorce Remedy: The Proven 7-Step Program for Saving Your Marriage*, (Simon & Schuster: New York City, 2002).

2. Nelson, Portia, "Autobiography in Five Short Chapters," *There's a Hole in My Sidewalk: The Romance of Self-Discovery*, (Atria Books/Beyond Words: New York City, 2012). Portia Nelson shares her autobiography in five short chapters.

3. Gorman, Michele, "Yogi Berra's Most Memorable Sayings," *Newsweek.com*, September 23, 2015. https://www.newsweek.com/most-memorable-yogi-isms-375661#:~:text=%22It%20ain't%20over%20till%20it's%20over.%22&text=%22We%20made%20too%20many%20wrong,d%C3%A9j%C3%A0%20vu%20all%20over%20again.%22.

Chapter Five

1. Cloud, Henry, 9 Things You Simply Must Do to Succeed in Love and Life: A Psychologist Learns from His Patients What Really Works and What Doesn't, (Thomas Nelson: Nashville, 2007). As a psychologist, Cloud probes the mystery of why some lives work and others don't. He gives nine practical, easy-to-grasp strategies to help readers discover behaviors and responses that successful individuals have in common.

2. Carter, Les and Minerth, Frank, The Anger Workbook: An Interactive Guide to Anger Management, (Thomas Nelson: Nashville, 2012). The good news is anger can be managed. In The Anger Workbook, Carter and Minerth offer a unique, thirteen-step interactive program that will help identify the best ways to handle anger. They also help understand how pride, fear, loneliness, and inferiority feed anger.

Part Two

Chapter Six

1. Love, *Patricia and Stosny, Steven, How to Improve Your Marriage Without Talking About It: Finding Love beyond Words,* (Harmony Publishing, 2008). This book is academic and difficult to read, but the truth is transformational. Love is not about better communication; it's about *connection*. If you feel connected, it's easy to communicate. This book is full of practical advice about the behaviors that improve marriages.

2. Burke, John, *No Perfect People Allowed: Creating a Come-as-You-Are*

Culture in the Church, (Zondervan: Grand Rapids, 2007). The church is facing its greatest challenge—and its greatest opportunity—in our postmodern, post-Christian world. God is drawing thousands of spiritually curious "imperfect people" to become his church—but how are we doing at welcoming them?

3. Patterson, Kerry, Grenny, Joseph, McMillan, Ron, Switzler, Al, and Maxfield, David, *Crucial Accountability: Tools for Resolving Violated Expectations, Broken Commitments, and Bad Behavior*, (McGraw Hill: New York City, 2013). Practical methods to hold people accountable and maintain the relationship.

Chapter Seven

1. Leman, Kevin and Pentak, William, *The Way of a Shepherd: Seven Secrets to Managing Productive People*, (Zondervan: Grand Rapids, 2004). Throughout the book, you'll learn how to infuse your work with meaning, no matter your role, title, industry, or size of your team. Uncover the tried-and-true best practices for how to engage, energize, and ignite your workforce.

2. The gender-specific tendencies described in the first two destructive strategies, anger and emotional intensity, do not always fall this way. Both men and women are capable of both. As a matter of fact, we have all probably been on both sides of all of these destructive choices.

3. Clarke, David E. and Clarke, William G., *Men Are Clams, Women Are Crowbars: Understand Your Differences and Make Them Work,* (Focus on the Family: Colorado Springs, 2019). David Clarke takes a fresh, relevant, and humorous approach to gender differences. He explains what you need to know to understand your differences and make the most of them. You can learn to improve communication by understanding why men and women think, talk, and behave so differently from each other.

Chapter Eight

1. Grenny, Joseph, Patterson, Kerry, Maxfield, David, McMillan, Ron, and Switzler, Al, *Influencer: The New Science of Leading Change*, (McGraw Hill: New York City, 2013). They combine the remarkable insights of behavioral scientists and business leaders with the astonishing stories of high-powered influencers from all walks of life. They give you strategies to increase your influence in your personal life, your business, and your world.

2. Clark, Chap with Clark, Dee, *Disconnected: Parenting Teens in a MySpace World,* (Baker Publishing Group: Ada, Michigan, 2007). Parents worry they don't have the understanding or training to be able to care for their kids in a world that is increasingly superficial, politicized, and

performance driven. In *Disconnected,* Chap and Dee Clark equip parents with a realistic parenting book that doesn't ignore the harsh realities of adolescent life. It builds a foundation for parents by taking them through the various developmental stages of their children.

Part Three

Chapter Nine

1. Miller, Sherod, Miller, Phyliss A., Nunnally, Elam W., and Wackman, Daniel B, *Couples Communication: Collaborative Marriage Skills*, (Interpersonal Communications, 2007. This is an invaluable resource because it breaks down why communication breaks down. The authors teach practical skills on how to listen accurately and speak clearly and constructively. They offer amazing techniques to reduce tension and resolve differences.

2. Patterson, Kerry, Grenny, Joseph, McMillian, Ron, and Switzler, Al, *Crucial Conversations: Tools for Talking When the Stakes are High,* (McGraw Hill, New York City, 2021). This book address why most conversation breaks down and gives practical tool to navigate difficult conversations.

Chapter Ten

1. Stone, Doublas and Heen, Sheila, *Thanks for the Feedback: The Science and Art of Receiving Feedback Well,* (Viking: New York City, 2014). Receiving feedback is so crucial yet so challenging because it sits at the junction of two conflicting human desires. We do want to learn and grow. And we also want to be accepted just as we are right now. They offer a compelling framework to help us take off-hand comments, annual evaluations, and unsolicited advice with curiosity and grace. This book addresses this tension head on and explains why getting feedback is so crucial yet so challenging.

2. Feldhahn, Shaunti *For Men Only* and Feldhahn, Jeff, *For Women Only,* (Multhomah Publishers: Colorado Springs, 2013) In these two books, the Feldhahns have unearthed a treasure chest of insights that are not only eye-opening, but also life-changing. These two tiny books are absolutely amazing in insights and practical tools.

3. McTiernan, John, dir. *Hunt for Red October*. Los Angeles, San Diego, and Port Angeles, Washington: Paramount Pictures, 1990, DVD.

Chapter Eleven

1. Davidson, Ph.D., Richard J., with Begly, Sharon, The Emotional Life of your Brain: How It's Unique Patterns Affect the Way You Think, Feel, and

Live – and How You Can Change Them, (Hudson Street Press: CITY, 2002), 200-214. Can't find this one in the chapter. Was it deleted?

2. Stosny, Steven, *Soar Above: How to Use the Most Profound Part of Your Brain Under Any Kind of Stress,* (Health Communications, Inc.: Deerfield Beach, Florida, 2016), Kindle Edition. Success in work, love, and life depends on developing habits that activate the powerful prefrontal cortex when we need it most. Unfortunately, under stress, the human brain tends to revert to emotional habits we developed when we were very young. He helps you learn how to switch to the adult brain automatically when things get tough and to soar above the impulse to make things worse.

3. Stosny, Steven, *Love Without Hurt: Turn Your Resentful, Angry, or Emotionally Abusive Relationship into a Compassionate, Loving One,* (De Capo Press: Boston, 2008). This is a wonderful resource to help understand anger, end the cycle of resentment, pain, and abuse, and develop a loving relationship. Dr. Stosny has been featured on national media for the revolutionary techniques he uses in his Compassion-Power and Boot Camp programs.

4. Smedes, Lewis B., *Forgive and Forget: Healing the Hurts We Don't Deserve,* (HarperOne: San Francisco, 2007). The 4 stages to forgiveness are practical, easy to understand, and life changing. The four steps are (the hurt, the hate, the healing, and the coming together).

5. Smedes, Lewis B., ibid.

6. Wilson, Jim, *How to Be Free from Bitterness and Other Essays on Christian Relationships,* (Canon Press: Moscow, Idaho, 2007). This short book is full of wonderful relational advice, but the essay on bitterness is especially helpful and worthy of your time.

Chapter Twelve

1. Johnson, Dr. Sue, *Hold Me Tight: Seven Conversations for a Lifetime of Love,* (Little Brown Spark: Boston, 2008). Dr. Johnson has a unique ability to explain extremely complicated ideas in understandable language. She teaches that the way to save and enrich a relationship is to reestablish a safe, emotional connection and preserve the attachment bond.

2. Kimmel, Tim, *Grace Based Parenting: Set Your family Tree,* (Thomas Nelson: Nashville, 2005). Discover a parenting style that nurtures a healthy family and displaces fear as a motivator for behavior. Learn how to meet your child's three driving, inner needs for security, significance, and strength with the invaluable gifts of love, purpose, and hope.

Made in the USA
Monee, IL
19 August 2023

41286421R10157